THE REAL JAMES DEAN

*Intimate Memories from
Those Who Knew Him Best*

Edited by
PETER L. WINKLER

Foreword by
George Stevens Jr.

CHICAGO
REVIEW
PRESS

An A Cappella Book

Published by Chicago Review Press Incorporated
814 North Franklin Street
Chicago, Illinois 60610
ISBN 978-1-61373-472-8

A list of credits and copyright notices for the individual pieces in this collection
can be found on pages 333–36.

Library of Congress Cataloging-In-Publication Data
Names: Winkler, Peter L., editor.
Title: The real James Dean : intimate memories from those who knew him best /
    edited by Peter L. Winkler ; foreword by George Stevens.
Description: Chicago, Illinois : Chicago Review Press, 2016. | Includes index.
Identifiers: LCCN 2015050679 (print) | LCCN 2016003409 (ebook) | ISBN
    9781613734728 (paperback) | ISBN 9781613734711 (pdf) | ISBN 9781613734742
    (epub) | ISBN 9781613734735 (kindle)
Subjects: LCSH: Dean, James, 1931–1955. | Motion picture actors and
    actresses—United States—Biography. | BISAC: BIOGRAPHY & AUTOBIOGRAPHY /
    Entertainment & Performing Arts. | PERFORMING ARTS / Film & Video /
    History & Criticism.
Classification: LCC PN2287.D33 R43 2016 (print) | LCC PN2287.D33 (ebook) |
    DDC 791.4302/8092—dc23
LC record available at http://lccn.loc.gov/2015050679

Cover design: John Yates at Stealworks
Cover image: Photofest
Interior design: Jonathan Hahn

Printed in the United States of America
5 4 3 2 1

"All of us were touched by Jimmy, and he was touched by greatness."
—Natalie Wood

CONTENTS

———◆———

FOREWORD

———◆———

Hᴇ ᴍᴀᴅᴇ ᴏɴʟʏ ᴛʜʀᴇᴇ ᴍᴏᴛɪᴏɴ ᴘɪᴄᴛᴜʀᴇꜱ, yet sixty years after his death he remains one of the world's iconic movie stars.

James Dean made his mark and left his legacy in only eighteen months. His premature death at twenty-four in a highway collision shocked the world, and conferred legendary status to a young man at the very beginning of what those who knew him expected would be a long and productive career.

I was on leave from the air force in March of 1955 when I went with my father to Hollywood's Egyptian Theatre to see *East of Eden* in its first week of release. He would soon start directing *Giant* and he wanted me to see the actor he was considering for the role of Jett Rink. I recall vividly my first impression of the young man with an agile gait and mysterious eyes, whom Elia Kazan had cast as Cal Trask in the film adaptation of John Steinbeck's novel. Knowing that my father had considered Alan Ladd and Montgomery Clift for the role of Jett, I was excited by the prospect of this mercurial twenty-four-year-old playing the pivotal character in *Giant*, a character required to age into his fifties on screen.

I met Jimmy Dean in Marfa, Texas, several months later. He was on the *Giant* set in his worn and dusty jeans, a work shirt and vest, wearing a soiled western hat. He had *become* Jett Rink and spent his idle time on the set mastering rope tricks. Jimmy was nearsighted, and working without glasses seemed to produce in his eyes a concentration and intensity that made the camera embrace him. He was compelling and he was unpredictable. He could be warm, entertaining, and fun to be with. And he could be diffident and inconsiderate of those around him. He could be brilliant and intriguing in front of the camera, and he could be unfocused and mannered in front of the camera.

I spent several months in the editing room during the final stages of *Giant*. One of Dean's finest moments on screen takes place in the office of Bick Benedict's gothic ranch house. Benedict, played by Rock Hudson, informs Jett that Bick's deceased sister, in a sentimental gesture, left a little parcel of land to him. Then Bick places an imposing stack of bills on the desk to buy the land back, wishing to keep his ranch whole. Jett studies the men in the room, forcing us to wonder what he is thinking, before saying to Bick, "You know something, Bick, I don't know but what it just might not be a pretty good idea to gamble along with old Madama. . . . Just keep what she give me. I'm sentimental too, Bick." He then rises, gives the men a crooked smile, and swings his rope in a little move, making a knot. As he approaches the door, he turns, saying, "See ya," and sweeps his right hand outward, Dean's signature gesture for Rink. Of course, those few acres make Jett Rink an oil tycoon.

My father, who covered scenes from many angles in order to have options in editing, selected a single take featuring Dean in that scene, and let it run uninterrupted for three minutes and forty-seven seconds in the final film because his performance was so compelling. Dean would sometimes stammer, repeat gestures, and insert pauses into other scenes, sapping them of energy, but with the coverage at hand my father was able to shape his performance and retain Dean's compelling characterization.

I visited the *Giant* set at the Warner Bros. studio in September of 1955. Jimmy had completed most of his work by then, but he dropped by that day for a visit. He talked enthusiastically about the Porsche 550 Spyder he had just purchased and his plans for racing it. When Jimmy was cast as Jett, he had driven a Porsche Super Speedster in some races in California, winning two prizes. My father understood the attraction of fine cars. He drove one of the first Mercedes-Benz 300SL Gullwing coupés. He sat down with Jimmy and they discussed their cars before my father told him that they were embarking on an ambitious film with a long shooting schedule, and while he had confidence in Jimmy's driving skill, if he were injured on the track he would jeopardize the efforts of the three hundred people who were working on the film. He said it was important that Jim not race his car during production. Despite his rebellious tendencies, Jimmy understood the situation and agreed. And he kept his word.

Now, on the set of *Giant* he told me that his new car, which he nicknamed "Little Bastard," was parked outside and asked if I'd like to go for a ride. We went out and admired the sleek gray machine with red racing seats. We climbed in; Jimmy fired it up and took off, driving faster through the narrow streets that ran between the tall soundstages than the studio police would have liked. It was an exciting ride, and Jimmy, with his tousled hair and clip-on sun lenses over his thick glasses, was steady at the wheel. I was twenty-three, a year younger than Jimmy, and I shared his sense of adventure, and the fast ride gave me no premonition of trouble.

When he finished shooting his last scene, he told my father that he was going to enter a race in Salinas, three hundred miles north of Los Angeles. My father recalled suggesting that he truck his Porsche up north rather than driving it on the highway. Jimmy said that was his plan. On the morning of his trip, however, he changed his mind, telling his mechanic that he wanted to gain experience driving his new car before the race.

A stunned world heard the news of Dean's fatal crash on September 30, 1955. The shock of his violent death initiated a concentrated and prolonged media frenzy, fueled by a growing base of Dean fans and bizarre rumors surrounding his death. The articles in this book reflect the passion and breadth of that feeling.

In *The Real James Dean: Intimate Memories from Those Who Knew Him Best*, Peter Winkler has assembled a comprehensive trove of what has been written over the decades about the young actor by his contemporaries. It offers Dean enthusiasts a unique anthology of articles, essays, and remembrances that demonstrate how he revealed himself in different ways to different people. Among the fascinations of this collection are the contradictions in the various accounts, each observer drawing his or her own portrait of the young actor, marked by differing perceptions and conflicting facts.

A touching reminiscence in Mr. Winkler's compilation is by Sanford Roth, the photographer who followed Jimmy in another car on his ill-fated drive to Salinas. Jimmy was familiar with Roth's book of photos of Paris, and said to him:

That book makes me realize I've never been anywhere. I want to be in Paris before this year is out. I want to see the Paris theater—to see Pierre Blanchard and Gérard Philipe. I want to see the great artists—to see Rome—to buy shoes and crazy clothes in Capri. I want to live!

James Dean never saw Paris—but he did earn a permanent place in the history of cinema and in the hearts of filmgoers the world over.

—GEORGE STEVENS JR.

INTRODUCTION: RESCUED MEMORIES

O N APRIL 8, 1954, few passersby would have recognized James Dean as he stood on the sidewalk outside his New York apartment. He held just a few essential belongings in a brown paper lunch bag tied with string while he waited for director Elia Kazan's limousine to take him to the airport. From there, he'd be whisked away to Warner Bros.' studio in Burbank, California, to commence shooting *East of Eden*, the first of his only three starring roles.

Prior to filming *East of Eden*, Dean had acted in one TV commercial, a little over thirty TV shows, three bit parts in films, and two Broadway plays. Apart from notices of his performances in the stage productions of *See the Jaguar* and *The Immoralist* and a few of the TV shows he appeared in, nothing else had been written about him. He was just one of many emerging actors who had yet to be called to the public's attention.

During the eighteen months he spent in Hollywood making *East of Eden*, *Rebel Without a Cause*, and *Giant*, Dean received relatively light press coverage. He reluctantly submitted himself to interviews with Hollywood gossip columnists, who did not devote much column space to him, and some of his comings and goings were noted in the *Hollywood Reporter* and *Variety*. Before his death, he was the subject of about a dozen magazine articles.

The floodgates suddenly opened when the release of *Rebel Without a Cause* rocketed Dean to stardom a month after his death. A year later, *Life* magazine titled their article about the phenomenal bereavement of the actor's devotees "Delirium Over Dead Star." Jim Backus, who portrayed Dean's father in *Rebel*, described the "mass hysteria" that erupted after Dean's death in personal terms in his autobiography, published three years later:

> I know, because I have literally received thousands of letters, mainly from teenagers, and they are still coming in by the sack full. These are usually three or four pages long. They are actually quite literate, and because they feel I was his "father," they pour out their hearts to me. They want to know everything about him . . . what he said . . . how we got along . . . and what he was like. Every single writer asks me to send something that belonged to Jimmy or that he even touched. They even beg for articles of clothing that I had worn in scenes with him, against which he might have brushed.

The editors of movie fan magazines like *Modern Screen* and *Photoplay*, as well as scandal rags like *Confidential* knock-off *Whisper*, were eager to exploit the seemingly insatiable demand of obsessive Dean fans for stories about their dead idol. They published 140 articles about him between 1955 and 1958.

A handful of these articles made worthwhile contributions to the literature about Dean, when some of his family, friends, and colleagues were solicited or seized the opportunity to share their reminiscences of him.

George Stevens, director of *Giant*; Natalie Wood, Dean's costar in *Rebel Without a Cause*; and Rolf Wütherich, Dean's mechanic, who rode with him on September 30, 1955, and survived the crash that killed him that day, wrote or affixed their names to ghostwritten features offering their impressions of Dean. Dean's girlfriends, Beverly Wills and Elizabeth Sheridan, came forward with stories to tell of his salad days in Hollywood and New York, when his stardom was anything but assured.

Several people close to James Dean were reportedly planning to write books about him, but only one came to fruition. William Bast, Dean's college roommate, wrote the first serious biography of Dean, based on his friendship with him during the last six years of his life. Bast's biography was serialized in *Photoplay*.

Director Nicholas Ray was profoundly affected by his collaborative relationship with Dean during the production of *Rebel Without a Cause*, and was devastated by his death. Two articles that he wrote, part of a projected book on the making of *Rebel* that he never completed, were published on the first anniversary of its release in late October 1956. In 1958, Jim Backus devoted an entire chapter to Dean in his autobiography, *Rocks on the Roof*—the first of his costars to do so.

With no more Dean films forthcoming after *Giant* to fuel Dean mania, his crowd of fans dispersed, turning their attention to living, breathing actors and pop phenomena like Elvis Presley. The flood of articles devoted to Dean slowed to a trickle, then dried up completely.

Twenty years later, post-Vietnam and post-Watergate America was mired in cultural stagnation and malaise. The response was not another countercultural upheaval like the one seen in the late '60s that soured and died after the election of Richard Nixon, the Manson murders, and the killing at the Rolling Stones concert at the Altamont Speedway in northern California.

There was instead a nostalgic revival of '50s pop culture as the teenagers from that era, now facing middle age, looked backward. The mid-'70s also saw the first revival of interest in James Dean, producing six biographies, a documentary, and a TV docudrama written and produced by William Bast. Dean became a star in the pop culture firmament, taking his rightful place alongside Marilyn and Elvis. His likeness began to adorn countless pieces of merchandise.

Dennis Hopper, who acted with Dean in *Rebel Without a Cause* and *Giant*, later commented on the ubiquity of his image: "I mean, I can go to Europe, I'm going to Sweden, I go into a nightclub, and there's James Dean, Humphrey Bogart, Marilyn Monroe on the wall. Going to Paris, there he is . . ."

Dean's newfound icon status was not lost on those of his contemporaries, including showbiz luminaries like Alec Guinness, Elia Kazan, Eartha Kitt, and Shelley Winters, who had neglected to write about him immediately after his death. Dean now loomed so large he threatened to eclipse lives he had passed through only briefly, reducing their estimable careers to a footnote to his legend. When it came time for them to write their memoirs in the autumn of their years, Dean's colleagues were obligated to devote some space to recalling their encounters with him, lest his absence seem a disappointing omission to fans hungrily perusing their books in search of new stories about their beloved idol.

In the six decades since his death, nearly everyone who knew Dean, however briefly, made sure to record their experiences with him in articles, interviews, and their autobiographies and memoirs.

Unfortunately, the brief commercial shelf life of books and the ephemeral nature of newspapers and magazines has meant that their recollections of Dean became relegated to fragile back issues of movie magazines, newspapers, and out-of-print books that are extremely hard to find, often available only at exorbitant collector's prices. Some of this material can be read only on microfiche or microfilm in libraries inaccessible to most readers.

They have not been reprinted since their original publication.

Until now.

The Real James Dean is the first book of its kind, a rich collection of articles, excerpts from showbiz autobiographies, and interviews in which many of the people whose lives were touched by Dean recall their indelible experiences with him in their own words.

Here you will find personal accounts of Dean from his father and grandmother; high school and college drama teachers; lovers (women *and* men); actors Raymond Massey (Dean's father in *East of Eden*), Jim Backus, Natalie Wood, Rock Hudson, and Mercedes McCambridge (Dean's costars in *Rebel Without a Cause* and *Giant*); directors Elia Kazan, Nicholas Ray, and George Stevens; gossip columnist Hedda Hopper; Rolf Wütherich; and a number of Dean's other friends and colleagues who recorded their impressions of him for posterity.

Misspellings in the original text of the pieces in this book have been corrected. Editor's notes correcting factual errors or supplying additional information appear in brackets or footnotes. *The Real James Dean* presents the articles from *Modern Screen* and *Photoplay* as they were first published, complete with their original epigraphs, introductions, and coming attractions–style previews. The original use of italics and capitals has also been reproduced.

—Peter L. Winkler
Valley Village, California
June 2015

I

James Dean — The Boy I Loved

Emma Woolen Dean

Emma Woolen Dean was James Dean's paternal grandmother. Her article recalling her beloved grandson Jimmy appeared in the March 1956 issue of *Photoplay*. —Ed.

When you voted him one of your favorites for a Photoplay Gold Medal Award, I knew you loved him, too. And I knew you would want to know him the way I did

NONE OF US WILL EVER FORGET that last family reunion we had with Jimmy in the spring of 1955. He had finished "East of Eden." He'd got his wish: he knew he was a good actor.

Jimmy had been to New York, then came here to Fairmount before returning to California. Everybody here was excited—not that Jimmy had to be an actor to be welcomed in Fairmount; he didn't. People here always liked him. But this was different. When "East of Eden" was at the drive-in, so many people went it made a traffic jam.

But, in spite of all the fanfare, Jimmy only wanted to be with his family. We all gathered out at my daughter Ortense's farm. Ortense and Marcus Winslow raised Jimmy after his mother died. Jimmy and Charlie— that's my husband—had just come back from the cemetery, where Jimmy had taken pictures of his great-grandfather's and great-great grandfather's graves. When they came in, Jimmy turned to Charlie and said, "Grampa, do you think you could do some auctioneering?"

Now my husband Charlie has always claimed his father was the best auctioneer living. So with us, what Jimmy said was kind of a little joke. When Jimmy was little, Charlie would hold him on his knee and auction him off to me, and I'd buy him and Jimmy would laugh.

Well, it ended up this time that Jimmy talked Charlie into auctioneering little Markie Winslow's dog right back to Markie. (Markie is Ortense's and Marcus' little boy.) We laughed, but didn't think anything about this little joke until the next day when Jimmy opened this "satchel" he'd had standing around. It turned out the satchel was a tape recorder. You should have seen my husband's face when Jimmy played it back! Charlie said, "Hey, you shouldn't have done that without telling me. I used some words there that maybe don't belong in polite society."

Well, Jimmy wouldn't give in. He said, "That's how I'm going to take you back to California with me—for now. But someday I'm going to have a nice house and I want you and Grandma to live with me."

That was our Jimmy. His family meant a lot to him and he meant even more to us. While we're not the ones to do much lollygagging around, kissing and hugging each other, it does seem that whenever we are going to be separated and have to see someone off, we all have tears running down our faces.

You might say we're a close-knit family. That's what comes from living in one place for so long. The first Deans came from around Lexington, Kentucky, and settled in Grant County, Indiana, about 1815. My family, the Woolens, and Jimmy's mother's family, the Wilsons, got here about the same time.

Mostly, we've been around Fairmount or Marion—sixty, seventy miles from Indianapolis—ever since. Charlie and I live on Washington Street, in Fairmount, but he still farms, as he has always done. Charlie's a great hand at having two or three things going at once. At various times he's been a stock buyer, run a livery stable, sold automobiles and raced a string of horses. We're not rich, but we're not poor, either. So long as I live, I'll always have a porch to sit on, a rocking chair to rock in and a clock that strikes.

We have three children, Ortense, Winton and Charles Nolan. I don't want to get a lot of "begats" into this, as in the Bible, but so as you can keep

James Dean, age eight. *Photofest*

all of us straight, I'd like to say that you couldn't ask for a nicer bunch of grandchildren and great grandchildren.

Ortense married Marcus Winslow and they have Joan and young Marcus. Winton married Mildred Wilson and Jimmy was born February 8, 1931. Charles Nolan married Mildred Miller and they have Joseph, David and Betsy Jane. Joan, who is now Mrs. Mayron Reece Peacock, gave us our first great-grandchildren, Gerrell Reese and Jane Ann.

They're all dear to us, but Jimmy was almost like a son in each of the families. We all tried to make it up to him for losing his mother.

I'll never forget the day Winton's letter came telling us that Mildred couldn't get well. They lived in Santa Monica where Winton was supervisor of the dental laboratory at the Veterans Hospital. Jimmy was just nine then. Winton asked if I could come out. Mildred, who was so young and lovely, had cancer. I took the letter to our doctor and he judged I'd be there six to eight weeks. I was gone seven, and when I brought Mildred's body back, Jimmy was with me, for after the services out there, I gave Winton the Winslows' message.

I said, I recall, "Now Winton, I want you to think this over carefully. If you see fit to let Jimmy come back to Fairmount, Ortense and Marcus would like to take him. They'll raise him for you, if you want." Having a boy on the farm would be nice. Joan was then their only child. Markie wasn't yet born.

Well, poor Winton just sat there and stared. At last he said, "It never occurred to me I might be separated from Jimmy."

But Winton knew what he faced. He had a living to earn and didn't have a single relative in California. At last he said, "You can't find a finer man than Marcus Winslow, and so far as choosing between the way my sister would mother Jimmy and how some housekeeper might take care of him, there's just no question."

Hard as it was, I've always felt Winton made the right choice, particularly since it turned out that he was drafted about eighteen months later.

It helped that the Winslow farm already was home to Jimmy. For a while, when Winton had worked in Marion, they had lived in a little cottage up beyond the Friends' Back Creek meeting house, on the corner of the farm.

And just to show you how Marcus and Ortense welcomed Jimmy, they even gave him their own room and moved across the hall. Ortense said, "He liked our bedroom set better. It was maple and that seemed right for a boy."

I don't mean to brag, but Ortense and Marcus are a daughter and son-in-law any woman would be proud to own. They do their share in the community, and besides their organizations, Ortense plays piano for the Friends' Sunday school and Marcus is interested in Earlham College, a Quaker school near here. Both are wise and gentle and have a great gift for loving. Theirs is like a Quaker home should be. You never hear a harsh word. Best of all, they are happy as well as good—and that's what Jimmy needed most after the shock of losing his mother.

Joan, too, made a great fuss over Jimmy, and so did her friends. Always, there were lots of young people around, for they all loved to come to the Winslow farm.

It's just two miles north of town and it's a beautiful place. Several farm magazines have used pictures of it on their covers and camera clubs come there for their outings. Every Winslow for generations has done something to improve it. The big square white "new" house, built in 1904, stands on a hill and the land rolls down to the farmyard with its white barns and sheds. A stand of timber along the creek sets off the buildings. In the near pasture, there's a big pond. Marcus ran an electric line out and strung lights so the kids could skate on winter nights. Summers there was always a picnic going.

Maybe the best way to tell you how Marcus and Jimmy got along would be to repeat what one of Jimmy's classmates said to me. "Ma Dean," he said, "I always envied Jimmy. My dad never took time to play with me, but Marcus was forever out there shooting baskets with Jimmy or passing a football or taking him hunting or showing him how to do stunts."

For Jimmy, it soon added up to health, happiness and that charge of energy which later was sort of able to break right through a movie screen. Seems like he could do anything. A professional figure skating teacher who happened into our town gave him a few lessons, then said Jimmy was as good a skater as he was. Jimmy also wanted to play basketball and, although he wasn't big and rangy like most boys that make the team, he was quick and sure of himself and turned out to be a good player.

One reason Jimmy could do so well was that he was a born mimic. Charlie and I used to laugh about it when he was a little shaver. Charlie and Jimmy always were awfully fond of each other. If Charlie sat with his knees crossed, Jimmy crossed his; if Charlie stretched out his legs, Jimmy did, too. It was more than just mocking Charlie's gestures. Even then, Jimmy seemed able to be another person.

He did right well with his 4-H projects. The first year he had baby chicks, the second a garden and then it was cattle. Eventually, his Guernsey bull won grand champion at the county fair.

But the funniest was Jimmy's pig. As a farm boy usually does, Jimmy got the runt of the litter. He bottle-fed it and it became his pet. There would be Jimmy and his dog, crossing the yard and that pig, running along behind, squealing and oinking and trying to keep up with them.

Marcus and Ortense saw that Jimmy had every advantage. He could draw and paint and work with clay. When Joan took dancing lessons, Jimmy got them, too. Ortense tried to teach him piano, but there was too much playing to be done outdoors for him to ever want to practice. Violin was no better, but when they got him a bass horn, Jimmy took to it. That and drums. Before he finished high school, he could play almost any instrument in the band.

He sure took after Charlie when it came to cars. Charlie bought his first car in 1911 and horrified the town by scorching along at 35 miles an hour. Jimmy learned to drive a tractor first, and then his bikes. He had a little boy's bicycle first, then his whizzer—a bike with a motor. A real noisy motor. You could hear Jimmy coming three miles away. Then he got to trading. Start an Indiana boy with a jackknife and he'll end up with a house and lot. Jimmy swapped his whizzer for a little foreign cycle and after that his motorcycles got larger and larger.

Clearest proof that Jimmy could do whatever he set his mind to was his marks in school. In grammar school, they called him Quiz Kid. It helped that he went to visit his father nearly every vacation, for then he'd stand up in class and tell about places he'd seen. In high school, it was a different story. Jimmy got the notion it was what he called "square" to study. Well, his senior year, Marcus had a talk with him. "You'll never get into college with such grades," Marcus told him. Well, sir, Jimmy got down to business. He stayed on the honor roll all year.

He had a hard time making up his mind whether he wanted to be an actor or a lawyer. Winton favored law, but he hadn't seen Jimmy in as many plays as the rest of us. Marcus, who always encouraged Jimmy in all he wanted to do, helped him decide on his school. First Jimmy wanted to go to Earlham, where Marcus went, but Marcus pointed out that if he wanted to act, he'd better go to California.

It was becoming plain to all of us that acting was the thing Jimmy was best at. He won declamatory contests, even a state one, but the thing that convinced us he was an actor was his appearance in a church play, called "To Them That Sleep in Darkness." Jimmy played the blind boy. Well, I'll tell you, I wished he wasn't quite so good at it. I cried all the way through.

Jimmy was in his glory when Joan got married to Reece Peacock. Markie was still a toddler, so it was Jimmy who was in the mischievous little brother position. It was during the war and rice was hard to get, but Jimmy found some. He went to store after store and saved it up for weeks. Then he tied stuff to their car. He sure fixed it up so they went clanking down the road.

I like to remember, too, the understanding Marcus and Jimmy reached before he left Fairmount. Jimmy wanted to earn his way, do

Emma Dean and her grandson, James Dean. *Photofest*

it all himself, but Marcus knew that would be difficult. So Marcus said, "Now Jimmy, I don't want you running up a board bill. Stay out of debt. If you get short, let me know." Winton, I understand, said the same.

It was nice that Jimmy could spend a year with his father. Winton had been five years a widower when he married Ethel Case in 1945. Jimmy lived with them that first year when he attended Santa Monica Junior College. Later he went to UCLA and then to New York to study at the Actors Studio.

Thanks to television, we felt we shared those New York days with Jimmy. We had to buy television sets as soon as he began getting parts in programs. Marcus and Ortense had one of the first sets around here, and then Charlie and I got one. The old grapevine got going every time Jimmy was on *Lux* or *Studio One* or some program like that. They'd announce it in school and the neighbors would come streaming in to watch.

It's hard for us to understand why Jimmy's life had to end so soon. Seemed like he was just beginning to give other people the same kind of pleasure he had always given his family.

One thing I'll always be glad of is that Jimmy did get that house he wanted and that he had a chance to show it to some of those closest to him. Last fall, Marcus and Ortense and Charles Nolan and his Mildred went out to see Winton and Jimmy. Marcus and Ortense had ended their visit and were driving back. They didn't know about Jimmy's accident until they got back to Fairmount.

Jimmy had wanted his father and Charles Nolan to see him race that day, but at the last minute, Charles Nolan decided he couldn't make it down to the racetrack and still start for Indiana the next morning. Jimmy had their tickets in his pocket when he was killed on the highway.

We never saw such a crowd as came to Jimmy's funeral. The ministers tried to comfort us. Rev. James DeWeerd, who was on the school board when Jimmy was in school came from Cincinnati. He's the one who said that Jimmy, in his few years, had lived as much as some people do by 90. Our own pastor, Xen Harvey, said this was only part of Jimmy's own great drama. The first act was life, the second death, and the third, which Jimmy was just entering, was the Hereafter.

We have found comfort, too, in all that our close neighbors have done for us and in the wonderful letters people we don't even know have written. Friends continue to send flowers. On his grave at Christmas, we counted fourteen wreaths, a cross, a vase of fresh flowers, a vase of bittersweet and a big basket of red roses. We are touched that Jimmy earned such devotion.

But the greatest comfort comes from our children's children. Whenever little Markie or Reecy draw me a picture, or when small Joe mimics a television star, or when the others give us their bright smiles, Charlie and I know that the spark which Jimmy had has not died. It's the little ones we must think of now.

When I stand on the hill by Jimmy's grave, I sometimes feel I can look one way and see the work done by all the Deans who have been here. Then I can look ahead and see the promise of those still to come. Sometimes it is comforting just to have lived so long in Indiana.

THE END

2

"My Jim Is a Tough Boy to Understand": James Dean's Father Talks About His Son

RICHARD MOORE

Winton Dean spoke to the press about his son only once, to writer Richard Moore, whose article about James Dean, "Lone Wolf," appeared in the August 1955 issue of Modern Screen *magazine. Buried within Moore's piece, Winton Dean's words spoke volumes about the gulf that separated father and son. Even though James Dean had already starred in two major Hollywood films and was costarring in the mammoth epic* Giant *when Moore interviewed him, Winton Dean remained perplexed by his son's choice of career, and was still waiting for him to "make his mark." —Ed.*

A T THIS POINT IN HIS LIFE James Byron Dean is living strictly for himself. He has no one to support, no one to please, no one in the world to cater to except James Byron Dean.

Although his father and stepmother live only eight or ten miles away from his Hollywood hideaway in the hills, he rarely visits them. Just why he isn't there more often is hard to tell.

Winton Dean, Jim's father, has what he thinks might be an adequate explanation for his son's behavior.

"I'll tell you this," he says. "My Jim is a tough boy to understand. At least, he is for me. But maybe that's because I don't understand actors, and he's always wanted to become one.

"Another reason is that we were separated for a long period of time, from when he was nine until he was eighteen. Those are the important, formative years when a boy and his father usually become close friends.

"Jim and I—well, we've never had that closeness. It's nobody's fault, really. Just circumstances. I came out to California in 1936 with Jim and his mother. Came right out here to Santa Monica. Worked in the Veterans Hospital, dental technician. Did the same thing back in Indiana. Back there I worked for the Veterans Hospital in Marion.

"A few years later, Jim's mother came down with cancer. She was only twenty-nine. The doctors told me it was hopeless. I didn't know what to do. How do you tell an eight-year-old boy his mother's going to die? I tried. In my own stumbling way I tried to prepare Jim for it. Tried to tell him about the sorrow that was coming. Many times I tried to tell the boy what was coming. I just couldn't make it.

"Jim's mother passed away before she was thirty. I was broken up. So was the boy. I couldn't look after him and work, too, so I sent him back to Indiana to live with my sister and her husband. They raised Jim on their farm. And what a fine job they did. In high school, you know, he was a standout athlete, specializing in track and basketball. Absolutely tops.

"When Jim came out here," Mr. Dean continues, "to go to Santa Monica College, he stayed with us—I was remarried by then—and we got along just fine. He was always crazy about acting, and I remember saying to him a couple of times, 'Jim, acting is a good hobby but why don't you study something substantial? Why don't you become a lawyer?' But no, it was acting with him all the way.

"Nowadays, he lives in a world we don't understand too well—the actors' world. We don't see too much of him. But he's a good boy, my Jim. A good boy, and I'm very proud of him. Not easy to understand. No, sir. He's not easy to understand. But he's all man, and he'll make his mark. Mind you, my boy will make his mark."

OUTTAKES

Life with Father

"When I finally met Jimmy's father," Rosenman recalled years later, "I understood how similar our emotional backgrounds had been. Jimmy's mother had been very encouraging, but she had married this rigid, stupid, dreadful man with an infantile jealousy of both his wife and his son—and of their closeness to one another. As for me, my father, too, was jealous—of my close relationship with his father—and I was virtually abandoned by him from a very early age. This common background brought Jimmy and me together.

"Well, then I met his father and I understood. His father was a monster, a person without any kind of sensitivity. Jimmy was doing everything in his career to get his father to like and approve of him, and his father never took the slightest interest.

"He was doing everything, for one person—his father. Not for a director, not for audiences, not even for himself. And his father never took the remotest interest."

—Leonard Rosenman, James Dean's friend, to Donald Spoto,
author of *Rebel: The Life and Legend of James Dean*
(New York: HarperCollins, 1996)

"I think, well, you see . . . my understanding of Jimmy was he was so desperate for familial love. He needed a father very badly and attached himself to many men as father figures, [Elia] Kazan and George Stevens, even George Stevens, who was a bad father to him. But there were others, Nick Ray became a father to him, and he needed that desperately."

—James Dean's friend, actor and director Mark Rydell on
Larry King Live, December 3, 2005

"When we [James Dean, Elizabeth Sheridan, and Bill Bast] hitchhiked to Indiana, his father came from California to meet him there on the farm. And—to fix his teeth. And they were so dear with each other, he and the father—shy and quiet and kind of almost getting to know each other. And we decided we'll let them alone."

—James Dean's girlfriend Elizabeth Sheridan on *Larry King Live*, December 3, 2005

3

My Case Study

James Dean

In the fall of 1948, Fairmount High School's new principal, Roland DuBois, assigned his students the task of writing a brief autobiography as a way of introducing themselves. James Dean's essay, "My Case Study," was preserved for posterity by Adeline Nall, his high school speech teacher and drama coach, who encouraged his pursuit of acting as a career. —Ed.

I, James Byron Dean, was born February 8, 1931, [in] Marion, Indiana. My parents, Winton Dean and Mildred Dean, formerly Mildred Wilson, and myself existed in the state of Indiana until I was six years of age.

Dad's work with the government caused a change, so Dad as a dental mechanic was transferred to California. There we lived, until the fourth year. Mom became ill and passed out of my life at the age of nine. I never knew the reason for Mom's death, in fact it still preys on my mind.

I had always lived such a talented life. I studied violin, played in concerts, tap-danced on theatre stages but most of all I like art, to mold and create things with my hands.

I came back to Indiana to live with my uncle. I lost the dancing and violin, but not the art. I think my life will be devoted to art and dramatics. And there are so many different fields of art it would be hard to foul up, and if I did, there are so many different things to do—farm, sports, science, geology, coaching, teaching music. I got it and I know if I better myself that there will be no match. A fellow must have confidence.

When living in California my young eyes experienced many things. It was also my luck to make three visiting trips to Indiana, going and coming a different route each time. I have been in almost every state west of Indiana. I remember all.

My hobby, or what I do in my spare time, is motorcycle. I know a lot about them mechanically and I love to ride. I have been in a few races and I have done well. I own a small cycle myself. When I'm not doing that I'm usually engaged in athletics, the heart beat of every American boy. As one strives to make a goal in a game there should be a goal in this crazy world for each of us. I hope I know where mine is, anyway, I'm after it.

I don't mind telling you, Mr. DuBois, this is the hardest subject to write about considering the information one knows of himself, I ever attempted.

4

Grant County's Own

Adeline Nall as told to Val Holley

Adeline Mart Nall taught speech and English in public schools for thirty-seven years, thirty-five of them at Fairmount High School in Fairmount, Indiana, where her star pupil was James Dean. Nall coached him in public speaking and drama, and helped prepare him to compete in an annual national forensics competition held in Longmont, Colorado, in 1949, where he gave a riveting performance of "A Madman's Manuscript," the lurid memoir of a lunatic found in Charles Dickens's *The Pickwick Papers*.

Though Dean snubbed her the last time he visited Fairmount, and told an interviewer that she was just a frustrated actress, Nall remained content to bask in the reflected glow of his stardom, proud of the role she played in his path to glory. She was unfailingly polite and generous with biographers, journalists, and fans of Dean who sought her out on their pilgrimages to Fairmount, and never tired of answering the inevitable question: "What was James Dean really like?"

"Jimmy, he's my life," she told a reporter in 1995, when she was confined to a wheelchair at the age of eighty-nine. Her room in the nursing home where she resided was a shrine to Dean, whom she hoped to meet again in heaven after her death.

"I remember one time when Jim was in high school," she said. "We were staging a play, and I cast him as an old man. He came to me and said, 'Mrs. Nall, you don't know anything about casting: I'm a perfect juvenile.'

"When I get to heaven, I'm going to say: 'Jim, look what you did in *Giant*. Do you still think I don't know anything about casting?'"

One hopes her wish was granted. Adeline Nall died on November 19, 1996, at the age of ninety. Her article recalling her former student James Dean was published in the fall 1989 issue of *Traces of Indiana and Midwestern History*. —Ed.

*Anyone who watched James Dean perform could tell that he
was good, but Adeline Nall had the insight and experience to
recognize that his talent was exceptional.*

Back in the Forties, Fairmount High was one of the few schools in
Indiana to require Beginning Speech for all students. Having to take it
whether they liked it or not, some of those kids had such stage fright that
I felt lucky simply to get them on their feet in front of the class! I had to
spoon-feed them.

With that background, it isn't surprising that some of the students in
my Advanced Speech class of 1948–49 weren't exactly what you would call
advanced. It was a small class—seven boys, and three girls. I think the boys
took the course because they thought it was a snap. But James Dean was a
top dramatic student as well as a top basketball player.

I sometimes grew weary of trying to interest students in speech contests. Jim's case was different. One day in Advanced Speech I read an
announcement of the Indiana statewide National Forensic League (NFL)
tournament. Even though no Indianapolis schools were in NFL, the competition would still be tough. Howe Military, Fort Wayne's Central High,
Hammond's Clark, and others with strong speech programs would all be
there.

Jim came to me after class and said, "If you want me to, I'll get a reading and enter that tournament." After perusing some catalogs, he asked me
to order "A Madman's Manuscript," a Dickensian monologue that, as he
told the *New York Times* after becoming a star, is "about this real gone cat
who knocks off several people." From the start, Jim had a natural feeling for
his selection's mood contrasts—the almost imperceptible drifting from san-
ity to madness and back again. Once he had learned it, I assigned the whole
class to give readings. To make it as simple as possible, I provided resource
material if necessary—even Psalms could be used. But my ulterior motive
was to allow Jim to practice during class time. Once another pupil blurted
out, "We only do what Jim wants to do!" Advanced Speech *did* seem to
revolve around the young Mr. Dean, but I would never have admitted it!

I remember listening from the rear of the room as Jim took his turn.
"Yes—a madman!" he cried. "How that word would have roused the terror

that used to come up on me sometimes, sending the blood hissing and tingling through my veins!" Jim's most outstanding trait in his later film career, the ability to concentrate, was already evident as he crouched in front of the class, losing himself completely in the role of the mad Englishman. "Hurrah for the madhouse! Oh, it's a rare place," he cackled.

"Madman" was way beyond most of the other students. Those who hadn't prepared for the assignment at all became restless. David Fox, a junior, began to jeer in low tones. This not only bothered Jim, but me as well. Then David started making sarcastic remarks, and Jim lost characterization. "All right, folks, I want it quiet in this room," I warned. Jim started from where he had been interrupted but found it difficult to get back in character. Another groan came from the back of the room, and, visibly angry, Jim stared menacingly at David. Just then the bell rang, and I was relieved to be saved by it. Our principal, Mr. DuBois, often told me I needed more discipline in my classes. I feared that a brawl between two of my students would be a poor reflection on me.

Unfortunately, Jim and David reached the classroom door at the same time. They started shouting abusively at each other: "Go on out of here, you two," I ordered. My heart nearly stopped beating when I heard a ruckus on the stairs, where the two combatants were punching and shoving each other. Waiting for them at the foot of the stairs was Mr. DuBois.

Suspended from school, Jim was barred from playing in a basketball game with Sweetser High. When he tried to buy a student ticket, he was told he was not a student. It must have frustrated him that his teammates squeaked by Sweetser without him, 43-42. Center Bob Cox was the top scorer against Sweetser, and that is significant because at the end of the season Cox, who had played eighteen games, barely edged out Jim, who had played only seventeen, as top season scorer.

When Jim returned to school, he seemed calm and held no visible grudge. But he did not forget. In the "Seniors' Last Will and Testaments" section of our yearbook, he bequeathed, "my short temper to David Fox."

The day of Jim's NFL tournament—Friday, 8 April 1949—was doubly special for me because my son, David Nall, a sophomore, left early that morning for Purdue to compete in the statewide Future Farmers of America (FFA) public speaking contest. Later on, Jim drove by my house to pick

James Dean (front row center) with his high school baseball team. *Photofest*

me up for the drive to Peru High, where his first round was set for 2 PM. He didn't seem nervous.

Jim performed as well in that first round as I had ever heard him. The most effective aspect of his rendition was the expression in his eyes. Near the startling finale, he hissed, "I kept my eyes carefully from him at first, for I knew what he little thought—that the light of madness gleamed from them like fire." Then the effect was chilling: "I turned my eyes upon him—I could not help it—I saw the sudden change that came upon him beneath my gaze. He was a bold man, but the color faded from his face, and he drew back his chair."

The judge for the first round was Frieda Bedwell of Terre Haute's Garfield High. "He does a fine job. I was deeply moved," she said. "I was especially impressed with the eerie expression in his eyes. They actually looked glassy, and mad at times." Her comments on his interpretation delighted us. We felt sure she had given him first place in the round. Jim left the room, but I stayed behind to deal with a problem. He had gone over the ten-minute limit. With his tendency to ad-lib, you could never tell if he would end within the allowable time. I had tried to get him to make strategic cuts in the text before this tournament. "But every part is necessary," he protested.

I asked Mrs. Bedwell if the reading had been too long. "Oh, no! I'm not one who feels that the time is so important," she answered. Even with her encouragement, I remained nervous about Jim exceeding the limit. But he was a temperamental artist, and I didn't press the issue. When the results of the first round were posted, we saw that our hunch had been right. He had come in first.

Since Purdue is farther from my home (southwest of Marion) than Peru, we got there before David. Jim waited with me to see how David had fared in the FFA contest. Finally, we heard the car horn as David drove up the road. We rushed to the front door, and Jim leapt over the three front porch steps. David ran toward us, arms raised high. "I won! I won!" he shouted. He hugged me and Jim, too, when he heard how well Jim had done. Needless to say, both boys were on Cloud Nine, and I, coach to one and mother to the other, was ecstatic. We made plans for Jim's final rounds at Peru the next day. "I guess you're not going to let a little ol' sophomore put anything over on you, are you, Jim?" I thought to myself.

As Jim rendered "Madman" during the final round, some of the people in the audience were startled at his intensity, especially since this was not a stage production with costumes or properties, but just a boy standing in the classroom. They were no longer just contestants waiting to take their turns or friends and family of participants. They had been transported from Peru High to England, watching Jim actually be the madman, bound in chains and threatening to snap the iron bars of his cell like a twig. The results were announced, and Jim was the state winner in Dramatic Declamation.

The Peru tournament was a qualifying contest for entry in the national meet in Longmont, Colorado, at the end of April. I was thrilled to contemplate the adventure of chaperoning Jim to Longmont and, since coaches at nationals usually served as judges, getting to judge the finest speech students in the nation. On 27 April, cheered on by a flock of Fairmount High boosters who were causing a scene at the Marion depot, Jim and I boarded a train for Chicago. En route, he described for me a memorable send-off the students had given him at the school that morning. Principal DuBois, apparently having forgiven him for punching David Fox, had planned it. The band was out on the front lawn playing, and the cheerleaders led a yell. The loyalty of his peers had so touched him that he cried as he told me about it.

In Chicago, we transferred to the Denver Zephyr, and after twenty-four hours and another transfer in Denver, we found ourselves signing in at Longmont High. The next morning 100 contestants from 24 states, accompanied by 39 coaches, were eager to go at it. I had a heady feeling of good luck because staring out at the world from the front page of the *Longmont Times-Call* was my picture.

I wanted to be carried along on the fearsome mood Jim sustained in his first round, but was distracted because he was going over the ten minutes. The Longmont judge was not as lenient as Mrs. Bedwell. "Young man," she said in her critique, "you do an excellent job with the 'Madman's Story.' But if I were to judge you with another equally good speaker, time would have to be an element in my decision. It might be splitting a hair, but I would have to use that against you." Whether or not Jim subsequently cut his reading I never knew, because I had to judge other contests in later rounds.

That evening, an outdoor western program was given in front of Longmont High's grandstand, with cowboy music, barbershop quartets, a German band, and square dancing. A huge bonfire illuminated the area, but nowhere could I find Jim. I went into the high school auditorium, where there was a dance going on, but he wasn't there. After the program, lists were posted of those who had made the semifinals the next morning. Jim's name was on the list. But where was he when we needed to talk over strategy? I phoned his host's home. The host had loaned Jim a car, and he had gone out on the town. It was probably innocent enough, but I was greatly disturbed that Jim wasn't concentrating on the one reason we had to come to Longmont: to win the contest.

The next day the *Longmont Times-Call* had done it again—this time, *Jim's* picture was on the front page! We had both sent in our pictures with the registration forms, but I have no idea why the newspaper chose our pictures to print. I thought for sure it was a harbinger of good luck. But it was not to be. When the finalists' names were posted, James Dean was not one of them. We learned he had placed sixth. Unfortunately, there were only five finalists in Dramatic Declaration.

To this day I can still see him huddled in his seat during the finals, heartsick that he was out of the running. The first place winner in Dramatic Declaration was Carolyn Parks of Santa Rosa, California. She was only a junior, and the next year she won first place again. Perhaps Jim couldn't have beaten this talented girl, but we both knew that he could have placed higher. In my opinion, goofing off the night before instead of rehearsing kept him out of the top five.

This sobering setback in Longmont turned out to be a crucial lesson for Jim. By teaching him the consequences of not concentrating, it helped him get where he eventually got in New York and Hollywood. By the time he found himself in front of a Warner Bros. camera, he had learned concentration. He wouldn't let anything distract him from his work. It's as if the westward journey to Longmont was just a warm-up for going all the way to the coast.

There were only a few days left in the school year when Jim and I returned from Longmont. He asked my advice on where to go to college. I made several suggestions. Earlham College had an excellent theater department. On a larger scale there were Northwestern and Iowa, both noted for their theater arts programs, but I suspected he had a yen for California. After graduation, that is where he went.

Jim told everybody in town that he planned to enroll at UCLA and take courses in dramatics. No one suspected he would ever make a career out of it. Maybe even he didn't realize it then. But I did tell him before he left that if he would send me a picture of himself from California, I would hang it on the wall in my home room. He had been my prize student—why shouldn't he be on display to inspire future groups of young thespians?

Both of us were involved in the theater that summer. After going to live with his father and stepmother in California, Jim joined the Experimental Workshop wing of the Santa Monica Theater Guild. "I wasn't in time to be cast in any production," he wrote his grandparents in Fairmount, "but my knowledge of the stage and the ability to design and paint sets won me the place of head stage manager for the next production of four one-act plays."

In Nashville, Indiana, the Brown County Playhouse opened for its first season that summer; I was at Indiana University working on my Masters degree in speech. For the premiere show, Dr. Norvelle, chairman of IU's speech department, chose "The Old Soak," a Broadway hit from 1922. I played the part of Matilda, wife of the chronically soused title character. The Playhouse stage was fashioned from an old barn, and the audience sat in folding chairs under a large tent.

The next time I saw Jim was right there at IU. He was visiting Indiana and drove down to see me while I devoted another summer towards my Master's. We strolled around the campus and saw the Memorial Theater and Little Theater. On the Little Theater stage we paused to catch up on the past year's events. Jim was perched up on the prompter's table, and I sat in an adjacent chair. Only the pit and work lights were on as he surveyed the darkened auditorium. Something about the way he looked at the empty seats, and his comments about the thrill of an audience, gave me the feeling that he really was meant to be an actor.

Jim didn't feel his year in college had helped him very much in achieving his theatrical aims. When he wondered aloud about coming to IU, I had a sudden idea. I knew Dr. Norvelle well enough to pop into his office whenever I needed advice or suggestions. So we walked over to his office, and, sure enough, he had a few minutes to talk with Jim.

I could hardly wait to hear what had been said. As we resumed our stroll I pestered Jim for the details. Dr. Norvelle had said he would be glad to welcome him to IU. That much of the interview Jim had liked. But Dr. Norvelle went on to encourage him to complete his education and get a teacher's certificate as a hedge against not making it as an actor. These weren't exactly the words my young friend wanted to hear. He wanted "to get there fast." The Korean War was on, and with "the army breathing down my neck," as he once put it to me, he didn't have time to make any detours as a teacher.

Jim averaged about one visit to Indiana per year after that. He stopped off as he moved across the country to New York in 1951, and he hitchhiked to Fairmount with two friends from New York in 1952. Both of those visits coincided with our annual junior class play, and each time Jim was more than happy to direct rehearsals, attempting to apply the Actors Studio techniques he had learned to my small-town high school students.

Sometimes he and I would talk about his struggles as an aspiring actor. I asked him if I was crazy to want to break into acting in New York myself. He said absolutely not—he knew from the way I taught that I could act as well.

In 1953 I was president of the Indiana Speech Association, an organization formed to promote and improve speech education. In that capacity I attended the Speech Association of America's annual convention in New York at year's end—but I had an ulterior motive for being there. I wanted a chance to see Jim, who was in rehearsals for an important new Broadway play.

Through Actors Equity I got the number of Jim's answering service and left word that I was in town. When he called late that night, he told me about his play, an adaptation of André Gide's *The Immoralist*. It was being produced by the indefatigable little giant of leggy Broadway extravaganzas, Billy Rose, and starred Geraldine Page and Louis Jourdan in the leading roles. He asked me if I wanted to come to the next day's rehearsal at the Ziegfeld Theater. I was floored by such an invitation. Nothing at the convention was as exciting as this!

I went to the theater on the morning of New Year's Eve. During the rehearsal, Jim would slip into the seat behind mine to whisper comments. Once he asked, "Are you learning anything?" Our roles as teacher and student were suddenly reversed. Now it was he who introduced me to new concepts and experiences. It meant a lot to me that he wanted me to learn.

For lunch, Jim, Geraldine Page, and I walked to a nearby delicatessen. It was cold and windy. Geraldine was wearing a cape. As we crossed the street, Jim nestled up to her, and she threw the flying cape around his shoulders.

The Immoralist had been adapted for the stage by the distinguished playwrights Ruth and Augustus Goetz. Late in the afternoon, Ruth Goetz sat down behind me. "I think your student has the soul of a true artist," she reflected. "When we first started rehearsing, I thought he was the most undisciplined boy I had ever seen. He seemed to be absolutely uncontrolled. But as I watched him develop in his role, I realized this young man is one of the most disciplined actors I have ever seen."

It was getting late in the day, and I had to catch my train to Indiana. Jim came over to me again and tried to persuade me to stay until the following Monday to meet his agent. He had told her about me, and now she wanted to see me. But I had commitments at home for the New Year's holiday. Besides, I didn't have enough money to last through the weekend.

The last time I ever saw Jim was in February 1955. He had recently completed his first big picture, *East of Eden*, and the press was saying he was going to be a sensation. *Life* magazine wanted to run a photo essay and assigned photographer Dennis Stock to take pictures of him in the setting of his hometown.

In his previous visits, Jim had always called on me at the school. But the days passed, and not once did he drop by. It seemed like he was ignoring me. I knew it was silly to let his absence bother me, but it kept eating away at my peace of mind.

Finally I could stand it no longer, so I drove over to Jim's grandparents' home to see him. When I got a couple of minutes to talk to him alone, I discovered he was quite preoccupied with the abrupt burden of his newly acquired stardom. "I'm sick of the way all these people follow me around," he grumbled.

"But Jim, that's part of the game. You have to have your public if you want to be in the acting profession. You should be delighted that they want to follow you." I tried to capture the rapport that had been second nature in our friendship.

"I guess the only way is to become a hermit," Jim continued in his small tirade. "That's what I'd like to be—a hermit. Then they couldn't touch me. They're all just a bunch of leeches."

I told him that in the movie business being considerate of persons who are attracted to you is part of being a star. "How do you know I'm a star?" he asked.

"You certainly are getting publicity. *East of Eden* has had a lot of press coverage." Our conversation became philosophical as I tried to remind him of old-fashioned values. He asked me what I meant by all this.

"Well, Jim," I concluded, "don't forget to be kind." Those turned out to be the last words I ever spoke to him.

The *Life* issue with Dennis Stock's photos hit the newsstands the first week of March. Instead of being pleased at the unprecedented national attention focused on Jim and Fairmount, I sank into a week's worth of the blues to think that the photos were taken during the only visit where Jim had failed to come see me.

In retrospect, I am sure that having Dennis Stock with him made a big difference in how relaxed Jim felt around the hometown folks. What would otherwise have been natural and easy interaction between us, if, say, we had been visiting in my classroom, might have been viewed by Jim as embarrassingly provincial in the presence of an outsider like Dennis, who was used to hobnobbing with the likes of Humphrey Bogart.

Furthermore, Jim's confusion and revulsion at the insincerity of Hollywood's star system, into which he had suddenly been thrust, cannot be overemphasized. On the one hand, he hated the lack of privacy that goes with celebrity, as our last conversation showed. On the other hand, he could easily feel slighted if he thought he was not treated with deference. Much later I learned he had been angry at the *Marion Leader-Tribune* on the last visit because of a perceived slight and refused to grant an interview. Fame and public adulation were things that might have taken him years to come to grips with had he lived. I just had the misfortune of last seeing him when he was in this unsettled state.

A month after its New York opening, *East of Eden* was on its way to Indiana. Jim had asked Warner Bros. to allow a special preview in his home county. This Indiana premiere would be a silver lining to the emotional clouds that had shadowed me ever since Jim's visit.

Drysdale Brannon and Ed Camp, editor and general manager, respectively, of the Marion newspapers, had been friends of mine for two decades. Both had keen eyes and ears for anything that would bring media attention to Marion. Joining forces with the manager of the theater, they orchestrated an opening that for Marion was quite a gala event. Dry and Ed suggested that I draw up the guest list. What an honor! Besides many good friends I included all of Jim's relatives that I could locate.

Just after school started on 5 April, I received a telegram from Jim. It read, "Would be honored if you would accept this wire as invitation to attend special screening my new Warner Bros. picture 'East of Eden' at Indiana State Theatre Marion April 5 10:00 AM. Although picture opens April 10 would like you to be one of first persons from Grant County to see it. Sincerely—Your former pupil James Dean."

The telegram sounded more like the public relations office at Warner Bros. than it did like vintage Jim Dean. But I was so touched to receive it that I cried. I managed to scribble a telegram message in reply: "It's almost more than I can take. I am so grateful—Speech class, seniors, your family with a few chosen friends will leave in 15 minutes for Marion. All my love—Adeline Nall."

I was excited as could be to see this movie that was such a triumph for Jim, but for some reason I was nervous, too. My lack of composure didn't go unnoticed. The next day the *Leader-Tribune* carried a gossipy little squib. "There was a question Tuesday," it teased, "as to which person was more nervous at the preview of 'East of Eden' at the Indiana Theater . . . John DeBoo, theater manager . . . or Adeline Nall, first drama teacher for the movie's star, Jim Dean of Fairmount . . . the consensus was that John won the contest . . . even if he did keep it under control better."

The house lights went down, and the drama of John Steinbeck's retelling of the Cain and Abel story in a modern setting unfolded on the screen. Many of the movements of the character Cal Trask—his funny laugh, the quick, jerky, springy walk and actions, and the sudden changes from frivolity to gloom—were all just like Jim used to do. His performance was beyond all that we Hoosiers had expected.

After the movie I stood to share my reactions with the audience. "He was so natural I felt as if I could just reach up and touch him," I extolled. "It's plain to see how well he has absorbed the art of acting."

For the official opening, the *Marion Chronicle-Tribune* carried a huge ad which trumpeted, "OK folks: here he is . . . Grant County's own James Dean in his first motion picture starring role." When you have a hometown celebrity, your advertising campaign can be somewhat different from others around the country.

Xen Harvey, minister of Fairmount Friends Church, couldn't attend but sent this kind note: "You took Jim Dean when no one else believed in him, trained him and took him all over the country as a speech student. I am sure that the work you did with Jim and the faith you had in his ability was the cornerstone of his success." Six months later Xen would preach at Jim's funeral service.

On the morning of Saturday, 1 October 1955, I was working at the desk of the famous Biltmore Hotel in New York. Two months earlier, on a leave of absence from Fairmount High, I had moved to New York to try my hand at acting—largely at Jim's urging. At about 9 AM the phone at the front counter rang. It was the personnel manager. He told me he had just read in the *New York Times* that Jim had been killed in a car crash in California the previous evening.

I remember feeling a chill shoot down my spine as I registered what I had just heard. It was a sensation I had experienced on stage before, and I told students that if you ever felt such a chill, you knew you were really into the part. But I didn't want to be into this part. Jim couldn't be dead, I said to myself, yet dreading that this was not a staged drama but a real-life tragedy. It was unbelievable! My mind went completely blank. Someone soon came to relieve me at the front desk, and I ran down the stairs to confront the *Times*. The bitter truth hit me hard. Jim was gone.

Sadness pervaded the halls back at Fairmount High. "The students feel they knew Jim well, because he spoke before them in convocations whenever he was home and visited many of the classrooms," said the school newspaper. "Because he was a Fairmount graduate, the students felt especially proud when he came back to the school, with his greatness never making them feel small or unimportant."

On 21 November 1955 I went to a staged reading of *Anna Christie* at the Phoenix Theater. I had seen in the *Times* that Geraldine Page would play the title role, and I remembered her fondly from the day I had lunch with her and Jim.

After the show, several people lined up backstage to congratulate Geraldine on her performance. She had brought a special illumination to the role, but that wasn't what I wanted to tell her. I knew she had admired Jim's talent and was very close to him, and I hoped she would remember me. When I got to her, I said, "I'm Adeline Nall from Indiana—Jim Dean's teacher." Tears filled her eyes. With several people in line behind me, it wasn't possible to have any extended conversation. We clasped hands for a few moments and I felt her warmth.

I did not carve out my niche in the American theater or earn the fame that would follow during my years in New York. But with Jim's sudden demise, fate decreed that I should have fame of a different nature once people began seeking his essence through me. Today, video crews record my recollections, school classes visit my home, college students writing research papers ask to interview me, and fans from all over the world track me down and show up on my doorstep. Juggling the demands of their unflagging curiosity has been almost a full-time job throughout the years.

There is a long-standing tension between Fairmount, which will never believe Jim was anything but an ordinary farm boy, and the fans and popular press, who interpret him as a misunderstood rebel, the ultimate in cool, perhaps with a death wish. I often feel caught in the middle of these two camps. To me, he was a great actor who learned a lot in just a few short years and whose remarkable technique was rooted in Hoosier culture. It still humbles me that it was my classroom to which this young genius came to be nurtured.

5

The Man Who Would Be 50: A Memory of James Dean

MRS. GENE NIELSON OWEN

James Dean's former college teacher Gene Owen offered her remembrance of him in this article published in the *Los Angeles Times Calendar* on February 8, 1981, the fiftieth anniversary of his birthday. That evening, ABC-TV aired the first episode of an eight-hour miniseries adaptation of John Steinbeck's novel *East of Eden*. —Ed.

AT SANTA MONICA COLLEGE I was James Dean's teacher and counselor. I met him shortly after he graduated from Fairmount (Ind.) High School, when he came to live with his father in Santa Monica the summer of 1949. He was 18 years old. He had six short years in which to accomplish all that he did.

A typical star-struck lad born in Marion, Ind., and raised in nearby Fairmount, his development at college began slowly. Jimmy (his only name to me) was fascinated by Hollywood and its activities, but his father, who had long lived in [the] Hollywood area and was much less enamored of it, strongly advised him to become a basketball coach. Jimmy was athletic and established a fine record in high school basketball. However, he was just of average height, had to wear glasses for short-sightedness and couldn't see far enough to hit a long basket. But with Indiana love-of-the-game and considerable zeal, he won a letter in the sport and was a delight to watch.

Ah, but it was acting and Hollywood which absorbed him. Again he was impeded by a limitation. His articulation was poor, he mashed his words and he was somewhat difficult to understand. In an interpretation class, someone pointed this out and blamed it on his Hoosier accent. Later, when we were alone in my office, Jimmy protested and removed the upper plate he wore across his hard palate for a dental problem.* Obviously it made some tongue positions difficult for certain sounds. To overcome this articulation problem, we launched a semester-long, extra-hour, oral interpretation of *Hamlet*. I told him that if anything would clear up fuzzy speech it would be the demanding soliloquies of Shakespeare. And so we began, on a one-to-one basis, what was to be a fascinating and revealing study for both of us.

Early I found that Jimmy was not a very good reader, but if complicated parts of the play were explained to him, as "this is what has happened, leading up to this," he would pursue the role of young Hamlet with intensity and originality. Although, as with all beginning actors, he immediately wanted to get into the longest Hamlet soliloquy, "Oh, what a rogue and peasant slave am I," I announced that we would begin at the beginning of the play, and that he would memorize each of Hamlet's soliloquies in turn, building up to that two-page speech he was so eager to attack.

At our next weekly meeting, he had learned Hamlet's poignant opening reply to his mother's remark at his seeming dejection due to his King-father's death. I read the cue for Jimmy and he began: "Seems, Madam, nay, it is. I know not seems." He finished with ". . . I have that within which passeth show . . ." In a dozen lines he had established a deeply disturbed young Hamlet which touched my heart. I had seen the play with every great actor in both England and America in the role, and I had never heard those lines expressed quite so well.

That was the beginning. On we went through the play, with Jimmy devouring every soliloquy, short and long, sharpening his articulation, and along the way developing and defining a vulnerable and troubled Hamlet that was artistry. Finally, Hamlet's dying speech was reached. ". . . The rest is silence." I finished Horatio's response through blurred vision: "Goodnight, sweet prince; and flights of angels sing thee to thy rest."

When James Dean died, I wept again for that young prince, whose rich creative effort had just begun. Multitudes of fans mourned his untimely

---

* When he was a child, James Dean accidentally knocked out his two front teeth while swinging on a trapeze in the barn on his aunt and uncle's farm. —Ed.

death; I grieved for the Hamlet we would never see.

Life ended for Jimmy at the intersection of U.S. 466 and State Highway 41, 19 miles east of Paso Robles at Cholame, population 5 then, and now only 65. The town is surrounded by a landscape of gentle hills and farmland, so like that of Jimmy's youth in Indiana. He and his mechanic were on an isolated road when he opened up his new Porsche preparatory to racing it at Salinas. Unexpectedly, a car appeared,

James Dean and an unidentified actor enjoy a good laugh on the set of *Rebel Without a Cause.*
Warner Bros./Photofest © Warner Bros.

making a left turn into the path of the race car. Swerving to avoid it, Jimmy turned his car sharply, rolling it over.* He died of a broken neck.

I think of Jimmy mostly as a person who laughed often and spontaneously. In a radio-workshop his ready laugh encouraged other performers in their live broadcasts. His response to comedy was so contagious that fellow students urged him to sit in on performances. At our home one evening, he literally fell off his chair and continued laughing on the floor at a remark made by my husband Hal. The guests ended up laughing more at Jimmy sitting helplessly on the floor, than at Hal's quip.

Another memory of Jimmy was his gleeful love of speed, reflected in his driving. He owned several motorbikes in his teen-age years in Fairmount, and drove them "full speed ahead" on country trails and dirt roads.

---

* James Dean's Porsche collided almost head-on with the car driven by Donald Turnupseed, who was beginning a left turn into Dean's lane when the accident happened. —Ed.

However, upon returning to California from New York, en route to a location in Salinas for the shooting of *East of Eden*, he bought his first car, a second-hand MG roadster. He came to the house to take me and my 10-year-old daughter, Barrie, for a ride. He immediately demonstrated the capacity of the car to turn "square corners." The quiet streets of the Pacific Palisades have never heard such squealing of tires.

Fans identified strongly with Jimmy's image of being his own person. He demonstrated this when he decided to leave UCLA, which he attended briefly after transferring from Santa Monica College, to establish his acting career in New York. On a stake of $200 from a perceptive minister-friend in Fairmount, Dean's quest began. He spent his first year in New York at chores in television. Finally, he was before the camera.

Almost immediately, he got a reputation among TV directors of "being difficult." He didn't snap out his lines, but deliberately delayed his response with "thinking" pauses. Some TV directors stopped hiring him because of this, but the thought process which swept across his expressive face became one of his most appealing characteristics.

"Don't be afraid to keep them waiting," was the advice Jimmy gave at a dinner party in our home to actor Richard Shannon. "Directors try to get you to save time, so they get credit for wrapping up a show with record speed. Don't do it! Make 'em wait! One director shouted at me, 'What in the hell are you doing over there by the window, Dean?' I shouted back, 'I'm trying to figure out a motivation for that stupid cross you gave me!'"

For the rest of Dean's brief life, he was to live out his independence and disregard for establishment standards. So solid had his reputation for rebellion become by the time of his death that when national magazine reporters discovered that Santa Monica College, not UCLA, was his major college, they came armed with leading questions: "Was he difficult to teach?" "Was he disruptive in the classroom?" I was so busy answering, "No. No!" that the Jimmy I knew never surfaced.

Hail to you, Jimmy, on the day of what would be your 50th birthday. You mattered while you were here. You made a lot of things easier for young performers who came after you, and through re-runs of your three films on television, you have enriched all of our lives.

6

There Was a Boy . . .

William Bast

Published in 1956, William Bast's book, *James Dean: A Biography*, was the first serious biography of the actor. It became an indispensable resource for succeeding Dean biographers. Bast's first-person account of the last six years of Dean's life—his journey from anonymity to stardom—is written from the vantage point of his close friendship with the actor that began when they were both students attending the University of California at Los Angeles. *Photoplay* magazine serialized a condensed version of Bast's biography in its September, October, and November 1956 issues. "There Was a Boy . . .", the title of Bast's three articles, was probably inspired by the lyrics of Eden Ahbez's song "Nature Boy," which became a hit when Nat King Cole recorded it in 1948, not long before Bast met Dean. The homoerotic overtones of the title and of Bast's articles, which are suffused with a romantic longing for Dean, may not have been apparent to readers in 1956, but were almost certainly intentional. Bast disclosed that he is gay and claimed that he was sexually intimate with Dean in *Surviving James Dean*, the revised edition of his biography, published in 2006. —Ed.

I knew him for such a short time—just six years. But that was all the time Jimmy had left to live

ON SEPTEMBER 30, 1955, the world was informed that the short but incredible career of James Dean had come to a tragic end on a lonely northern California highway. One year prior to that date James Dean was a comparatively obscure actor and was hardly known to the public. Now, almost one year after his death, he stands on the threshold of immortality.

James Dean's life was by all means filled with excitement and turbulence. It is the fascinating tale of a young man who propelled himself violently through a few short years, in search of fulfillment, love, and understanding. It is a legend filled with the profundity and gentleness that was the boy himself.

Jimmy was my closest and most constant friend during the six years before his death. Most of that time we shared the living expenses involved in the struggle to gain recognition in the theatre, and we were seldom out of touch with each other. In my peculiar position of having known him so long and having shared so many experiences with him, I find it hard to comprehend the full significance of what happened to the school chum I came to call my friend. Just three years ago he was just my crazy roommate who, like all the kids we knew, was trying to make a mark for himself. He was known only to a limited group of people and his name meant nothing to the man on the street. Now, there isn't a day that goes by that I don't hear his name on the lips of some stranger passing on the street, that I don't hear stories of how many of his fans are still writing letters of devotion to the Hollywood columnists, that I don't see his picture in the window of some store in a small town, that I don't see his name headlining the double feature at a neighborhood movie house, that I don't feel the strong and memorable impression he made on the people who knew him, worked with him, or admired him. I still find it hard to believe that they are all referring to the same Jimmy Dean I knew so well. Perhaps, I often think, they are referring to the Jimmy Dean they came to know only briefly, only partially, on the screen, on a sound stage, or in a rehearsal hall. And perhaps, I wonder, it isn't the same Jimmy Dean at all.

In 1949, the Theatre Arts Department of the University of California at Los Angeles was a busy place. Stage productions were at a peak. The acting, it seemed, had never been so fine. World War II had ended a few years before and the departmental heads were enthusiastically utilizing the more mature talents of the many recently returned GIs. Unfortunately, the younger students who hadn't participated in the war, and who hadn't as yet matured, were being sidestepped. The gap of years between the regular students and those on the GI Bill created cliques within the drama department.

In this atmosphere, the slouched, unimpressive figure of James Dean drew no attention. The sandy-haired boy, completely withdrawn behind his horned-rimmed glasses, was a new student who had just transferred from Santa Monica City College. His major was Law and his minor was Theatre Arts. He had been pledged to Sigma Nu fraternity and was "living in" near the campus. He had some knowledge of motion picture projectors and, with the help of the campus employment agency, was able to bear the financial burden of fraternity and college life by acting as projectionist for classes using visual education. His clothes were few and modest, and his manner was mild and unnoticeable. He did not mingle freely and, as a result, did not become a part of any particular clique. It was impossible for him to make friends with these people who were so impressed with their own self-importance, as he later put it. So he withdrew from the society of the Theatre Arts Department and tried very hard to fit in with his fraternity brothers. Jimmy was not happy at UCLA.

The department was doing a production of "Macbeth." Somehow, Jimmy had been cast in the role of young *Prince Malcolm*. One night, during a late rehearsal, I was introduced to him in the Green Room— which, in theatre circles, is a gathering place backstage, sort of a reception room where actors get together before or after a show. As I recall, Jimmy made no impression on me at all. He was quiet, almost sullen, and seemed to resent the fact that he had been asked to work in the show.

When "Macbeth" opened and started its two-week run, the reviews in *Spotlight*, the Theatre Arts Department's newspaper, were not kind. As for Jimmy's performance, it said only, "*Malcolm* (James Dean) failed to show any growth, and would have made a hollow king." It was true that Jimmy's acting was not good. His Indiana twang made Shakespeare's immortal lines sound more like they had been written by Mark Twain and were being delivered by Herb Shriner.* It was obvious that James Dean was not one of UCLA's outstanding acting talents. As a matter of fact, it seemed that it would have been wise for some close friend to advise him to forget

---

* Radio and TV humorist Herb Shriner (1918–1970) was known for his folksy monologues, which were usually about his home state of Indiana. He was often compared to Will Rogers. —Ed.

James Dean played Malcolm in a UCLA Theatre Arts Department production of Shakespeare's *Macbeth*. From left: Paul McKim, James Wasson, and James Dean.
Photofest

any theatrical aspirations. No, indeed, James Dean just didn't have it—not then, at any rate.

Among some of the more dedicated actors on campus, there was a feeling that UCLA was not providing enough in the way of acting guidance and training. The regular classes were considered totally inadequate, in the light of the upsurge of a "new school" of acting that was emanating from far-off New York. I had briefly met James Whitmore, who had just won an Academy Award nomination for his acting in "Battleground." Noting the dissatisfaction on campus, it occurred to me that Whitmore, a graduate of the Actor's Wing in New York, might be able to solve our problem.

Whitmore, himself, had found that Hollywood was completely lacking any type of acting school in which he could continue his studies and was, as a result, greatly interested in such a project. He suggested that I invite eight or nine people from UCLA whom I felt would be seriously interested in pursuing their drama studies more intensely. He insisted, however, that we were not to consider him a teacher, but merely someone who was there to guide us and learn with us. As carefully as possible, I selected the students whom I felt would most appreciate and benefit from this advance training.

During the UCLA run of "Macbeth," a Hollywood agent saw Jimmy and approached him with the proposition of representing him.* The idea

---

* James Dean's first agent, Isabel Draesemer, never saw him perform in *Macbeth*. Dean was introduced to her by another one of her clients, James Bellah, who was Dean's pledge brother at UCLA. —Ed.

of an honest-to-goodness agent, regardless of how unimportant he was, believing he had a potential, so flattered Jimmy's ego that he decided it was an actor's life for him from then on. This new dedication, coupled with the fact that Jimmy and I had become good friends, convinced me that he should be invited to join the Whitmore class.

Jimmy completed the group of nine. We began to meet several times a week in a room above the Brentwood Country Mart. The first meeting found us all tense and anxious. An air of quiet excitement hung over the group. We were about to hear the magic words that would reveal to us the secret of acting. It didn't take Whitmore long to dispel all that nonsense and plunge us headlong into serious and intense study. So, listening attentively, and reading faithfully from our copies of Stanislavsky's *An Actor Prepares*, we waited for something to happen.

About this time, Jimmy confided to me that he was finding it increasingly difficult to tolerate his fraternity brothers. It seems they suffered from the slightly dated and provincial attitude that there was definitely something wrong with anyone who was interested in the theatre. Considering Jimmy's hyper-sensitivity to the subject, it was no wonder that he was rubbed the wrong way by the jibes of a fraternity brother one night during a stag party. Jimmy took the snide remarks as an insult and the affair ended in a fistfight. It was with mutual sentiments that Jimmy and his fraternity brothers parted company. Since both of us were then in search of living quarters, we decided to combine forces and find a place together.

Eventually, we found a three-room apartment which had been constructed on top of an apartment building near the beach in Santa Monica. It was artfully done—a place, we felt sure, where budding young artists could grow. Although it was too expensive for our limited budgets, we were unable to resist its charm, and so we moved in.

"The Penthouse," as we called it, was the scene of Jimmy's intellectual awakening. Living in such close quarters, it didn't take me long to discover that my friend was greatly lacking in plain old everyday knowledge. It was amazing how little he actually knew about art, literature, music, history, politics, and the like. I think it was the excitement over the Whitmore acting group and his new agent that made Jimmy want to start learning more about everything. He wanted to be completely prepared for anything life might present. He had often expressed a desire to grow intellectually, to broaden his scope of understanding, but had never actually started on an all-out campaign.

We would read, sometimes to each other, then we'd discuss what we had read with other members of the group or with friends. Sometimes, with our girls, we would read from Stanislavsky, Henry Miller, or Kenneth Patchen. Jimmy tried very hard to perfect his diction by reading aloud from various plays, acting out every part himself. He kept a dictionary at hand to look up any word he didn't know.

So it went for several months.

Those were the lean months. Jimmy had no income, and I was barely able to scrape together enough for food and rent from a part-time job as an usher at CBS. Somehow we managed, in spite of the fact that our combined resources rarely exceeded $30 a week. Each month, when rent time rolled around, there was a scramble to gather together the few dollars that people owed to either of us and to borrow whatever we were lacking.

When we first moved in, the electricity had not been turned on and we were forced to use candlelight for several nights. However, the effect was so pleasing, we decided to dedicate at least one night a week exclusively to the use of candles. Thus we had the inspirational effect of candlelight and, at the same time, saved on our electricity. Sometimes on "Lightless Fridays," a group of us would lounge around the apartment, listening to classical music and learning to identify the selections. The mood was warm and friendly, and there was always the feeling that something important was happening to every one of us.

Food was very often a serious problem. I remember once, shortly after we had paid the rent and we were both flat broke, sitting down to a dinner consisting of dry oatmeal mixed to taste with mayonnaise or jam. One successful scheme we used to keep from starving was to invite several friends up for dinner, then pool the few pennies we all had, and prepare rice or spaghetti dishes. Times were hard, but fortunately we were able to keep laughing—at least most of the time.

However, Jimmy was subject to frequent periods of depression and would slip off into a silent mood at least once a day. During these periods, I found it impossible to communicate with him, and I soon learned to ignore him or avoid him completely. Sometimes he would sit quietly thinking for hours; other times he would read or draw, making only occasional grunting noises when a question was put to him. Very often he would take long walks late at night, mostly to the amusement pier in Venice, a few miles away, where he would watch and study the people. But, invariably, he would snap to after a few hours and never acknowledge the fact that he had caused anyone concern or offense. Jimmy's moods ended as abruptly as they started.

It must have been an act of God that made my mother decide to pay me a visit about this time. When she arrived from the East, we invited her to stay with us in our modest quarters. Her arrival was like a ray of heavenly sunlight. As soon as she saw our barren larder, she headed for the local supermarket where she bought everything in sight. She cooked sumptuous meals for us and saw to it that the apartment was clean.

Jimmy liked Mother at first, but soon he became uncomfortable. He was always embarrassed when people did things for him. He disliked the feeling of obligation that goes with the acceptance of a favor. He knew he was in no position to repay her with tokens of kindness or appreciation. He hadn't matured enough to realize that her payment came in the form of seeing him well-fed, clean, and happy.

One rainy day, Mother decided to stay in, clean the apartment, and fix a fine dinner for that evening. Jimmy also remained in the apartment the whole day. When I returned from work that evening, I found Mother in tears. Jimmy, it seems, had spent the entire day working sullenly on a mobile he was constructing. He had not spoken to her all day and he'd only grunted in response to her questions and attempts at conversation. It was all very upsetting for Mother, who didn't even know what the crazy thing was Jimmy had been building. She had not experienced his moods before and was under the impression that she had offended him. Jimmy didn't seem to feel remiss, nor did he apologize. Instead, he slumped into his chair at dinner and shoveled her carefully prepared meal into his mouth with boorish abandon. During the remainder of her visit, Mother avoided staying in the apartment alone with Jimmy.

When she left, we drove her to the depot. While she was checking her luggage, Jimmy disappeared for a few moments. When he returned, he presented her with a box of candy, for Mother's Day, which he had bought with his last dollar. Included with the gift was a photograph of himself which she had admired. He had signed the picture: "To my second mother—Love, Jimmy." Knowing that his mother had died when Jimmy was only nine, Mother was deeply touched, although somewhat confused by his seemingly sudden switch in attitude. It wasn't until a few years later, when I explained that it was simply Jimmy's nature to be moody and that he had really liked her very much, that she understood. Neither of us knew then that she was to be the first in a series of "second mothers" for Jimmy.

Up to that point, the only job Jimmy's agent had been able to get him was a television commercial in which he danced around a jukebox with a girl and another boy. He got $30 for that first professional job, and didn't talk much about it. The money didn't last long and, after several weeks of waiting and hoping for something else to come up, Jimmy took the situation into his own hands. He went back to the studio where the TV commercial had been filmed and asked if there was anything else on the fire in which they could use him. He read for them and was assigned a role in a full-length television feature. He was to play young John, the Baptist,* in an Easter film called, "Hill Number One."

About a week before he was to start the film, while in the Whitmore class, Jimmy suddenly seemed to get the message—the "golden secret"— which, I feel, started him on the road to becoming a true artist. Jimmy and I were doing an impromptu scene, set up by Whitmore. Secretly, Whitmore told me I was to play a jeweler who had repaired a watch Jimmy had brought in and I had since learned that the watch was stolen. It was my job to detain Jimmy until the police could arrive. Jimmy was told, without my knowledge, that he must get the watch at any cost and catch a train out of town in ten minutes in order to avoid being caught by the police.

We tried the scene several times, but it was flat and uninteresting. Each time, either I gave the watch to Jimmy, or he left without it, neither of us putting up much of a fight. Whitmore finally stopped us and talked about the singleness of purpose in a scene such as this and how one could achieve that attitude through intense concentration. He spoke of a type of concentration we had never imagined possible. His explanation seemed to hit Jimmy right where it was supposed to.

---

* Dean played the role of John the Apostle in "Hill Number One." —Ed.

We tried the scene again. At first, the noticeable change that came over Jimmy was almost frightening. With grim determination he set himself to the desperate task of getting the watch. Nothing else in the world mattered to him. The more he insisted, the more I refused. The more demanding and insulting he became, the more emphatic I became in my refusal. The fist fight that resulted had to be broken up by Whitmore and the others.

When it was over, Jimmy and I were both amazed, and we felt refreshed, as though we had just been given a shock treatment. From that moment on, everything he heard, everything he read, everything he did seemed to have new meaning for Jimmy. Until then he had *understood* everything, but now he was able to apply it. For the first time, acting made sense to him.

Jimmy carried this newly acquired understanding with him into the filming of "Hill Number One." When the picture was released on television Easter weekend, the reviews of his acting were filled with praise. His agent had contacted several producers and asked them to watch the film. They were impressed with Jimmy, but, as is so often the case, that was as far as it went. Jimmy had hoped for more than praise and he was terribly disappointed when the jobs didn't start rolling in. After all, he insisted, shouldn't an actor who has proven his worth be employed? He still had to learn that this is one of the most heartbreaking aspects of the acting profession.

Before long, Jimmy was out of money again and needed a job. I was still working as an usher at CBS in Hollywood and, after much persuasion, I was able to convince my boss to hire Jimmy. Although he had taught sports at a small military academy near Los Angeles one summer, Jimmy found it impossible to conform to the regimentation of an usher's life. He resented wearing the uniform—the "monkey suit," as he called it—and refused to take the directives of the head ushers with appropriate seriousness. As a result, unprecedented as it was at CBS, Jimmy was released after one short week, during which he had managed to provoke the wrath of every one of his superiors. After that, I just smiled blandly when they would sneeringly refer to him as "your friend, Dean." Having committed the unpardonable sin of introducing the corruptive influence of James Dean into the orderly, well-organized pattern of the CBS machine, I had to remain constantly on guard, lest I make another dreadful mistake. Jimmy accepted his dubious notoriety with devilish glee and gracefully lapsed into the status of being unemployed.

He began dating Beverly Wills, daughter of the noted comedienne, Joan Davis. I had introduced them at CBS, where Beverly was acting on the radio show, *Junior Miss*. They soon found that they had a great deal in common, mostly their love for sports, and started spending much time together. Beverly introduced Jimmy to the world of young Hollywood, where he found new interests and excitement in meeting and getting to know up-and-coming stars like Debbie Reynolds. However, there was one serious flaw in the relationship, Beverly's mother. Jimmy's lack of social grace and his candid frankness unnerved Joan Davis so much, there was constant friction between them. It soon became apparent that Jimmy's relationship with Beverly was destined to be short-lived.

Going with a girl like Beverly made money more important to Jimmy. He was forced to take a part-time job parking cars in the lot next to CBS. Since his hours were irregular and flexible, he was able to search for acting jobs on the side. Most of the CBS radio directors and producers parked their cars in the lot, and Jimmy soon got to know them. Eventually, one or two of them discovered he was an actor and decided to give him a chance on their shows. He did a few bit parts on several dramatic radio shows and even got a walk-on in one Alan Young TV show. He also arranged for interviews at the major studios, through a friend who had done some bit roles in movies, and managed to snare bit parts in "Sailor Beware," starring Martin and Lewis[*]; "Has Anybody Seen my Gal?" starring Rock Hudson; and "Fixed Bayonets!," starring Richard Basehart.

In spite of the jobs he seemed to be getting, Jimmy was dissatisfied and impatient. The Whitmore classes had adjourned for the summer, he had broken off with Beverly, and he was becoming increasingly restless. His personal life didn't seem to have any order. He had recently met several established actors and directors, such as David Wayne and Budd Boetticher, whom he found intellectually stimulating. Their strong influence on Jimmy prompted him to delve even deeper into the realms of the abstract and the esoteric. What he found made him eager for more and greater sources of truth and wisdom. Hollywood didn't hold the answer for him and he knew it. He wanted to soar, but he didn't know how.

---

[*] Dean Martin and Jerry Lewis.—Ed.

A great boredom set in. Through some of his newly acquired friends, Jimmy was introduced to the plush life on [the] Sunset Strip. He had little to do but loll around the pool at the Sunset Plaza where some friends of his were staying and make clever talk with the "Strip Set."*

It would be completely wrong, however, to say that Jimmy did not grow during this period. He was an attentive listener and had a tenacious memory. He picked up a great deal from the people with whom he was associating, and he made it a point to study in detail any subjects they discussed which were unfamiliar to him. In an amazingly short time he became well-versed in the subjects of modern art, contemporary literature, and progressive classical music. But, the shallow veneer of Strip life eventually wore thin, and his boredom grew and grew. There was more than this waiting for James Dean and, somewhere in the back of his mind, he knew it. That was the reason he made the decision that was to change the pattern of his life so radically.

Clockwise from top: Bill Bast, James Dean, Debbie Reynolds, Beverly Wills, and Lugene Sanders at Wills's eighteenth birthday party on August 5, 1951.
Courtesy of Paul Huson

Next month, Bill Bast will tell of Jimmy Dean's move to New York, of his intense struggle to find acting jobs, the new, influential people he met, and the little-known facts behind the events leading up to the biggest break of his career.

*Part II of "There Was a Boy" in
October Photoplay
On Sale September 6*

---

* The most important of Dean's Sunset Strip friends was Rogers Brackett, an account executive for a major advertising agency with show business connections. Dean lived with Brackett, who was gay, in Los Angeles and New York. See chapter 14, "Life With Rogers: James Dean's Gay Mentor Tells All." —Ed.

7

There Was a Boy . . . Part II

WILLIAM BAST

Photoplay published the second part of Bill Bast's account of the last six years of his friend James Dean's life in their October 1956 issue. —Ed.

It was during his early years in New York that Jimmy Dean found some of the answers to the self-doubts that tortured him. It was there that he started on the road that led to fame — and tragedy

WHAT HAS GONE BEFORE: In the first installment of this absorbing story, Bill Bast, who was James Dean's close friend and roommate, told how Jimmy came to UCLA and became seriously interested in acting. He showed that Jimmy was a restless, searching youth, eager to improve his mind as well as his acting ability, and revealed how Jimmy's early association with Hollywood made him decide to move to New York to pursue his acting career. But, even though Jimmy made progress, the threat of loneliness was ever-present, connecting the past with the present, sowing the seeds of his personal tragedy.

Late in 1951, equipped with only a few radio, TV, and movie credits, his meager belongings, a pocketful of change, and a short list of future contacts, James Dean slipped quietly out of Hollywood and headed for New

York. He had barely started his career, and had only begun to develop his mind. But his mental appetite had been whetted, and he was off to a strange new place where he felt he would find much nourishment for both his career and his mind.

The first few months in New York were mildly successful ones for Jimmy. He utilized his handful of contacts and, through them, was able to secure several bit parts on radio and TV programs. Jane Deacy, then of the Louis Shurr office, became his new agent, and in a realistic way she made his future look promising. Slowly, Jimmy found new friends among the actors who hung out at Cromwell's drugstore in the RCA Building and at Walgreen's in the Paramount Building. Financially, things seemed to be in order, to the extent that he even bought himself a new suit, the first in years. Like his new suit, New York fit Jimmy very well. He was glad he had come East.

I had been offered a job in New York, but upon my arrival, I found it had been filled. Since Jimmy was the only person I really knew in town, I contacted him immediately. Over coffee at Walgreen's he briefed me on the New York situation. We stopped by Louis Shurr's office, where he introduced me and kidded with the agents and office girls. Then he made a quick phone call and we left to meet someone very important.

Jimmy had met Elizabeth (Dizzy) Sheridan a month or so before, and was completely captivated by her warmth, charm, and alert mind. Dizzy, the daughter of pianist Frank Sheridan, was a dancer—or, that is, she aspired to be a dancer. Alone in New York, she had taken a part-time job as an usherette at the Paris motion-picture theatre, and was existing solely on her small salary. Somehow, she scraped together enough to study dance, her first love, and on rare occasions to go horseback riding, her second love. Dizzy had a wonderful sense of humor and was easy to know. It was understandable that she and Jimmy got on so well.

That afternoon, Dizzy, Jimmy and I took a walk through the zoo in Central Park, where it was decided that Jimmy and I should find an apartment to share. Jimmy had been staying temporarily with a friend and had been thinking of moving.

Apartment-hunting in New York, as any New Yorker will attest, is a fatiguing and complex chore. After less than one hour of looking, we gave up the struggle and compromised by taking a single room with bath at the

Iroquois Hotel on 44th Street. The quarters were cramped, the rent was too high for our pocketbooks, but it put an end to a search that could have gone on for weeks.

Several members of Jimmy's special circle of friends were living next-door at New York's famous old theatrical hotel, the Algonquin. Most of the people in the group were well established in the theater or TV, and their acceptance of him was very gratifying to Jimmy. Prominent in the group was composer Alec Wilder, who wrote "Songs Were Made to Sing While We're Young." Alec had gained Jimmy's respect and admiration and was responsible for slowly reactivating his interest in music and literature. Gradually, Jimmy began looking to both Alec Wilder and Rogers Brackett, another member of the group in whom he had a great deal of confidence, for advice and guidance.

The summer months crept on us and with them came the annual theatre and television disease, the summer hiatus. It is the time when many of the regular TV shows go off the air and the theatre becomes less active, leading actors to either sweat out hungrily the muggy New York summer, or to take jobs in summer stock companies out of town. Jimmy decided not to try stock, but to remain in town and take his chances at getting work.

As the weeks went by and the work failed to materialize, Jimmy became more and more depressed. Summer in New York can be that way when you are not eating regularly. In an effort to offer him some relief, Rogers Brackett invited Jimmy for a weekend at the home of some friends who lived up the Hudson River. The thought of a refreshing weekend in the country appealed to Jimmy, and he accepted gratefully.

That was the first of several weekends he was to spend at the home of Lemuel and Shirley Ayers. Lem Ayers was a rising young Broadway producer, then working on plans for a fall production. Jimmy liked the Ayerses and, during his visits, he would spend his time puttering in their garden and listening attentively to the inside conversations about Lem's forthcoming production of N. Richard Nash's "See the Jaguar." As time went on, the Ayerses came to like the quiet young man who came for occasional weekends. They were not aware, however, that somewhere in the back of Jimmy's mind there glimmered a hope, a dream for the near future, which very much involved them.

The weekends in the country made the days between in the city more bearable, but in spite of the relief, Jimmy's despondency over the lack of work continued. He tried to spend his free time reading and studying. Even in his darkest hours he remained very active, meeting and getting to know new people, finding new and unusual things around New York, and discovering a little more about himself each day.

New York seemed to stimulate Jimmy's mind to a point where it was more alert than it had ever been. One day, during a period when he had been reading a lot of modern literature, he asked me to suggest something in the classic vein to read. He seemed especially interested in Greek philosophy and drama, so I suggested he start with Plato. That night he turned up with a volume of Plato's works and began reading a section on Democratic Education. After an hour or so, he closed the book and offered to treat me to a cooling beer at a bar nearby. I knew Jimmy was an expert bluff artist, especially when he was in a corner, but I had never seen as vivid an example as I was about to get.

As chance had it, we ran into a friend of Jimmy's at the bar. The man was a writer for *Life* magazine and was apparently well-educated. In less than five minutes, Jimmy had him deep in a discussion of Plato's philosophy. Although he had read a mere twenty pages or so, Jimmy talked with the authority and enthusiasm of an expert. I am confident that when that man left the bar, he was thoroughly convinced Jimmy was a scholar of Platonic philosophy. However, I had discovered the secret of Jimmy's little game: let the other fellow do most of the talking and you will learn what he thinks you already know.

One day in the office of his agent, Jane Deacy, Jimmy met an intense young actress named Chris White. Over coffee he learned that Chris had written a scene with which she wanted to audition for the famous Actors Studio. They agreed to do the scene together and began rehearsing immediately. Often they would come up to our hotel room and, using my objective criticism and direction, they shaped the scene with loving care and caution.

By the time audition day rolled around, Jimmy and Chris had the scene beautifully molded. Frightened and nervous, they took their humble offering before what they considered the mighty High Priests of their craft. As I recall, they were two of the fifteen—out of the hundred and fifty who auditioned—who were accepted into the Studio. Jimmy was then reputedly the youngest member of The Actors Studio. He was twenty-one, and he belonged.

Late in August, the Ayerses invited Jimmy on a ten-day boat cruise to Cape Cod, stipulating that he was to act as a member of the crew. Jimmy had long been interested in boats and eagerly snatched at the opportunity to learn more about them. And, indeed, by the time he returned he had absorbed most of the basic rudiments of boating and navigation. For weeks thereafter he talked enthusiastically of boats and boating, but he avoided discussing the social aspects of the trip.

Out of a growing awareness that he needed people and had to exist in a world full of them, Jimmy had begun to develop a knack for compliment-ing their egos. This he accomplished by taking a deep and sincere interest in the things they liked most. By the time he took the boat trip, he had matured enough to realize that—in order to win the favor of the others on board—being friendly and genial, yet remaining true to his own character, was a simpler and wiser way to enjoy himself and to be enjoyed. When he returned, it was obvious that all had gone well and that he was due to hear more from the Ayerses.

Just before Jimmy left on the boat trip, we decided to give up our hotel room and accept the kind offer of a girl with whom we had studied at UCLA. So, in Jimmy's absence, I moved our possessions into the large apartment the girl had been subletting and was turning over to us for the remainder of the summer. The arrangement seemed ideal, but we had hardly moved in when the people from whom the girl had been subletting returned from Europe and demanded their apartment. Helpless, we were forced to find a smaller place uptown.

The night before we moved out of the large apartment we were partic-ularly broke, due to the advance-rent payment we had to make on the new place. Jimmy, Dizzy Sheridan and I had between us less than a dollar on which to eat. So, like scavengers, we took all the leftovers from the refriger-ator and made with them a soupy stew into which we dumped a half-pack-age of stale spaghetti. As we sat eating the mess, not one of us said a word.

All in all, that summer in New York was a torturous one. I had secured a low-paying job at CBS, but Jimmy was still suffering from the pressures of being unemployed. We had taken to pooling the little I had, the very little Dizzy had, and the occasional few dollars Jimmy picked up by taking jobs on TV quiz programs on which they would throw pies in his face. Still there was barely enough to manage the bare necessities, such as food, rent, and cigarettes. It was no wonder, then, that about four o'clock one morning over coffee in a hamburger joint, Jimmy, Dizzy and I came to the conclusion that we'd had it and decided to get away from it all. After a moment's further consideration, we packed a suitcase, gathered together the ten dollars we had between us (it was payday) and headed for the bus terminal, where we boarded a bus for New Jersey. Once there, we got off and hitchhiked the rest of the way to Indiana, where we visited the farm on which Jimmy had been raised.

The two wholesome weeks we spent on the farm brought the kind of relief our tired souls required. The Winslows, Jimmy's aunt and uncle, opened their home and their hearts to us. Mom, as Jimmy called his aunt Ortense, saw to it that we had plenty of delicious home-cooked food, and Marcus, his uncle, gave us the run of their serenely beautiful and efficiently clean, modern farm.

After all the years of seeing Jimmy alone and without a family, it was a wonderful thing to watch him touch once again the gentle roots of his early years. He discussed the farm and its problems at great length with Marcus, learning from his uncle the complications of farming in our present economic structure. Marcus seemed to beam with silent pride as Jimmy listened attentively, seeing in him for the first time a matured and developed young man who had, only a few short years before, left his household a mere boy.

Ortense was touched by Jimmy's compassion and concern over her increased pain from the arthritis that had begun to gnaw at her hands. To Dizzy and me, Jimmy expressed a strong desire to offer the Winslows, someday when he made his fortune, the opportunity to move to a drier climate where Mom's arthritis would not pain her as much.

Jimmy also spent many hours talking to and explaining things to little Markie, who is his cousin and the youngest of the Winslow children. Whenever he detected traces of his own character in Markie, Jimmy would expand with a secret pride and fond remembrance of his own boyhood days in Fairmont. He tried, in the brief time allotted, to encourage little Markie in all that he felt was important.

Jimmy took us to his old high school where, with a bit of his ego showing and the flourish of his own special brand of bravado, he took over for a few days. His dramatics teacher was more than pleased to see him, and turned her classroom over to the three of us. Jimmy spoke on the art of acting, Dizzy demonstrated modern dance techniques, and I got in my quarter's worth by talking on TV directing and writing. None of us was really enough of a master of his craft to warrant this display of unabashed authoritative lecturing, but it was greatly rewarding to us to have those youngsters pay such close attention and regard us with so much awe. After a year of trying in vain to convince the New York professional world of our capabilities, it was a wonderful boost to have so many people accept us as masters of all we were trying to accomplish.

After too short a time, a call from New York for Jimmy brought our bliss to an end. We had slept well, been fed well, and had been accepted; we could ask for no more. Three grateful, refreshed young people were driven to the highway and deposited there to hitch a ride eight hundred miles back to the city, back to the task of finding their ways.

Our return brought with it great excitement. Shortly after we got back, Jimmy was asked to read for a leading role in Lem Ayers' fall production of "See the Jaguar." Jimmy had little hopes of getting the part, since another actor, who had been reading it during the auditions for the show's backers, was almost set for the role. But it was the dream he'd had in the back of his mind all these months, and he was determined to do his best to make it come true.

His nerves were showing the night he went to read. He had no clean shirt, so I lent him one of mine. He was unable to manipulate his hands to tie his tie, so Dizzy took over for him. We agreed to meet him at the Paris Theatre after the audition. I went to the theater with Dizzy and tried to concentrate on a movie while Dizzy worked out her hours. By the time she got off, Jimmy had not arrived, so we walked in the direction of the place where he had gone to read. We were halfway there when we saw him walking down the street toward us. We stopped, afraid to know the answer, and tried to discern from his expression what had happened. His face told

Arthur Kennedy (left) and
James Dean in the play
See the Jaguar, which ran
for only five performances
in December 1952.
Photofest

the story. No one said a word; we just stood there laughing and crying like three crazy, grateful little kids. After many intense months of clinging to a slippery handful of faith and hope, the littlest part of a dream come true can be an exulting experience.

All of Jimmy's hopes were riding on that play. It was the first time he had been afforded the opportunity to work closely with top professional talent, and he meant to absorb as much as possible. Immediately, he allowed himself to fall under the complete influence of his director and the star, Arthur Kennedy, and carefully followed their advice. The only difficulty he encountered was in trying to sing the folk song Alec Wilder had composed for the play. Jimmy was practically tone-deaf and had to be coached every evening by Dizzy or me, until at last he almost had it. During the four weeks of rehearsal, every thought he had, every conscious moment was devoted to his role. He was determined to make the most of this, his first experience on Broadway.

Opening night in New York was especially tense for him. The out-of-town reviews of the play had been bad. Most of the critics panned the script, but they had been favorable toward Jimmy. His concern on opening night was, therefore not as much for his singular success as it was for the over-all success of the show.

Anyone who saw his performance can attest that Jimmy did beautifully. He played a young boy whose mother had locked him in a smokehouse for many years in order to spare him from the cruelty of the outside world, and his portrayal was filled with sensitivity and pathos. The whole audience seemed to respond sympathetically and intensely to Jimmy's acting. Backstage after the show, his dressing room was crowded with friends and well-wishers. Jimmy's heart was filled with pride and gratitude. He had done well and he knew it.

The New York critics, however, did not like the script, even though they praised the acting highly, and the play closed after only five performances. However, as a result of his favorable notices, job offers started coming in for Jimmy almost immediately. The recognition and ensuing activity took the edge off his disappointment over the show's closing. He was assigned several TV roles and got calls from the motion picture studios. One such call was an offer to fly to Hollywood to make a screen test. Jimmy declined, insisting that a test could be made in New York, if they really wanted to test him. He had no desire to return to Hollywood, even to make a screen test. Ultimately the idea for the test was dropped, and Jimmy continued doing television work and auditioning for Broadway plays.

Several months went by without any major incidents. Jimmy continued to work, a little more regularly now, and studied even more intensely. He moved back to the Iroquois where he spent much of his time reading and learning to play the recorder, a flute-like instrument. Often he would sit in the window of his small room, piping out the sad strains of the folk tunes Alec Wilder had written for him to practice. Dizzy had gone off to dance at some place on Trinidad, and although Jimmy dated frequently, there was for a time no one to take her place. His anxieties were less than they had been during the past two years, but still he appeared to be waiting for something.

Shortly after I left New York to write for a TV show in Hollywood, Jimmy was cast in "The Immoralist." I later learned from him that all had gone well in the early stages of rehearsal, but that the experience had ended badly. The out-of-town opening had proved Jimmy to be a highlight, but the show to be in need of rewriting and redirecting. A new director was brought in to take over and Jimmy's part was drastically cut down. He had always shown a son-like attachment to any director in whom he had faith and confidence, but, either deliberately or unintentionally, this new director abused his confidence. As Jimmy related it, the director turned on him one day when he asked for guidance in his role. The experience so shattered Jimmy that he left the rehearsal for several hours.

Because of the cutting of his part and his disillusionment by the director, Jimmy gave his quitting notice the night the show opened in New York. In spite of the behind-the-scenes difficulties, the reviews of the show praised Jimmy's performance highly. Jimmy settled down to fill out his contract and, once again, waited.

There is a point in the lives of men destined to be famous when Fate steps in and offers the perfect circumstance or vehicle to help them on their way to greatness. Once this opportunity has been afforded him, however, a man must assume the responsibility for following through and proving his worth. As James Dean prepared for his moment, another man—an active man with a power and greatness of his own—was preparing another of his many projects, a screenplay which he planned to direct. The lives of the two men had crossed occasionally, but briefly. To Elia Kazan, James Dean was an actor, a member of the Actors Studio, another actor to be watched and catalogued for future reference. To James Dean, Elia Kazan was a master of his craft, a champion of his school, a maker of his destiny.

It would have been normal procedure for any good agent to submit Jimmy's name for a role in Elia Kazan's production of "East of Eden." But Jane Deacy isn't merely any good agent. She is an intelligent woman with an acute eye for just the right thing, and when she read the screenplay for "Eden," she knew it was just the right thing for her client, James Dean. So, in her own style (which shall remain a professional secret), she gave Fate a gentle nudge and nursed the situation, convincing all concerned that "Eden" was the perfect vehicle for Jimmy's talent. Kazan was familiar with

Jimmy's work at the Studio and had been impressed by him in the "The Immoralist." He liked Jimmy and was soon convinced that he would fit the role of *Cal* in his forthcoming production at Warner Bros. Jimmy was signed to do the part, then Fate stepped back to let him do the rest.

As a boy, Jimmy had had several motorcycles. In the years away from his home in Indiana, he grew to miss the thrill, the sweet sensation of whizzing along the roads and highways. As his pocketbook fattened, he found he had enough to warrant the purchase of such a luxury. New York is hardly a perfect place for motorcycling, but any place will do in a pinch, and Jimmy was in a pinch. He buzzed around town from appointment to appointment, storing the cycle in the entrance-way of his apartment building when he wasn't using it. When people pointed fingers and called him "Brando-imitator," he didn't hear them. He knew what his motorcycle meant to him—they didn't.

But, as it is so often with things you love, you get hurt by them. The week he was signed to do the role in "Eden," Jimmy took a bad spill on the motorcycle, scraping himself seriously. Kazan had several strong words to say about the incident and concluded by instructing Jimmy to "stay off that motorcycle." So, instead of cycling across the country to Hollywood as he had planned, Jimmy reluctantly stored the motorcycle, packed a few things, boarded a plane, and bade farewell to New York, the city he had come to love for all it had given him.

As he sat on the plane, watching the land between New York and Indiana beneath him, his dreams of the future were strange and unnerving. But they were not nearly as fantastic as the reality into which he was speeding.

Next month, Bill Bast tells about Jimmy Dean's triumphant return to Hollywood, of his determination to live his own life on his own terms, of the people and events that had a strong influence on him, and the real truth behind the rumors that: he is still alive; or he committed suicide.

Concluding "There Was a Boy" in
November Photoplay
On Sale October 4

8

---◆---

There Was a Boy . . . Part III

WILLIAM BAST

Photoplay published the final installment of Bill Bast's story of the last six years of his friend James Dean's life in their November 1956 issue. —Ed.

"Death," Jimmy Dean said, "is the only thing I respect. It's the only thing that has any dignity." Strange words for a brilliantly successful young boy to utter, but the moods that evoked the words were stranger still. Before you read this third and final installment of Jimmy's life story, we suggest you read the editorial piece on this same page, finish the story, and then reach your own conclusions. Did Jimmy Dean have a premonition of death? Or was he obsessed with thoughts of dying?

WHEN I LEFT NEW YORK to return to Hollywood late in 1953, James Dean presented me with a collection of short stories by André Maurois. The inscription read, "To Bill: While in the aura of metaphysical whoo-haaas, ebb away your displeasures on this. May flights of harpies escort your winged trip of vengeance." Since leaving Hollywood almost two years previously, we had both come to look westward with a vengeful eye. My turn to revisit the city of make-believe came first, and in a manner of speaking Jimmy envied me for it. Several months later, when his turn finally did come, Jimmy collected for himself a whole armada of screaming harpies to help protect him from the individuality-debasing influences of the publicity capital of the world.

Jimmy felt deeply that he, like many other enterprising young hopefuls, had suffered too many indignities while running the gamut of the accepted methods of breaking into movies. Too many doors had been slammed in his face. Too many casting directors and agents had treated him with disinterest and disrespect. Too many unpleasant people in positions of influence and authority had demanded of him too much flattering attention. Two years before he had not been wise enough, aware enough, confident enough, to know better than to play along with their degrading games. He had been a hopeful, naïve boy who believed in those foolish prescribed methods for getting ahead in movieland. But he had grown a good deal in New York, and he returned to Hollywood much taller and much stronger.

He arrived in Hollywood in an enviable position. He was there to take a starring role in Elia Kazan's newest and most promising masterpiece, "East of Eden." His only desire was to make the picture and return to New York and the Broadway stage. He didn't need Hollywood and, perhaps, Hollywood didn't need him. But he had found out one very important thing about himself which gave him the advantage: He was a competent and talented actor and had, as far as Hollywood was concerned, a saleable commodity. If they were willing to pay for his best, he was willing to sell it.

But *talent* was all he intended to sell them. He had established a rigid set of standards and values, most of them adhering passionately to individual integrity and basic honesty. He was determined to have no truck with the dishonest nonsense so prevalent in glamorville. There would be no great publicity campaign for James Dean, no star-studded crown to wear as a false laurel wreath, no blind acceptance of shallow standards, no falling into the trap of believing that stardom brought with it fulfillment and completion. His aim had been for a long time higher than Hollywood and he didn't mean to lose sight of his ultimate goal: to be a fine and accomplished artist. He knew he had a long way to go and a lot to learn before his day of arrival.

The level of Jimmy's standards had been set so high that the constant application of them would have been nearly impossible for anyone. He must have known he would falter and stumble, make mistakes, but he would pick himself up again and learn from those mistakes. His ideals were right and worth fighting for, and he was dedicated to that proposition. And along the way, he would not permit Hollywood to bury him in the permanent grave of stagnation as it had done to so many before him. Hollywood would have to accept him on his terms, or not accept him at all. About this he was adamant.

Early on the morning after he arrived, he came to my apartment and announced that he was taking me with him to the desert where he intended to get a suntan, as per Kazan's instructions. Within an hour we were on the road to my favorite desert retreat, Borrego Springs, about one hundred miles beyond Palm Springs.

Understandably, Jimmy was excited about doing his first movie, especially since it was to be directed by Kazan, for whom he had a great deal of admiration. He told me of the plans for the film and chuckled at one point over a comment Kazan had made. It was the director's feeling that the role Jimmy was to play could very well put him in the running for an Oscar in the next year's Academy Awards race.

In our younger, more critical days we had often joked about the Academy of Motion Picture Arts and Sciences and their yearly Oscar presentations as being chauvinistic, heavily influenced by studio prejudices and politics, too often ruled by saccharine sentimentality, and generally lacking the objectivity so necessary in criticizing art. It was natural, therefore, for me to ask him what his reaction would be to winning an Oscar. He admitted that he was not really concerned with the matter, but that he felt he would only win the award as a result of giving a performance that was too obviously good to be ignored. In that instance, he would accept it for exactly what it was—an honest prize won in a fair game.

But he felt strongly that they would dislike him so intensely in Hollywood that they would never vote him an Oscar, unless public opinion, for some reason or other, were to force them. Noting the Academy's decision to grant him an award next March due to the strong public reaction to their neglect of him in last year's race, I can only marvel, though sadly, at Jimmy's astute perception.*

---

* The Academy of Motion Picture Arts and Sciences did not give James Dean a posthumous Academy Award. —Ed

Immediately upon our return from the desert we went to Famous Artists, the agency that was to handle Jimmy's affairs on the West Coast. Bearded and shabbily dressed, we were led into Dick Clayton's office, where Jimmy met for the first time the young agent who was to become his friend and advisor. Jimmy had had over a week to mull and brood about the Hollywood situation, so Dick, being his first contact with the town that was a potential threat to him, got the full brunt of his defensive attitude. As best he could, Dick, a charming guy with an easy manner for handling temperaments, tried to show Jimmy that he was on his side, but Jimmy did nothing to ease the strain. After about an hour of discussing the plans and procedures for starting the film, we left Dick, who must have felt he surely had a problem on his hands. Outside Jimmy remarked, "Nice guy. Guess I've got him worried." It was his intention not to give Dick Clayton trouble, but slowly to invest in him his trust and confidence. He was not going to make it easy for anyone. This time they would all have to earn his confidence.

For a while it was as though Hollywood was a new place for Jimmy. There were few, if any, old friends to look up, and no ties to re-establish. He floundered a bit at first, meeting new people and adjusting to a new life. With the help of Dick Clayton he found a bright red MG, a great improvement over the 1937 car he had owned several years before, and gradually began finding his way around movietown again. He started dating some of the young starlets he met. Karen Sharpe, whom he had known before, and Terry Moore went out with him frequently.

Jimmy spread out and enjoyed himself for a few weeks, as if he were ridding himself in as short a time as possible of a natural desire to sop up some of the old, and once unattainable, superficial glitter of Hollywood. By the time filming started on "Eden," he had had it and seemed ready to settle down to the serious task of creating a character.

It was during the filming of "Eden" that Jimmy met Pier Angeli. The strong fascination they had for one another developed into something fine and beautiful. Jimmy sought her out and tried to spend much of his time with her. When I asked him about her, he replied that she was a sensitive girl with a wonderful mind, someone who understood him and with whom he could be at ease, but, he insisted, it did not go beyond that. "Methinks thou dost protest too much" kept running through my mind as he denied the press's implications that there was something more serious than just friendship behind their relationship.

There was something in his manner of underplaying it that indicated a deeper attachment than he would have cared to have had known. About most matters he could be flip, but about matters of consequence he was often shy and guarded. It is a known fact that Pier's mother openly objected to the relationship and made things very difficult for them. They say that when Pier married Vic Damone, Jimmy stood across from the church and cried. I do not know this to be true, but if he loved her, it is something he might have done. When Jimmy loved, he loved completely, and when he lost the object of his love, he suffered completely.

As soon as "Eden" was completed, word started to seep out that Warner Bros. had a great new star in James Dean. The studio screenings and audience previews were drawing the best reactions, and it was becoming a matter of great excitement around town. Hollywood was abuzz with the name of James Dean. Jimmy's anxieties mounted as the release date on the picture drew near. Consequently, he snatched at a chance to return to New York to do a live TV broadcast and to study. He seemed to feel an ominous foreboding of the sensational fame that was to come out of his first picture, and was hoping to maintain a degree of objective sensibility and rationality about the situation by getting away from Hollywood, a place where one can too easily begin to believe what one hears about oneself.

In New York Jimmy touched once again the fibers of those things that were really important to him. He studied acting, singing, dancing, drums, doing occasional roles on TV. Due to contract stipulations, he was not free to leave Hollywood for Broadway, as he had wished, but was being held for more picture work. So, while in New York, he absorbed enough of the creative atmosphere from which he, as an artist, had emerged to last him through the trying days ahead in Hollywood. He was determined, at least, to return to New York after each picture to reaffirm himself. It was with reluctance again that he left the big city to return for the preparations of his next film, "Rebel Without a Cause."

Jimmy had long been a motorcycle enthusiast, having owned several different bikes in Indiana as a boy. He had a new motorcycle in Hollywood and was proud of it, since it was by far the finest he had ever owned. He was a good cyclist and took pride in demonstrating the fact. Often he could be seen roaring down [the] Sunset Strip in the direction of Googie's, a favorite restaurant with the young film actors.

Kazan and Warner Bros. had warned him to stay off the bike while making a picture. The studio's investment was too great to risk an accident which might delay filming for weeks or months at a tremendous cost. But they had no jurisdiction over him when he was not filming, so he mounted his motorcycle and breezed through town, enjoying the sensation of liberation that every cyclist must know and appreciate.

Ella Logan, a close friend of Kazan's who often visited him at work, developed a fear of Jimmy's craze for motorcycling soon after they met on the set of "Eden." Ella is not only a remarkable performer and fascinating personality, but also a woman intensely interested in creative young people. She was immediately drawn to Jimmy and admired in him all the dynamic force and sensitive beauty that so many others had misinterpreted as arrogance and an anti-social attitude. It was at one of the impromptu parties at her home in Brentwood, where she often invited young people like Jimmy, Sammy Davis, Jr., [and] Marlon Brando, that she asked Brando to speak to Jimmy about the motorcycle. As he was leaving, Brando advised Jimmy to give up the motorcycle, pointing out that an actor with half a face was no actor at all. Jimmy seemed to shrug the incident off. Ella feared the battle was lost, but a short time later Jimmy informed her that he had disposed of the bike because it was too dangerous. For a time, Ella and most of his close friends were relieved.

Then, just prior to the making of "Rebel," he bought his first real sports car, a German-built Porsche. He took it to Palm Springs one weekend and entered the road races, winning first place in the amateur class the first day, and third place in the professional class the second day. It was the first time he had ever raced a car and he brought his trophies home to Hollywood and displayed them with enthusiasm. It was apparent that sports cars were going to replace motorcycles in his life.

It was at this point that most of Jimmy's friends realized that to make him give up sports cars would be as futile as making him give up motorcycles had been. There would soon be something else, equally dangerous, he would find to take the place of the thrill he got from defying death in a racing car.

For a long time Jimmy had been addicted to the ecstatic pleasure he derived from the frenzy of speed and the emotional excitement of taunting death. Although he had a normal degree of the fear of dying, he intellectualized that in death there was great dignity and nobility. He reasoned that death was ultimate and undeniable Truth. It was, he claimed, the only thing he completely respected. And he, like the bullfighter he wished someday to be, seemed to have a morbid fascination for the things he feared the most. There was nothing any of his friends could ever have done to change his attitude.

During the filming of "Rebel," Jimmy slipped into a different way of life. Perhaps it was the essence of the role he was to play, or the mental unrest of the more complex characters of the movie's story that made him want to re-experience the sensations of being lost, unwanted, and different from the norm. Or, perhaps, it was not so much a matter of study and research, but more a definite and strong feeling he had that he, too, belonged partly to that portion of humanity that is lost, alone, and confused. In either case, as he once put it to Ella Logan, "I like you, Ella. You're good. But, you know, I like bad people, too. I guess that's because I'm so damn curious to know what makes them bad."

By "bad" I don't think he meant precisely "evil." People with odd viewpoints and strange modes of existence always intrigued him. It was probably more in the sense of "different" or "unusual" that he used the word "bad," but at some point during his early Quaker background, he must have learned to associate "bad" with those actions not conforming to the normal and accepted patterns of conduct.

He met and befriended Maila Nurmi, famous for her *Vampira* role on TV. Maila is a compassionate girl who understood him and tried to help him where she could. Their relationship, contrary to unfortunate rumor, was strictly one of friendship and intellectual rapport. With Maila and several of their mutual friends Jimmy started what has been dubbed "the night watch." In the cool damp hours of early morning, life in Hollywood, as in any other place, assumes a weird but enticing perspective. The world becomes a place where lonely and frightened souls can be free and secure, having shut out the terrifying life of daytime. It is a place where misery is understood, but forgotten, where sorrow is inherent, but ignored. It is an

Elizabeth Taylor was James Dean's confidant while they filmed *Giant*.
She became inconsolable after he was killed in an auto accident.
Warner Bros./Photofest © Warner Bros.

easier place to live, if you are afraid, or if you do not belong. From this
place, then, was bred the spirit of the character Jimmy was creating in
"Rebel Without a Cause."

By the time the filming of "Rebel" was finished, Jimmy was already
steeped in preparations for George Stevens' next film, "Giant." He had
come to know Stevens and the other people in the office as a result of
hanging around during his off-hours at Warners. One day, after reading
the "Giant" screenplay which Stevens had given him, Jimmy confided to
Stevens that he would like to play the part of *Jett Rink*. He was surprised to
learn that he had actually been considered for the role. As Stevens tells it,
"Jimmy seemed amazed that we wanted him for the part and didn't seem

to expect it." When Stevens asked if he felt he could handle the age change from eighteen to fifty, Jimmy affirmed that he was sure he could do it well. He was assigned to do the role and began to learn how to be a Texan.

As he was with most people, Jimmy was inconsistent in his attitude toward Elizabeth Taylor when they first met shortly before the start of "Giant." The day they were introduced Jimmy was charming, even to the point of taking Liz for a ride in his new Porsche. His whole approach was contrary to everything she had been braced to expect from him. She went away thinking people were crazy for calling him an anti-social oddball. The next time she saw him she approached him in her usual friendly manner, expecting from him the same warm reaction she got the first day. Instead, she was surprised when Jimmy glared at her over the upper rim of his glasses, muttered something to himself, and strode off as though he hadn't seen her. As would anyone, she took this as a personal affront. It was not until they were in Texas on location that she succeeded in finding out the truth about the mystery of Jimmy's behavior.

At dinner in a Texas country club one night, Liz found herself seated at the table alone with Jimmy. After a long, deadly, unbearable pause, she turned to him and pointedly stated, "You don't like me, do you?" Jimmy began to chuckle. "I like that," he replied. The simple directness of her challenge had the kind of honesty he appreciated. For the rest of the evening they talked in a free and easy way and, for the first time since they had met, Jimmy let Liz pass through the tightly guarded protective shell he often put up around himself. After that, Liz stopped taking offense at what he did and stopped feeling hurt when he was moody around her. She had discovered that his moods and actions were simply a part of his complex nature and were not meant to be taken personally by those who were unfortunate enough to be around at the time.

Sanford Roth, the still photographer on "Giant," is an internationally respected artist, having done photographic essays on many of the world's most famous artists and intellects. As he slipped around the set getting shots of the cast, he noticed that Jimmy kept on him the same suspicious, wary eye he kept on Warner Bros.' publicity people. Studying Jimmy at close range, Sandy began to see in him the same qualities he had come to know in so many of the other artists with whom he had worked.

Finally Sandy approached Jimmy and informed him that he would like to be his friend. In plain terms Sandy explained that he did not need Jimmy for anything, that he was, in his own right, an artist of some repute, and a man of sufficient means. He made it very clear that he wanted to be a friend solely because he admired Jimmy's talent and respected his way of thinking. Once again the directness of the approach so appealed to Jimmy that he responded almost immediately. It was not long before both Sandy and his wife came to occupy a prominent position in Jimmy's life.

When Jimmy discovered in the Roths a source of intellectual stimulation and growth, he developed a great spiritual need for them; when he discovered in them a source of love and comradeship as well, he developed a great psychological need for them. The Roths are people in their middle years, but their lives are so filled with work and growth that they have and probably will always have a perpetual youth about them. They understood Jimmy's insatiable curiosity and desire for knowledge and they offered him what they had. He began spending much time with them, dropping in at their home, raiding the refrigerator, playing with Luis, their Siamese cat, and discussing things, all sorts of things, with Sandy and Beulah, who have an abundance of enthusiasm for everything worthwhile. The pattern of the "second mothers" was repeating itself, and little by little he came to regard them as a family.

The work on "Giant" was coming to a close. Jimmy was once again thinking of the future. There was another road race at Salinas. There was time to make a trip back to New York before starting on "Somebody Up There Likes Me" at Metro [Metro-Goldwyn-Mayer]. There were thoughts on his mind of a long-delayed voyage to Europe, of another Broadway play, of all the studying he wanted to do before he could become a director or a writer, of the possibilities of a production company of his own. So many things, and so little time. It seemed to be the story of his life.

A few weeks before the finish of "Giant" Liz Taylor went out and bought Jimmy a tiny Siamese kitten. She had noticed how exceptionally well he got on with the Roths' unusual Siamese cat, Luis, and how well Luis got on with Jimmy, and she wanted to do something nice for Jimmy. She presented it to him in her dressing room on the set and watched as Jimmy, speechless with gratitude, fondled the little creature.

In the days that followed Jimmy grew to love little Marcus, as he dubbed him. Here for the first time in many years he had a being he could love and be loved by, with less of a risk of losing that love. He was attentive to the point of driving home from the studio at lunch to feed Marcus and be with him for a while. He even began getting in at more reasonable hours to be able to spend more time with the pet he loved so much. He rigged a long cord with a knot at the end which hung from the two-story ceiling of his rustic living room, and sat by the hour chuckling at his little friend as the kitten would smack the knot with his terrible little paw, stalk it like a lion stalking its prey, cling to it and swing like a miniature feline *Tarzan*, and be thrown in a tumble to the floor, where he would shake his dazed little head and prepare for another attack. For all the amusement and affection Marcus gave Jimmy, Jimmy, in turn, gave Marcus his love and attention.

It was a shock to the Roths when Jimmy announced, a few days after the finish of "Giant," that he had given Marcus away. When they asked him why, he replied that he was too concerned for his friend and realized that he led such a strange and unpredictable life that some night he might just never come home again. "Then," he asked, "what would happen to Marcus?" Less than a week after he gave Marcus away, Jimmy died near Paso Robles, California, never to return home again.

Jimmy is gone now, and I miss him. All of his friends miss him. Millions of his admirers and fans, who came to know him through motion pictures, miss him. But there is no need for me to eulogize him, to sing out praises to him. There is no need to extol his virtues, and no need to hide his errors. He was here with us for a while, but now he is gone. Let us be content to have known him, if even for so short a time. Let his art be his memorial. Let his immortality be the tribute to his life. Let the silent love of those who knew him be a lasting symbol of the beauty of his soul.

In his "Divine Comedy" the great classic poet Dante said, "Sorrow remarries us to God." I am content to know that Jimmy is at peace in the consummation of a marriage that, it seems to me, took place the day he was born.

THE END

YOU'LL SEE: James Dean in "Giant," a George Stevens Production for Warner Bros.

9

---◆---

The Great White Way

JOHN GILMORE

John Gilmore's scabrous recollections of his friendship with James Dean contrast starkly with the gauzy romantic portrait of the actor presented by William Bast. Like Bast, Gilmore is one of only three men who openly admitted to having been sexually intimate with James Dean. The handsome seventeen-year-old actor was eating breakfast in a Manhattan drugstore one morning in May 1953 when Dean seemingly stumbled across its threshold and into his life. Curious about the book on bullfighting he saw Gilmore reading, Dean sat down next to him and began leafing through it. It was the beginning of what Gilmore calls a sporadic but intense friendship. They shared interests in art, bullfighting, motorcycles, and an off-kilter view of the world tinged with black humor.

"Eventually I was to feel as though I were mother, brother, lover to him," Gilmore later wrote in *The Real James Dean*, a memoir of his friendship with Dean, published in 1975.

In *Laid Bare: A Memoir of Wrecked Lives and the Hollywood Death Trip* (1997), Gilmore writes about his encounters not only with James Dean, but with a veritable who's who of pop culture, including Brigitte Bardot, Lenny Bruce, William S. Burroughs, Jane Fonda, Dennis Hopper, Janis Joplin, Jayne Mansfield, Steve McQueen, Hank Williams, and Ed Wood Jr.

"The Great White Way" is the first of two chapters in *Laid Bare* that Gilmore devoted to his memories of Dean. —Ed.

I REMEMBER LOOKING AT JAMES DEAN one day when he and I had been hanging around in New York—he was standing in the rain with his head tipped back and water running down his face. He reminded me of the famous circus clown, Emmett Kelly. Dean's eyes had the same look as the clown's: not funny or cheerful, more a sort of distant craziness, a controlled kind of craziness that kept you from knowing what he was thinking.

The first time I saw Dean he looked like a small scarecrow. I was at the counter in a drugstore at 47th and Broadway when he shambled in behind a guy I knew from Hollywood. Dean lurched into the place as though he'd tripped on the door sill and was struggling for balance. With that shock of hair standing out like straw, his hands jammed into the pockets of baggy trousers, and a checkered jacket that hung on him big and had leather patches sewn around the cuffs, Dean seemed like a burlesque character. He was all hunched down into himself, squinting through his brown-framed glasses.

The other guy, Ray Curry, introduced us, but Jimmy hung too far back for a handshake, so I nodded. He said nothing, just stood there staring suspiciously and bending slightly forward as though from a stomach ache. I was also wearing glasses, and he asked if I was near-sighted or far-sighted. I told him I was far-sighted. "You're lucky," he said, sitting on a stool. He glanced at what I'd ordered and asked the waitress to bring him the same: orange juice, coffee, an English muffin. Curry told her he'd have that also, then went to make phone calls with a big safety pin. You could stick the point into a mouthpiece, touch the clasp to the nickel or dime slot, and presto—a dial tone. Not every pay phone fooled so easily, but the drugstore and a booth in the Museum of Modern Art never failed to plug through free of charge.

While waiting for the juice, Jimmy twirled the stool between us, wanting to say something important. "Eyes can be a drag," he said. He'd been in a Broadway play, lost his glasses and had trouble seeing the other actors if they "got out of reach." He had seen them "only as shapes" and couldn't see how they were looking at him.

I asked him how he had managed to play it, and he said he had related to the scene in his mind, as opposed to "what the hams were doing on the stage." I asked him what the play was, and he said it was "a shit-fucker with

Arthur Kennedy."* He didn't say anything else about it, which I figured meant it had been a rotten experience.

Leaning closer, he eyed the book I had open on the counter, Barnaby Conrad's *Matador*. "Why are you reading a book about bullfighting?" he asked. I told him I liked it. Had I read Hemingway's *Death in the Afternoon*? he wanted to know. "Now that's a fucking book about bullfighting," he said. Of course I'd read it, I told him. In fact, I had a copy at my apartment. He asked where I lived and I said, "Around the corner on 48th off Eighth."

"What've you got," he asked, "a room? You got to come here to eat?"

I said, "No, there's a kitchen—part of one main room, and a bedroom."

"What about a bathroom?" he asked. "You got one in the hall?"

"It's in the apartment," I said. "A shower—no tub, you know."

"It's better to take a shower," he said, laughing, "or you start playing with your dick . . . So, no shit," he continued, "What's it cost?" I told him what I paid on a weekly basis, and he asked, "You live there by yourself?"

"Right now," I said and Jimmy nodded, logging in the information. When he asked to take a look at the Conrad book, I said, "It's a novel," and he said he knew it was fiction. He knew the book. I slid it down the counter and he picked it up. He held the book open in one hand. He hunched over the pages, touching the paper like someone reading Braille. His lips moved quickly, and he'd glance off as if remembering something or mouthing lines.

That was how the friendship began: without wanting to know if I'd finished reading the book, he asked to borrow it. I remember the way he was holding it and looking at me with his mouth slightly moving with whatever thoughts were spinning in his head.

There would come a time when we'd talk about other books—Arthur Rimbaud's *A Season in Hell* and Garcia Lorca's plays. I loaned Jimmy my

---

* Arthur Kennedy and Constance Ford starred in N. Richard Nash's play *See the Jaguar*, which ran from December 3 to December 6, 1952, at the Cort Theatre in New York. James Dean played the role of Wally Wilkins, a backcountry teenager whose mother kept him locked in an icehouse to protect him from the cruelties of the world outside. —Ed.

copy of *The Psychology of Interpersonal Relations*, and when we tried discuss-ing the book, I could tell he hadn't read it. I tricked him on it; he didn't say anything at first, but later told me he hadn't had time, finally confessing that he read "slow." He said, "It takes me a while to get the gist of the whole thing." It was because he thought in "circles," he said, grinning.

I'd soon find out about his reading disability. Eager to talk about books, he'd absorb what was said, taking it in and quite consciously making it his own. An amazing trick, his sponging whatever you knew about a subject, kind of shaking it around with what he'd learned elsewhere and piecing together a rather original, persuasive presentation.

It took him a long time to actually read pages. He thought in pictures, not in words. Reading was an excruciating chore, and though he'd profess to be an avid reader—a "cosmolite," as he once put it—he rarely cracked a book. And yet he could evolve a spontaneous performance from what he'd heard and made his own.

In acting, Dean had to "swallow the script," as he put it, "take it into the stomach and fart it out." Without digesting the words, he'd mumble and stumble and say he was figuring out "motivations" and character—all of which was a ruse, of course, to hide the reading problem. He had to have the full play inside himself before he could relate to any of the parts. This would later create some serious problems for Jimmy, as his work became spotty, a collection of ticks and mannerisms that seemed to be jumping out of the picture. You'd be watching him pop through a series of bits like corn on a hot pan, and you wouldn't be taking in the character. At moments he'd appear as an isolated figure in a river of rush-hour traffic. "He'll have to control the idiosyncratic impulses," a television director said, "or go for a one-man show."

The 47th Street drugstore provided thick pats of butter with its muf-fins, and Jimmy helped himself to all the butter on his plate as well as Cur-ry's, heaping it on the muffin, which he ate with one hand, sucking each finger clean afterwards. He'd gone down to Tijuana from L.A., he said, to see the bullfights, and the American matador Sidney Franklin had given him a cape during the filming of a movie there.

"Why did he give it to you?" I asked. Jimmy said he'd mentioned a par-ticular matador by name and used the correct Spanish pronunciation, which

is what had earned him the cape. I said I'd seen that bullfighter gored less
than a year before, not fatally, but bad enough to put him out of the ring.

"He was probably high as a kite," Jimmy said, and slid the book back
to me. He asked if I'd seen the horn go into the matador, and I said it all
happened so fast I didn't actually see the horn sticking him. But he was on
the ground in a second, and the bull was going for him.

I talked to Curry a few minutes after Jimmy walked out, hands in his
pockets again, a cigarette dangling from his lips. Curry said they had met
working as extras on a picture on the coast, and that Jimmy was a hot
actor now. I could see Jimmy through the window, waiting near the curb,
his head craned back as he looked up at the building. "He's an oddball,"
Curry said. "We're going to smoke some reefers with this spade drummer
he knows . . ." When Curry joined him on the sidewalk, Jimmy glanced
back and gave a little nod, holding up two fingers. I didn't know what he
meant by that.

The drugstore wasn't a popular theatrical hangout like Cromwell's
Pharmacy a few blocks away, but was right in the heart of the "the Great
White Way." An acting school and dance studio were nearby, and performers ran in and out swapping news, grabbing lunch or coffee. The play
Jimmy had worked in, *See the Jaguar*, had closed after six performances,
but gained him a rush of television work. One actress from the drugstore
said he'd been "the best thing in a bad play," but was "an asshole in every
other way it's possible to be."

When I saw him again he was drinking coffee and dunking a Baby
Ruth candy bar in the cup. He had a small cloth bag of dance togs from a
class he'd taken with Eartha Kitt. I said I'd met her in L.A. at the home of
Alfredo de la Vega when she was doing the Broadway revue *New Faces of
1952*. Jimmy said, "Shucks, I know that old queen. He wanted to suck my
cock." Grinning, he said, "He must've wanted to suck yours."

Jimmy learned I'd bought an old Norton motorcycle and began talking
about his high school days in Indiana, how he'd built a bike, then started
putting together a hot-rod. But he'd gone to L.A., and he said, "I should've
come straight here instead of getting groped by everyone out there."

Once we went to a 42nd Street movie theater to see *A Place in the Sun*,
and I slept through the last part the second time through. When I woke,

Jimmy was staring at the screen, missing nothing, his jaw muscles working as he chewed popcorn and Milk Duds, mixing them together. Other times he'd stuff his mouth with more than he could chew comfortably, and he'd gag and spit it out. A couple of times he flexed his lower jaw to loosen the bridge of his three false teeth.

His eyes were bloodshot as we left the theater, and he didn't say much on the walk to Seventh Avenue. Then he began talking about Montgomery Clift's performance, and how Clift had managed to keep his work consistent even though we knew it was "all busted up" by the continuity of a movie. But it was "pure," and Jimmy brought up a particular piece of sculpture at the museum that he considered "perfect," with open ends, the same as Clift's acting in the George Stevens movie.

In a cafeteria near Broadway, we used the men's room before getting in line and Jimmy laughed about some holes in the wall between the urinal and toilet. He asked if I knew what the holes were for. I said I had a fair idea, and he said, "Do you know how to tell a sissy by his eyes?" I said I didn't know. He said, "Because he's got highballs!" I grinned, but I didn't really get the joke. I'd never heard it before and I've never heard it since, so I suspected it was something he'd made up on the spot, clowning around—even throwing in a little dance step that had nothing to do with what he was saying.

Jimmy squinted at the holes in the partition and touched them. He said they had been drilled, not cut into the divider with a knife or some other tool. "Someone's come in here and drilled these holes!" he announced. Had somebody brought a brace and bit into the john, he wondered, sat there drilling holes with his pants down around his ankles as a cover in case someone came in? It seemed to matter very much to Jimmy how the thing had been done.

The all-night cafeteria was hot and stuffy, and Jimmy drank coffee and smoked one cigarette after the other, lighting each new one from the butt of what he'd puffed down to his fingers. He hadn't told me where he was staying, even though I'd asked, and after a couple of these cafeteria sessions, he told me about "the flake and the chick," a situation he'd extricated himself from as quickly as possible. He said they were baggage—"over-freight," is how he put it—that he couldn't "drag any further." He'd met the guy at UCLA drama school though the guy had switched over to writing since then. They had roomed together on the Coast, and then the guy followed him to New York, Jimmy said, where the chick he'd known hooked up with them. He said if one of them should die or "kill themselves," he'd be stuck with carrying the other farther than he wanted to. Laughing, he asked if I'd seen dead bodies in my travels, and I said only my grandmother in the coffin. He wanted to know what the coffin had looked like, and I said I couldn't remember exactly except the rails were shiny like the handlebars on my bicycle, and a different color than the casket. I asked him why he wanted to know, and he dropped the subject.

I didn't know what his intentions were or why he'd ask things like that. I only knew he wanted to be the "most important actor in New York." He'd lean toward me and tap his finger on the cafeteria table and say, "I'm going to be the most important actor in town."

Another time in the cafeteria I said that getting pulled into the Army could blow a pretty serious hole in someone's career. I knew a little about trying to get into Special Services, being an actor and doing shows in the service, but Jimmy said one could beat the draft by claiming to have bisexual tendencies, "which includes having homosexual tendencies," he said, but one had to be careful about being branded a queer. The Selective Service wasn't dumb, he said, pointing out that by telling them you were a bisexual they'd think you were trying to hide the real facts from them. "It's like saying you've got only a little bit of leprosy," he said. He hadn't been drafted yet because he was below 1-A due to his eyesight, but he was above 4-F because he wasn't blind.

"They're not going to make you prove it by asking you to suck someone's dick," he said.

On our way out he flirted with a woman at the cash register. He told some joke I didn't hear, and they were both laughing. Then, some time later in the drug store on 47th, he approached the waitress with the same playfulness, and suddenly she called him a jerk for acting up. It was as though she'd knocked the air out of him, and the brief incident bothered him a lot longer than it should have. He seemed to carry it around, a kind of nagging confusion he was working into some unnecessary grudge.

In Cromwell's he described the cartoon of a man in a small box who didn't like the world. He said it was the same as "an emotional prison" that few could escape. You had to "close up" and pull back in order to discover the truth about something, he said.

Jimmy also seemed to inhabit his own world, yet gathered me into that same world as though into a conspiracy against an "outside" he perceived better than I did. If you weren't paying attention, he could take you in without your knowing it. Eartha Kitt and I talked later about Jimmy's knack for pulling people into tightly episodic, one-on-one relationships that had a way of running disconcertingly, if not disturbingly, deep. He had few pretensions and seemed to demand that you join him to form some single purpose.

Maybe that's what intrigued me most about him. Eartha said she couldn't remember going through any sort of "figuring out" of how he'd climbed into her life, or whether she liked him or not. "He was just suddenly there," she said. "I felt he'd always been there—one of the strangest friendships I've experienced . . ."

I'd learn later that the intense, sporadic friendships Jimmy imposed upon certain people would be like replenishing rest stops—emotional banks from which he'd make withdrawals during bad times. Then he'd retreat to his box, maybe sticking his head out and making faces at the world.

Jimmy had his share of detractors, those who'd say, "Oh, shit, here comes that little bastard . . . Let's get out of here before he sees us." Of course, a couple years later these same people would rally around as his closest buddies, with tales to unspool like the ball on a runaway kite.

I'd met a girl named Miriam Conley who lived at the Barbizon hotel for women. For a few weeks I'd been taking her on my motorcycle for modeling jobs, and a couple of times we had lunch in Central Park. We were walking my bike along the trail on the Fifth Avenue side one day and saw Jimmy on a bench with another actor, Martin Landau. They were sitting at opposite ends of the bench, having some sort of argument. Jimmy was eating peanuts and had a camera strapped around his neck. He said he was taking pictures of the monkey—I thought he was kidding Landau, who looked angry.

As we talked, Jimmy tossed peanuts at Miriam, throwing basketball shots to sink them down the front of her low-cut blouse. She laughed, caught some and threw them back. Jimmy thought that was great fun, and giggled while Landau looked resentful and kept urging Jimmy to leave. He stood up, tried to pull Jimmy by the arm, but Jimmy said "No," mouthing the word exaggeratedly and repeating it, rolling his eyes and acting silly.

Disgusted, Landau said, "Okay, okay," and walked away. Though they were friends, Jimmy shook his head and looked at us, saying, "Who was *that* guy? Some flake, man!"

Miriam had never met Jimmy, but she'd seen him on television and knew about the Broadway play and a radio interview where he'd talked about Aztec Indians. He wasn't at all shy about her flirting, and began to joke around, jumping up on the benches and almost falling. Pulling his jacket over his face to look headless, he ran lopsidedly up the path, calling out, "Ichabod Crane! Ichabod Crane! I want you!"

He collided with a woman and nearly knocked her over, scattering her packages on the ground. She was angry for a moment, but had to laugh as Jimmy, still headless, scuttled around picking them up for her.

The monkey house was a metal building with a tunnel through the center, bordered by cages. Jimmy was serious about taking pictures of the monkeys, and one in particular, a dark, noisy monkey that kept reaching frantically through the bars. Miriam said she'd heard of monkeys biting, and Jimmy gave the monkey a peanut, breaking the shell open with his own teeth. He wanted Miriam to be in the shot with the monkey, but then teased her by grabbing her hand and pretending to stick it into the cage. She squealed and laughed. He took pictures of the ceilings and walls because, he said, the light was "dancing" up there. I sat outside on the bike watching them, Miriam giggling in a kind of false voice while Jimmy's attention focused on the monkey and whatever he was seeing through the camera.

I know Miriam saw Jimmy again and snuck him into her room at the Barbizon, strictly against regulations. I'd made it upstairs to the Barbizon lounge with her, and we'd neck when no one was up there but I hadn't been to her room. She once said she wanted to "kiss it and take it into my mouth," and unzipped my pants. She put her head on my lap and I placed her coat over her head. A woman walked by and I said Miriam had been tired and fallen asleep.

Once heading down 8th Avenue, Jimmy told me Miriam had gone down on him and "gives pretty good head." I said I already knew that, and he said, "I hope you're not hung up on the chick . . ."

I wasn't, but I wanted to know if he'd fucked her, figuring he'd tell me if he had. He'd told me about a couple of girls I didn't know, one of whom worked at the Actors Studio. But he said he hadn't fucked Miriam, because she'd said she was saving herself for marriage.

"That's a crock," I said. She'd mentioned a guy from Wisconsin who had gotten her pregnant and that she'd had a "dusting and scraping job" at Bellevue.

"They all fucking lie, man," Jimmy said. "Females lie." He talked about the girl he'd been seeing and staying with "half the time," together with the roommate he'd had in L.A. He said he should've played a trick on them by turning into a hermaphrodite.

In the late spring, he'd met a waiter who worked in a little Greenwich Avenue cafe. He slept on a slab door with a Japanese neck rest and, along with Jimmy, wore a motorcycle jacket and even a pair of black leather pants while visiting the bars along Third Avenue.

"These weirdos are fucking and torturing each other," Jimmy told me. He said he'd sleep on a stack of sofa cushions in the waiter's studio after wandering around. At night, when he was troubled, he'd amble through the city, hanging out in 24-hour diners, or he'd go to the 42nd Street movies and fantasize about acting the roles on the screen.

One night he called me, upset because he'd seen a dead guy loaded into a paddy wagon. He said the man's hand had been sticking up as if reaching for something.

Not long after we met, I'd been working on lines for a play, and I'd just fallen asleep when I heard someone knocking on the door of my 48th Street apartment. When I opened the door, Jimmy seemed surprised that I'd been asleep. He was holding his greasy hands up in front of him and said he'd been downstairs working on my motorcycle. I was on the third floor facing the street, across from a fire station, and I kept it chained to a pipe in a small alley between the buildings where the garbage cans were lined up. He said my carburetor wasn't original and that someone had "jockeyed it around getting it on the engine." "You do that?" he asked. I told him it had been like that when I'd bought it.

"A bad idea," he said, "using spacers like that." A friend in Santa Monica had used a part that wasn't stock and the bike leaked gas. "Burned the bike up," Jimmy said. He asked if I'd ever rebuilt a carburetor for a Norton, and I said I hadn't. He said it wasn't hard, then asked if he could use the sink.

After washing his hands, he stood in the middle of the room looking around at the walls. He said, "Where's the bullfight pictures?"

I'd told him of my photographs, and he said he thought I'd have them all over the walls. When I brought out the box I kept them in, he got down on the floor and went through all of them, studying each one, even turning them sideways. We were still there when daylight came. He found a picture of the matador we'd talked about, and mumbled something about men with mirror swords and eyes dripping blood, flowing capes and pinpoints of death in their pores . . . He said it was from a Mexican poem, but I imagined he composed it on the spot.

Again he wanted to talk about the matador I'd seen gored, and again I told him what I remembered—the horn hooking and nailing the bull-fighter. He wanted to borrow the photo to put on his wall—"as soon as I get a wall," he added.

Once walking along 42nd Street, looking at the whores and nuts and movie placards—one for Brando's *The Men*—Jimmy said he had a snap-shot of Brando with a cock in his mouth. The photo, however, has never been proven to be of Brando. He had another picture showing Brando in a room with a porthole window behind him. Jimmy mentioned the shot had been taken in a room on West 68th Street and, grinning, said, "I've got the place—the same apartment." Someone he met through Marty Lan-dau, who'd worked out at Terry Hunt's with Brando, had given Jimmy the address of the apartment in the Brando photo. Jimmy said he'd dogged the manager of the building until the place became vacant. He believed it was the same apartment, the same porthole windows. "By the way," he said, "I've found out that Brando's fucked around with a couple of guys from Terry Hunt's, and one of them says Marlon keeps rolling over onto his stomach . . . So he loves taking it up the ass," Jimmy said, joking. He made a circle with his thumb and finger, then left saying he had a rehearsal in less than twenty minutes.

Later, Jimmy said he was sorry I was just a fan of bullfighting and didn't seriously consider doing it. Again, I took that as a joke, but he claimed that bullfighting was something he'd have to do someday—learn to work the cape and face a bull. "Maybe one about this size," he said, grinning, his hand held waist high.

He said he could see it—it was there, a speck in the back of his mind. He said it was a "black hole burned in one of those old-time photographs." He said whenever "the chick" said she was sick, he could smell the bull's breath. It was like "getting married or dying," he said. "Your life opens up in that one moment, and that's when you're the most complete you can be . . ."

The idea of cramming everything into one moment obsessed Jimmy. It was one of the ideas that nearly drove Eartha Kitt nuts. "He couldn't let go," she said later. He'd latched onto Eartha as a soul mate; there was nothing sexual between them. "We were like brother and sister," she said. Jimmy was convinced Eartha had "special powers" and knowledge she could deliver to him by some kind of osmosis if he hung around long enough. She had "a sense of magic, and the answers," he said, "were locked up in her." He'd badger her into long discussions, and while she enjoyed his friendship, she said at times it was almost painful for her. He'd devise some theory he knew she'd disagree with. "He'd play the devil's advocate. People had to get shook up. Sleepers had to wake up."

He was inclined to learn a little, she said, and then attempt "to teach the instructor." If Eartha thought he was wrong about something, he'd insist she didn't understand what he was trying to say: "It was one-sided. Jimmy wanted me to prove to him or demonstrate how he wasn't right. He believed that if I understood what he was trying to say, then I would agree with him." He'd go to great lengths to meet with her at such times and try to make her understand his ideas.

Such as his theory of "synchronization." He sensed moments in Eartha's performances when it seemed to him that everything she knew was fused directly into the moment. Even things that had nothing to do with performing, he thought, translated directly into one energy force—a magic connection. This moment of fusion was "synchronization."

He phoned her one night to meet him at the cafeteria. Jimmy had a small flask he used to spike the coffee, cup after cup, chain-smoking and sipping so intensely, she said, "he seemed to buzz with electricity . . . sparks flying off him."

The flask held brandy. He'd been told "by the gang Marlon hung around with at Terry Hunt's gym" that Marlon Brando drank hardly at all, but when he had to get to the meaning of something, he drank brandy. Jimmy wanted to learn everything and compress what he knew into one energy force representing "something perfect." He had to dance and sing, learn photography and bullfighting, because he knew that what he'd learn could come through in some other way, would make up qualities he would project as an artist—as an actor.

She told him she understood, "But whether or not all that can be 'fused' into a whole, some performance or art as a single energy, I didn't know. My logic inclines to say it can't, because life doesn't operate on single notes. It's a whole symphony." When she tried to tell him the "lessons of living" were orchestrated by God, Jimmy laughed.

"What bullshit!" he said. There was no God—there was only art, only the composer, the creator of the symphony.

"And God created him who creates the symphony," Eartha said. Jimmy laughed again. "He said I was passing the buck—shirking things off and not taking credit for my own perfection. He said that was why people go around walking in pig crap all the time . . . He didn't think I understood or was using my real knowledge to get at the answers he needed.

"He wasn't playing in anyone else's symphony," Eartha said. "He was a loner, a solo player, and those meetings with him were excruciating and frustrating and trying . . ."

A few years later, photographer Roy Schatt, from whom Jimmy had wanted to learn, displayed portraits of Jimmy in Rienzi's, a West Fourth Street coffeehouse, and told me Jimmy had bugged him mercilessly. "He was a miserable runt who was a genius at posturing in a different guise for almost everyone he came in contact with." Schatt said, "Alone and left alone, he was just that—miserable, a squinty-eyed runt. But he was like an electric bulb—you plug him in and there's all this light, a battery or something inside him, generating this incredible light . . . He wanted me to teach him everything about photography. I don't know why. I was the photographer. He was the subject, but he wanted to be as proficient as me. I said, 'What for? All you're interested in is yourself!'"

Jimmy's relationship with me was more fundamental. He told television director James Sheldon, whom I met through Jimmy, that I was a "kid iconoclast," a Rimbaud on a beat-up motorcycle. And others, particularly later in Hollywood, would say, "He's one of Jimmy's people—art-for-art's-sake." Jimmy's association with the Actors Studio was minimal; he was disliked by members of the board, and especially by Lee Strasberg.

Jimmy said that Strasberg was a "very ugly man" who kept no mirrors in his house for fear of chancing unexpectedly upon his own reflection. Neither Montgomery Clift nor Brando was affiliated with the Studio, and Jimmy felt that it was unnecessary for a talent such as his own to be criticized by the "ugly man" who had a "personal vindictiveness" toward Jimmy while favoring others who kowtowed to Strasberg's opinions or who fucked or sucked the members of the board. Jimmy said that Strasberg's ideas were "nothing more than personal opinions," and paraphrasing Nietzsche, Jimmy said, "It wasn't that they were true, only that they were held as being true." The instructor's opinions were, Jimmy said, "mostly hot air and hog shit." He mimicked Strasberg's self-importance; even the roundness of the man's bald head seemed to glint from Jimmy's impersonations. The voice was Strasberg's, mouthing silly, nonsensical statements or stodgy platitudes. "He sits there in this posture, this ugly man who is married to an ugly woman," Jimmy said, "and farts out these opinions while half of the people in the place run around goosing each other."

Jimmy delighted in the few times I became sarcastic and blasphemous, and he'd encourage me to get drunk and shoot my mouth off about people. James Sheldon said, "Dean aligns himself with the castigated. Point someone out as a mainstream reject or someone so wounded in some way they have a terrible negative attitude—a creep—and Jimmy goes out of his way to get close to that person. In that way you'll be caught off-balance."

Jimmy worked the angle of shock. He'd stir up ridiculous situations to upset people. Once he suggested I dress up as a girl before we went to visit some people. "The flake and the chick'll be there," he said, and he'd introduce me as a girl he'd met, and tell them we were "getting serious—going together." At the party he'd find out I was a guy. He'd be very upset and we'd fake a heated argument, but then we'd kiss and make up. The making up, he said, would "get them to the quick."

He asked me, "You ever had something to do with a guy, or just fooling around?" All I'd told him at the time was that when I was fifteen I'd gone to a Hollywood party at the Garden of Allah, and Tyrone Power, who was drunk, had squeezed my hand, patted me on the head, kissed me and said I was the most beautiful boy he had seen in a long time. Since then I'd gotten regular propositions, but I'd never had an affair with a guy. I'd just been experimenting and trying to get around.

Jimmy said the idea of us going to the party—me as a girl—was a "great idea." We talked a little about people being bisexual, and he said he didn't think there was any such thing. If someone really needed emotional support from a male, he would probably be homosexual, but if he needed the support from a woman, then he'd be "more heterosexual."

That season in New York, Jimmy began to deliberately shift his relationships. He was finding new supporters while breaking away from people who were no longer tolerant of his "bad boy" pranks. James Sheldon liked Jimmy, worked with him and helped him, but even Sheldon was taking a dim view of Jimmy's behavior. "He's changing for the worse," Sheldon told me, "and he can't even see it."

Meanwhile, John Hodiak was on Broadway in *The Caine Mutiny Court-Martial*, and I managed to join him in a restaurant one night after the performance. We'd talked briefly on the phone, and his voice had sounded far away. He was excellent on stage, but he had changed. He didn't look quite like he had in Hollywood.

With him was an attractive actress, Joan Lorring, who teased me for eating the bread and part of the salad John hadn't finished, even though he'd invited me to take it. "The kid doesn't have any money," he told Loring, and then asked how one could expect an actor to have any self-determining abilities? I reminded him of what he'd told me about the power of positive thinking. He said success was an illusory state of mind, "a figment of the imagination . . . Success is simply one dog eating at the other dog until one is dead and the other one full." Then he said, "You go out and look for another dog," and they began to laugh. There were hard lines around his mouth, and he was losing his hair.

A few days later, Jimmy came to my apartment wanting me to teach him how to fence in an hour or two. I said it couldn't be done, but tried to show him how to hold a foil, as one would hold a bird, firmly but carefully. But he clutched at it, his moves sudden and jerky, and he couldn't bend one of his fingers. He was still in Eartha's body-movement class, and though she'd said the fencing was a good idea, Jimmy quickly lost interest in it. I didn't know why he'd wanted to learn.

Another time he asked if I had any marijuana. He wanted to get high and was sorry Curry wasn't around because he always had grass. I had cheese and soda crackers and a quart of beer, and Jimmy drank that quickly. He was restless and edgy, and seemed trapped in the space of the apartment. I'd been fooling around with a painting, a view from my window of the corner drugstore and the firehouse across the street. "There's no people in the picture," Jimmy said. I said I hadn't painted any into it yet. He said if it was his painting he'd leave it empty.

I put on Alex North's music from *A Streetcar Named Desire*, but it only made him jumpy. He couldn't sit still, bracing and tensing his shoulders and squinting through his glasses at everything. At one point, staring at me, he said, "If you put on a wig and dress you could play a chick." He made several phone calls, drank the beer and made faces because he didn't like the taste of it. Did I have anything else to eat, he wanted to know, something like cake or cookies? I said I didn't, but suggested going out somewhere.

"Like where?" he asked. He said he was starving. His belt was full of holes, he said. He was lying. James Dean never went without a meal in New York.

There was a pretty good French cafe on Ninth Avenue, but Jimmy said he didn't know much about French food, and he was broke to boot. He then said James Sheldon knew "all the French stuff," and had suggested dinner a couple of times. "Sheldon's got money," Jimmy said, and he could pay for the dinners.

He phoned Sheldon, who knew the restaurant and would be waiting in front for us. Spirits lifted, Jimmy bounced down the stairs. But by the time we walked over there, his mood had changed again. He sat hunched and guarded at the table, suspicious of what Sheldon had ordered. Once he tasted it, though, he dug in, wolfing the food down. He soaked the crepe with a sweet syrup before eating it, almost floating it, as Sheldon stared at him and said, "You're going to eat that?"

Jimmy picked up the crepe in his hand and squeezed it until the filling oozed out. He thought that was very funny, and at one point Sheldon said, "You're a knucklehead!" and rubbed Jimmy's head—one of those Dutch-uncle rubs, and said again, "This guy's a knucklehead!"

Sheldon ordered another bottle of wine, though he drank little of it. Embarrassed by our behavior, he paid the check and left early. Jimmy wouldn't leave until he had eaten all the crepes and bread, and finished the second bottle. As we walked back toward 8th Avenue, he told me he'd been in a show with actress Irene Vernon. They had been eating somewhere when she complained about the greasy potatoes; they were "swimming in grease," she'd said. Jimmy thought that was funny, but Irene was upset that the grease was spreading to the other food. He removed the potatoes from her plate, he said, and put them into a water glass where they could "swim properly," then used a napkin to wipe up the grease from her dish. She could spread the other parts of her meal, he told her, onto the place where the potatoes had been.

Heading north again, we stopped at Jerry's Tavern, drank beers and were smashed by the time we got to my place. And because the conversation got around to sex with guys as well as girls, I told him about the time an actor friend, Bill Smith, had driven up to a dude ranch where I worked, and how we'd stayed overnight at a country club. It had surprised me, I told Jimmy, when the actor showed me his cock in the room, how big he could get it.

I said I wasn't sure what I thought about seeing him like that. Jimmy wanted to know if I'd been in the sack with the producers I'd met, and I said no—except for a couple of them, but I hadn't liked it. It was something like the experience of a young relative of mine going down on me, having failed to persuade me to have sex with him from behind. "Butt-fucking him," Jimmy said. I said yes, and Jimmy asked me in a serious voice, almost like he was a doctor, if I'd wanted to suck the actor's cock. He went on to inquire whether I'd experienced any sort of pain. "Be honest with me," he said, "be as honest as all the days." What did I feel about the guy's cock, "because it seems to stand out in my mind." He laughed at the unintended pun, and asked me how come I hadn't done it?

I said the guy had surprised me and I had been scared. I said I couldn't say more about it than I already had.

Jimmy said it was probably possible for him to have a relationship with a guy, too—to have a physical exchange without it being labeled "homosexual," because he felt that something like that, like what the actor and I had come close to, was simply an extension of the friendship. "Just going to the edge of the friendship or sort of beyond it," Jimmy said. He didn't think any kind of sexual experience would push him or anyone else in one direction or the other.

He wanted to know if I had sucked my relative's cock, and I said I'd done that once or twice. That was what he'd done to me, had me shoot in his mouth, and fuck him in the ass. Jimmy asked me about another producer and how it had felt to have him kissing me. I said I hadn't liked it.

"Have you tasted jizz?" Jimmy asked. Did I know what it tasted like? "Sure, I know what it tastes like," I said, and told him I'd said—having tasted my own on my finger. Jimmy said, "You're like a little girl who puts her finger in her pussy and then licks it off." He said, well, did I like the taste?

I laughed and he laughed, too. I answered no, I'd had to spit it out. He said, "Is that why you were scared of that guy's dick, because you didn't want to have that stuff in your mouth?" That was the question he'd been driving at. That's what he wanted to know. It made me feel nervous, and I said, "I don't know . . . What about you?"

He didn't answer, but began to giggle. He said, "I'm not active. I'm passive. You are passive too, from what you have said to me . . ." But active and passive were terms that depended on what a person happens to be doing, he said. With my relative I was being passive, but by fucking him I could be said to be active, but only if it was what I wanted to do. He said it all depended on how it happened, and on what the person wanted. It was all about circumstances—the nature of the "interpersonal relationship," he said.

He was lying on my bed with his head hanging over the edge, and I was sitting in the wicker chair. At one point I tried to get up, but I was too drunk and ended up on the floor near Jimmy. I reached up and touched his head, then pulled on his hair. He said, "Man, you know more than just being kissed by Tyrone Power. You know things like I do, because you've been through the same shit . . ."

After talking for a few minutes more, there was a strange sort of vibration in the air, a kind of intimacy that was electric and exciting. He put his finger on my lower lip and started to giggle. Then he turned his head around and was sitting facing me, and he put his hand behind my neck and pulled my face toward his, putting his lips on mine. It was the first time I had ever really been kissed by another guy. He said, "Come up on the bed before I break my neck." I moved up on the bed and lay alongside of him and he kissed me again. Our teeth touched, stuck together in a strange way. I remember closing my upper row of teeth down onto his lower row, so that I could almost bite his bottom teeth by closing my mouth. I felt his tongue against the edge of my upper teeth, and then I opened my mouth and he put his tongue in my mouth, pushing it against my tongue. I put my hands up at the sides of my face and we stayed like that for a few seconds until we backed up onto the bed. He kissed me on the neck and bit—though not really hard—into the skin between my neck and collarbone, and then he was laying on top of me.

He said, "Can you be fucked?"

"Jesus!" I said. "I don't think so."

He said, "I want to try to fuck you. We can try it if you want to." He wanted me to put my arms around him—which I felt funny doing—and to hold him. He wanted me to kiss him while he moved his lower body against me, and to keep kissing him. He wanted to suck my nipples and leaned his face over and kissed me on the side. Again he bit me, and this time it felt sharp. He was holding himself and he said, "Am I going to fuck you?"

I said, "I guess we can try to. I don't how know successful it will be." At that I replaced his hand with my hand. We tried to fuck but it wasn't going to work. I tried to go down on him, but his cock was big and made me gag and choke. I didn't know what we could do. It wasn't going to work. Whatever the hell it was that had sparked such a situation between us was just going to be all bound up by the impossibility of getting it across.

This part of the friendship stayed in the background over the next few weeks, as if it had occurred in another dimension and required no actual attention from us. For me, the physical thing was awkward. Though I doubted that either of us got much satisfaction out of it, the memory of it somehow held a wonder or excitement—and yet it still scared me. For Jimmy, the *idea* of doing it seemed more intriguing than whatever we actually did.

Caught up in our own ambitions, what we shared wasn't an affair by far, and what has been written about our friendship in books and magazines over the years is mostly mistaken. One book describes the relationship as "salacious" and "lustful," but it wasn't. It was a period of exploration. It wasn't so much a physical thing. I'd run into Jimmy and there would be an energy between us, even in the company of others, like a dark-haired girl he was seeing named Barbara Glenn, a young actress who cared sincerely for him, and whom he really liked.

Like one night in Jerry's, Jimmy was across from me in the booth, and we were joking around and drinking, and for a second our eyes met and that look was there, but just for a second. It was like something had run or flown across a screen—the bursting noise of a bunch of birds taking wing, so fast that unless you knew what it was, you wouldn't have seen it. But the feeling was there, and if either one of us had been a girl, we'd have gotten into a love affair, though it wouldn't have lasted.

Early that fall we were goofing around at a party on 45th Street, around the corner from the Algonquin and Iroquois. Jimmy had done another show with James Sheldon, who showed up briefly at the party. He said that he and Jimmy were momentarily at odds. It had something to do with Jimmy's attitude: the more work he got, the more he seemed to antagonize those he worked with. Playwright William Inge didn't want Jimmy in a particular production, because, he said, "his moods are so unpredictable and he scares the pants right off me."

At the party, in an apartment above a manufacturing loft, Jimmy was hiding in the kitchen. We were eating crackers and potato chips and drinking soda mixed with wine. I was watching Jimmy trying to open a can of salmon with a bottle opener when a young black actor named Billy Gunn joined us, prattling on about the Actors Studio, Geraldine Page and a play adaptation of André Gide's novel *The Immoralist*. Jimmy played dumb. He'd landed a good role in the same show, but pretended to know nothing about Geraldine Page starring in the play with Louis Jourdan. Jimmy's part was that of a homosexual Arab houseboy, and Billy Gunn had been signed to understudy the same character. Gunn didn't know Jimmy except to nod hello at casting calls, and Jimmy once said, "He's got some good reefers, when he's got 'em."

In the kitchen, Gunn bragged about landing the understudy, and Jimmy just said, "Oh, yeah?" and "What play's that? Who's in it?" The fact that Jimmy was signed for the role hadn't been announced, but he finally told Gunn. "They're keeping it a secret," he said, "in case they have to fire such an asshole as me before we get into rehearsals."

"That's okay with me," Gunn said. "If they do, I'll go on in your place!"

He left the kitchen, and Jimmy stared after him and said, "What a fucking jerk, man." But Gunn would become one of the few people Jimmy was friendly with that winter—part of Jimmy's "uptown" group. Jimmy was still seeing Barbara, hanging out with her sometimes, but kept us all pretty separate from one another. If two of us who knew him appeared in the same setting, he'd sort of shrink up, or start acting up, pulling some kind of stunt.

Barbara and I shared a sort of troubled distance, because she thought Jimmy was paying more attention to me than he was to her, and that he turned to me to discuss more serious ideas. Billy Gunn and I were friends, though. We'd have coffee at Cromwell's or the Museum of Modern Art. Billy talked about wanting to be a painter and a writer as well as an actor.

I felt relieved that Jimmy had signed for *The Immoralist*, because I was afraid to tell him about the play John Van Druten was putting together. The playwright told my agent he saw something in me of the boy he'd written in *I Remember Mama*—the character Nels—whom I'd played in stock. The play was projected for the following season, and with Van Druten's support the role was within my grasp. Yet it was a role Jimmy would have been right for if the Gide play weren't taking him out of circulation.

At another party, Jimmy introduced me to a Park Avenue art dealer named Fredrick Delius—like the composer—and we joked about him looking "remarkably life-like." Jimmy had met him at a show he'd gone to with Leonard Rosenman, a musician friend, and Delius invited us to his gallery. Apart from free snacks, Jimmy wanted to show me two works—an old Spanish painting of Saint Sebastian with all the arrows sticking in him, and a portrait of Rimbaud "in drag" by a French Symbolist painter.

From a smaller room with a table and chairs off the main gallery, you could look directly at the painting of Saint Sebastian, almost life-size, bound to a tree, hands tied, head tilted back slightly with his eyes raised toward heaven as arrows pierced various parts of his body. Jimmy remained in a chair, smoking and staring, entranced by the painting while Delius showed me his latest acquisitions. The portrait of Rimbaud, he said, had been shipped to another gallery, but what he showed me was a peculiar work showing the Virgin Mary holding the infant Christ. The baby's face looked wrinkled and strained, its teeth like an old person's. The Virgin was how I imagined an embalmed Jean Harlow might have looked. As I stared at the painting in a kind of awe, I felt Delius' hand moving across my rump, and he tried to kiss the back of my neck. He whispered something in some other language, and I moved away. He implored me to come back for dinner, and I said I'd let him know. As I walked away from him, he said weakly, "I can help you . . . I can be influential . . . You can ask Jimmy if I am not sincere."

Jimmy had dozed off, chin resting on the folds of his sweater, which was spotted with cigarette ash. His eyelids were slightly open and the whites of his eyes were visible behind his glasses. He wasn't interested in the proposal Delius had made to me. "He's an old queen," Jimmy said. "He's okay, and who gives a shit?" The man had wanted to fly him to Spain to see the bullfights, he said, then added, "Fat chance." He wanted to talk about the bulls again, the gorings and the funerals of matadors, until the dialogue settled on how long it would take Saint Sebastian to die from those arrows. One sticking in his lower abdomen must have pierced organs, Jimmy said, and he had to be bleeding inside. "That'd kill him," he said with certainty. He talked about being hanged—about suffocation—and was trying to imagine being guillotined, and whether the eyes fluttered with any last-second sight.

Jimmy's talk of death, dying and dismemberment wasn't as exciting or interesting to me as it was to him. It was never morose, though, and at times he tended to become almost ecstatic. Things became important and purposeful to him, and his whole attention seemed to focus on particular details, like the arrow in Saint Sebastian's lower abdomen. Nothing else mattered.

I stayed at the gallery a couple of times on a couch in the alcove. After dinner at an elegant Italian restaurant, we drank old vintage wine like water. We listened to Tagliavini records, and Delius gave me a black-silk Chinese

James Dean in rehearsal with the cast of *The Immoralist*, the second
Broadway production he appeared in, in 1954. From left: Geraldine Page,
Louis Jourdan, James Dean, and David J. Stewart. *Photofest*

robe with dragons on it. He said I was like Louise Brooks—like Lulu—and
he wanted to kiss my stomach and thighs. He cried until I undressed and
wore the new black robe. I was very drunk and Delius wound up fucking
me on the couch, under the painting of Saint Sebastian. I remember afterwards sitting on the toilet in the huge white bathroom, the black silk and
dragons shining on the tile and the fluid of the man coming out of me.

The company for *The Immoralist* was having a terrible time with Jimmy's
"uncommunicative behavior," as they put it. He'd read slowly and sullenly,
and with little apparent comprehension. What no one seemed to know was
that until he'd committed the script to memory, he was unable to formulate
what he'd say, so he'd mutter and mumble and make up words, or simply fill
in the blanks with speech that had nothing to do with the scene.

Jimmy had other people read his parts until he knew the thing by
heart. He couldn't deal with a new page, and it took him ages to finish a

paragraph. He preferred simple books with pictures, and poetry, and if he'd heard it enough he could repeat it like a talking bird.

Louis Jourdan complained that "Dean mutters obscenities!" Even then, it was not until Jimmy experienced the language of the play in rehearsals that he could get involved, and that didn't happen until almost the opening-night performance.

Frustration ran fever pitch. Other actors found Jimmy intolerable, impossible to work with. There were serious arguments that escalated to the point of almost getting him fired. But Geraldine Page rescued him by threatening to walk out if Jimmy was dismissed. She insisted he'd be fine by opening night. The truth was that he'd confided in her and made her swear she'd not repeat what he told her. Geraldine told me a few years later, "In some peculiar way, Jimmy's difficulties in dealing with the printed page somehow bypassed some other part of him, triggering the most intense concentration of any actor I've worked with. He was like a cat that jumps a great distance without the need to know how far he has to jump."

He attended rehearsals as though a reluctant viewer rather than an actor, wandering around the stage, turning his back to others or mumbling so nobody understood. Louis Jourdan said working with "this monster" was the worst experience he'd had in theater.

The play was opening in Philadelphia for the out-of-town tryout when one of Jimmy's ex-roommates told me he wanted to talk to me. He said he was very upset about the breakup of his friendship with Jimmy. I met him for coffee, but wound up drinking beer. He believed Jimmy was a very lonely individual. "I thought I was a maladjusted, miserable, lonely bastard," he said, "but Jimmy takes the cake." He pointed out that Jimmy couldn't be his friend, and he couldn't be my friend. I wasn't sure I understood what he was saying. "He goes through people as fast as he does underwear," he said, "if he even bothers to put it on half the time." He toasted Jimmy's forthcoming success in the play, saying, "He'll steal the show, you know. Don't underestimate my lost friend, James Dean."

He told me that Jimmy's mother had given him the middle name Byron after the crippled poet, Lord Byron, because she somehow "knew" that Jimmy would grow up a cripple or have a crippled soul. It was fitting, he said, since both Byron and Jimmy *were* cripples.

"Jimmy has said, himself, that it's best to be a cripple," the young man continued. "Has he told you about his ball-game theory?"

I said no. He summed it up, saying that when someone is hurt in the ball game, he's called to the sidelines. "From that position, one is offered a vantage point of the whole playing field that can't be appreciated when one is in the game. The injured one on the sidelines," he said, "sees more and knows more than those on the field . . ."

He then told me that Jimmy was seeking in others the mother he lost as a child. "Though to these same people," he said, "he can be harmful, if not destructive." He said that it resulted from the fact that it was impossible for anyone else to fill in for Jimmy's dead mother. "No one can," he said, "and in the role he forces upon you, you'll always fail our troubled boy."

Attempting to tell me how much he had been through with Jimmy, he said he was leaving New York in despair, having thrown up his hands. He said, "Once Jimmy has finished with a person, that person ceases to exist. Finis! Kaput!"

The real reason for our meeting came out when he asked me if Jimmy and I had been sleeping together. People were saying things. Was that the reason Jimmy was being so hurtful to his friends? "Are you lovers?" he asked, with a kind of weak smile. At that, I finished our conversation.

"You're a sad character, you know?" I said. "You'd be enough to drive anyone to the sidelines."

He raised his glass in a mock toast. "The playing field is yours," he said, "and with it all the blessings and the curses."

I didn't see Jimmy's ex-pal again in New York. The play went well in Philadelphia, then successfully opened on Broadway. When the opening-night curtain dropped at eleven o'clock, Jimmy had delivered a masterful performance—as well as his three-weeks notice. Everyone was stunned, including his most patient supporter, Geraldine. She said, "It was the most unheard-of set of circumstances I'd ever witnessed."

Jimmy told no one of his secret plans to dump the play. Not even Geraldine knew the whole truth, though she had played an unwitting part in the chain of events. A writer she knew, Paul Osborn, was doing a screen adaptation of John Steinbeck's novel *East of Eden* for Elia Kazan and Warner Bros. Geraldine had talked a great deal about Jimmy's antics, but stressed his peculiar intensity during rehearsals. After Osborn went to the Philadelphia tryouts, he realized Jimmy was the perfect actor for the part of the boyish troublemaker in Steinbeck's story.

Osborn told Kazan, and the director went to take a look at Jimmy. "I got to know him," Kazan said, "and he was an absolutely rotten person. Right away, he was a real cocker and an asshole. But he was the most perfect fucking actor for that part—all bound up in himself with his neurotic problems, lashing out at inappropriate moments. A sulker, an asshole, but absolutely perfect for the role. There wasn't any question in my mind that he'd bring it off—all he had to do was be himself. The problem I faced was convincing Warner Bros. that I should go with an unknown, starring him in the movie."

I hadn't seen Jimmy since he'd left for Philadelphia, but I went to the play after it opened at the Royale Theater in New York. He kept talking about plans that were in the works, and he said he couldn't tell anyone why he'd given his notice on opening night. In one scene, he did a seductive dance as the homosexual houseboy enticing Louis Jourdan. Using a pair of scissors like castanets, Jimmy improvised the snipping sounds to accompany his dance. "It was the strings, man," Jimmy told me, "and Louis Jourdan didn't even know what was going on." Jimmy was snipping away at the invisible strings binding Jourdan's character to the safe middle-class morality he'd left abroad. In the blaze of the Middle Eastern desert, surrounded by rampant sexuality, Jourdan becomes helpless, and with each coaxing step of the dance, Jimmy's snipping cut more and more at the man's hopeless respectability. The rigid European gives in, then finally commits suicide.

Jimmy told me his thoughts about the scissors when he called with a vague, muttered story about money being hidden in his apartment. He was going out of town on something important and had to alert me that he might need a favor, someone to get into his apartment and take care of a couple of things, maybe send something out of town. I later learned that he'd called Billy Gunn, and a girl named Chris White who worked at the Actors Studio, with a similar story. It was his way of saying "See you later" without giving away any secrets. Kazan had warned him not to talk to anyone about the movie until they had completed tests in New York, and until the studio had rubber-stamped the director's decision. With hardly anyone knowing it, Jimmy had fulfilled his prophecy—he had become the most important actor in town.

Though we'd get together in Hollywood, that was the last time I talked to him in New York. Soon, with most of his clothes and belongings stuffed into paper sacks, Jimmy was on a plane heading west "to shake the shit out of Hollywood . . ."

10

Blindside

JOHN GILMORE

John Gilmore has written extensively about his intimate friendship with James Dean during the last two years of the actor's life. "Blindside" is the second of two chapters in his 1997 memoir *Laid Bare* that Gilmore devoted to his memories of Dean. —Ed.

JIMMY'S FASCINATION WITH THE SPILLED BLOOD OF MATADORS escalated during his brief year-and-a-half of stardom. He'd stage endurance trials of bodily pain, sticking himself with safety pins and staying up for days on end, while quickly skipping over whatever emotional anguish happened to get tangled up in his relationships, which bottomed out one after the other.

From those lean and hungry days in New York to his sudden success, a part of Jimmy tried desperately to undermine his fame—as if any Hollywood foundations were cast indestructibly. He could not twist himself free of the emotions surrounding his mother's early death, and he clung to these painful memories as one might perpetually clutch a child's jack with sharpened points in one's palm. He sought to remain constantly aware of the pain. The image of his mother's coffin was indelibly etched in his mind—the idea of dwelling in caskets in general obsessed him—and this was somehow mixed up with his own sexual ambiguities.

He was not a homosexual, but dallied in it as an "opportunistic explorer," as he called himself on occasion, engaging in heterosexual sex for similar reasons. One of his early so-called romances was with the young actress Pier Angeli, under contract to Warner Bros. Way back in her past, controlled by a zealously Catholic mother, Pier had developed a constant, though out-wardly unseen, morbid streak that caught Jimmy's attention immediately. The kind of "delightful romance" the fans so gullibly chased was conjured up between them by the studio publicity department. So little has been shown of Pier's gloomy side that any revelation seems a shock, except to those who were exposed to Pier's escalating mental turmoil and drug use.

The trouble was there long before her "discovery" by screenwriter Stew-art Stern, who also wrote the script for *Rebel Without a Cause*. Something churning in this incredibly lovely young woman with the dark doe eyes—and a nature so wildly sexual that she sought to be punished for her defi-ance of those past Catholic bonds—would eventually push Pier to suicide.*

Even though she believed committing suicide was a sin, she still hoped that she'd find peace in a death she'd bring about herself. Never having found happiness or joy, she gambled for everlasting solitude. She claimed that the only love she knew, which had cut her to the quick, was the love she'd experienced for James Dean, though he could never have given her what she needed.

Jimmy had become an "overnight star," the envy of everyone in Holly-wood. Many were so bitterly jealous of his success that it would eventually poison their own careers. Within only months of Jimmy's death, Steve McQueen in New York would be looking at it as a personal convenience. And back in Hollywood later that same year, I'd be living with Dennis Hopper in a small house off Laurel Canyon, and he'd be chain-smoking reefers and saying that "cosmic configurations" had manipulated fates so that Dennis, another Warners contract player who'd acted in the shadow of Jimmy, had by Dean's sudden death been given a "mantle" to fill. I said to Dennis, "You worked in *Rebel* and you worked in *Giant*, but you didn't know Jimmy. You didn't know him."

Dennis said, "But fate knows us both, and fate makes the decisions, not Warner Bros. I'm the one to play the empty parts Jimmy left." I thought, "You might play the roles, pal, but you'll never fill in for Jimmy."

There was something similar about the people Jimmy shared himself with. Together they functioned as a refuge, a kind of cove into which he

---

* Though widely reported as a suicide, Pier Angeli's death on September 10, 1971, from barbiturate intoxication was officially determined to be accidental. —Ed.

could escape for varying periods of time—minutes, hours, a phone call, a fast ride, whatever he required. It was not the person, but the "sanctuary." (I'd heard him use the word two or three times, imitating Charles Laughton in *The Hunchback of Notre Dame*.) To Jimmy, people were almost interchangeable. From Eartha Kitt and other celebrities to Rolf Wütherich—the young auto mechanic who accompanied Jimmy on his last ride—the qualities that attracted him would gradually rise to the surface, converging. Getting a clear picture of Steve McQueen, Natalie Wood, Jack Nicholson, Jane Fonda, Warren Beatty or Dennis Hopper was an easy task compared to even focusing on Dean. The work he did will always be there. He proved in the very short time he had that he was one of this century's consummate artists. The other side is in shadow—the flesh and blood Dean has been dead more than four decades now, and only exists in the memory of a group of people who are rapidly dying off themselves. Jimmy—the mercurial clown who dances, sparks, outwits and is outwitted, and who never stands still—was in search of "the moment of truth," not as it was or as others saw it, but as he wanted it to be.

It was this "glorious" compulsion that found wings in the racing that led to his death. He had to go further than the others, and finally to surpass himself. "Dying," he told me, "is at the vanguard of limits. It's a symbol like a stop sign. It's an implication and a matter of interpretation . . . If you're chicken, you can't make the discoveries."

I hadn't seen Jimmy in about a year. I'd come back to Hollywood from New York with John Darrow, to work out a contract with Paramount. I was about to be drafted into the Army, but volunteered for induction instead, signing up for paratrooper school. I was doing okay in the Army until I got picked up and accused of going AWOL, and was stuck in the old stockade at Fort Ord, across the bay from Monterey. After a summary court-martial, I was back in the stockade instead of being sent overseas. I talked to the chaplain and a couple of army shrinks who stressed the necessity of being candid. I remembered that Jimmy had told the draft board he was "afraid of being inducted," afraid of his own "inner inclinations" toward other guys. When I told them I'd had some bisexual experiences, they claimed I could be emotionally unsuited for military training and urged I be discharged.

At first I decided to use what G.I. Bill money I got to go to France and study painting. But instead of living in a garret in Paris, I was soon back in

Beverly Hills with a black 1947 Jaguar sedan and an apartment on Canon
Drive. I was acting in *Season in the Sun* at the Geller Playhouse and seeing
a blonde carhop at Jack's Drive-in on the Strip. She was a part-time artist
and movie extra with big breasts and a skinny waist. She introduced me to
the blonde actress Irish McCalla, who was taller than I was. Irish and I got
along beautifully. She wanted to paint, and we talked about art. Though
she was starring in the television series *Sheena, Queen of the Jungle*, she
didn't talk that much about acting; it was like she didn't really want to do it.

Through another agent, I got a few jobs while going to the Geller
Workshop Theater. The Jaguar quit on me, and I sold it and got a rig-
id-frame BSA motorcycle, cheaper than a car. I dumped the ascot and the
fancy vests and started hanging around in a leather jacket.

I'd wanted to see action in the Army. Too late for Korea, I had still
hoped there'd be something else—somewhere, some battle I'd be able to
sink my teeth into. I even thought of joining the French Foreign Legion
since the U.S. Army had stamped me a misfit. I kept thinking about the
poet Alan Seeger and his love of combat, the glory and sense of immediacy
he'd experienced in battle and written about in his diary and letters. It was
something Jimmy and I talked about in New York. He'd read and reread
Seeger's poem "I Have a Rendezvous with Death," and he'd recite it—once
stoned on pot from Billy Gunn. But what I was after wasn't verse so much
as a rendezvous with fortune.

Sally Kellerman was still in Hollywood High School, as was a cousin
of hers, Hooper Dunbar, a very lean, pretty-faced boy acting in Hollywood
High plays the same as Sally, while also studying modern dance. We met in
a bookshop on Hollywood Boulevard and started hanging around together.
His body was like a slim girl's, and I was attracted to him, though he'd had
no experience with boys.

One spring day, I pulled into Googie's* parking lot on my bike and
saw Jimmy sitting on the seat of his own bike, a Triumph. He was wearing an expensive black leather bike jacket with a fur collar, and tan cow-
hide gloves. A photographer named Phil Stern was taking pictures of him.

---

* Designed by futuristic L.A. architect John Lautner, Googie's was an all-night coffee
shop located next to Schwab's Pharmacy on Sunset Boulevard in Hollywood. —Ed.

Jack Simmons (left) and James Dean take a break from shooting a screen test for *Rebel Without a Cause*. Simmons (who originally tested for the role of Plato, which went to Sal Mineo) played a member of the gang that harasses Jim Stark (Dean) in *Rebel*. *Warner Bros./Photofest © Warner Bros.*

Jimmy had clip-on sunglasses over his regular glasses and stared at me as I stopped in a space near his bike. He gave a little salute and said, "Hey, *atado*, what's happening, man?"

He seemed cool and distant, untrusting maybe, but that disappeared during our first few talks. He was running around with an odd bird named Jack Simmons, who held a reputation as "one of the most notorious faggots in Hollywood."

Jack has been described as being an "unknown" screwball who attached himself to Jimmy after the making of *East of Eden*. Actually, when *Life* magazine's huge spread on Jimmy had run the previous March, Jack had made up his mind to meet Jimmy and become his closest friend. Begging and badgering his way onto the Warners lot, Jack had succeeded in cornering his newfound idol, and laying himself down as Jimmy's personal doormat.

"What's 'atado'? What's 'atado'?" Jack asked me.

Then later he said, "It's got to do with a fucking bull. Tying it up or using a rope so it means some kind of state of *peace*—what bullshit! Why does he call you *that*?"

Rarely quoted, Jack would remain a "mysterious character" in Jimmy's history, with most of the tidbits coming from another mutual friend, Maila Nurmi, the would-be actress and self-professed "witch" who called herself Vampira at the time. Dressing in black like Morticia of the Addams Family, Maila hosted a television show of old spooky movies—the forerunner of many late-night TV horror gimmicks to come. While Simmons was reticent, Vampira freely concocted stories about Jimmy after his death, crediting herself via movie magazines and other publications as having been a lover of Jimmy's. She created publicity for herself and her television show, and unwanted notoriety for Jack, who was chauffeuring Maila around in an old black hearse. It was through Jack's possessive attachment to Jimmy that Maila was briefly ushered in as part of the "night watch," as we were called—or, by some columnists, the "crew of creeps."

Many of the all-night jams at Googie's, the bikes and stunts, were construed by reporters as crazy antics to shock and deride Hollywood. Jimmy was reveling in the publicity, creating a language of physical and psychological impact, a dangerous image that radiated from the screen and tabloid papers. The stories read, "The crazy kid is going to kill himself." It was a fear shared by the studio. Jimmy loved it.

Enhancing the public's curiosity were Vampira's innuendoes to the press about the "romance" between her and Jimmy, which he'd chuckle over. Most of all, however, it was the "morbid" appearance of his "crew," which included myself, that kept the bad publicity cooking. No one knew where it would lead or what Jimmy intended to do with these "jackals" he'd gathered around himself.

Jimmy's penchant for secrecy kept Jack Simmons initially half-ignorant of the relationship we'd shared in New York. At the same time, Jimmy showed no more than a passing curiosity about the fact that Jack and I had been friendly two years before. He did ask, "Did you and Jack get anything going?" I said no, absolutely not. Jimmy said, "He's a very nervous guy," and laughed. He asked how we met, and I told him it was in front of the Tropical Village, a gay bar on the boardwalk at Santa Monica. Jack had long dark hair and a big hook nose in those days. They called him "the Hawk," and when I met him he was wearing pink bathing trunks, cut high on the sides, and some sort of Indian beaded belt. He had on a pair of white sunglasses and was trying to dance with Rock Hudson or George Nader. The bar was usually jammed on weekends, and it wouldn't have been unusual to spot Hudson or George Nader or Dan Dailey dancing somewhere deep in the place. Someone I'd worked with on a show invited me in for a sandwich, and Jack stopped me on the boardwalk. He said he recognized me and wanted to buy me a drink. I said it wasn't a good idea because I wasn't even seventeen yet, and the whole place might get into a jam. He insisted on a Dr. Pepper and we talked outside the bar. After that, he was chasing me, calling at night, driving me places I'd have to be, but he never seriously tried to put the make on me.

Then he'd had his nose bobbed and combed his hair like Jimmy, who'd landed him a small part in *Rebel*. While the "New Star" halo was shining over Jimmy, it was people like Jack—as well as myself—who puzzled Hollywood. A reject, tabbed a pitiful fringe-nut in Hollywood's substratum, Jack had captured Jimmy's interest with an unwavering, dog-like devotion. Like myself, he wasn't one of those "fat numb people" who criticized Jimmy, but quickly became a member of the crew with whom Jimmy surrounded himself, "frequenting Sunset Boulevard's night hangouts, racing cars and motorcycles, and what gaucheries Dean doesn't think up, these sycophants do . . ." It was a very short-lived moment, long-remembered by Hollywood.

Jack would later claim that he was in love with Jimmy—the only love of his life, he'd say—and even decades later he'd break down and sob over Jimmy's death. Jack said he had not only lost his "one true love," but his "soul as well." Years later, Jack would try to purify his relationship with Jimmy, even telling writer Val Holley, "I never touched his organs," by which, of course, he meant Jimmy's cock.

One night in Googie's, Jimmy said that the line he wanted on his tombstone was from the poet Alan Seeger's diary about "one crowded hour of glorious life" being "worth an age without a name." A telegram was quickly sent to Jack Warner, suggesting an engraved headstone. The front office didn't appreciate the prank and promptly clamped down on Jimmy's reckless motorcycle racing around the studio lot. They began to keep tabs on the "oddballs" Jimmy was palling around with. These "tabs," actually file cards, soon became a sort of blackball list of potentially troublesome people—those who might cost the studio unnecessary expense. Following Dean's death, the word "unnecessary" would be changed to "grievous."

The night the telegram was sent, I ran into Irish McCalla in Googie's. She was in a front booth with a couple of people while Jimmy and the crew were in the usual rear booth. We were heading out when Irish looked up at me and then at Jimmy, and I said, "Hey, this is Irish McCalla, who's Sheena, Queen of the Jungle." Jimmy took her hand as if to shake it, but brought her up out of the booth. She was much taller than him and he started to giggle. She was still holding his hand as he mumbled something to her, bowing a little in mock-acknowledgment of her station as Queen of the Jungle. Then Jimmy said, "I'm gonna come swing in your tree, Sheena." She said that would be all right with her, as she had a lot of slack in the vines. I remember her looking at me and grinning.

When Jimmy asked your opinion, or how something might be "handled from a different perspective," as he'd put it, he was really seeking approval for something he'd already figured out. If you were critical of his unvoiced decision, or showed that you were no longer at ease with his antics, then you would be cast into the chorus of what he called "inconsequential grownups" and no longer of service to him.

People like Eartha Kitt and others whose particular intelligence or talents he valued were allowed to be critical of his behavior, but they could never be members of the "night watch." We were, as one writer put it, "the small handful of malcontents quite isolated from the mainstream, whose necessity to Jimmy so disturbs the studio front office that these hangers-on encouraging his rebelliousness are being noted in a way that assures what is called 'blackballing' in Hollywood . . ."

Jack's apartment was just west of Fairfax, an old second-floor building with a large living room separated from a dining room by a serving divider, where a pair of Jimmy's old boots sat enshrined inside a clear plastic box.

An unmade double bed was in the living room, and another bed and several stacks of boxes occupied the bedroom where Jimmy stayed when he didn't want to be chased down. Jack volunteered some ambiguous statements about his closeness to Jimmy, hinting at sex—"I won't say yes and I won't say no," he chirped. Even then, he claimed that he both loved and worshipped Jimmy, but that they were "friends first." It was bewildering to many, how important Jack was to Jimmy, over and above any of the members of the *Rebel* cast. Jimmy even suggested that Jack play Sal Mineo's role and had Jack tested for the part, though Jack, being not nearly as experienced an actor as Sal, would certainly have had a difficult time with it.

The test was shot one night on location during a break for another setup, and I'd ridden over with Jack in the hearse. It was the scene in the mansion with Sal and Natalie Wood, and tension quickly developed between Jack and Jimmy and myself. After the filming, Jack drove me to Hamburger Hamlet on the Strip, where we would later be met by Jimmy and Rolf Wütherich. They drove over in Jimmy's Porsche Speedster, at moments hitting seventy miles an hour along Sunset.

Jimmy drank milk at Hamburger Hamlet. He didn't smoke that night, complaining about a sore throat. The two of us talked about bikes for a while. Jack hardly spoke. After Jimmy left for his apartment on Sunset Plaza Drive, Jack said Jimmy had told him that he'd met me through James Sheldon—which wasn't accurate. I said I'd met Sheldon through Jimmy. That was the end of the conversation, though Jack wanted me to come to his place that night and talk to him. I said I couldn't. I had an interview first thing in the morning and I wanted to get to sleep. He asked me to meet him and Maila at Googie's the next day, and I said I'd call him, or talk to Jimmy. That upset him.

For days, Jack kept calling me and trying in every way he could to get me to talk about Jimmy and New York. Everything he said seemed to be an attempt to pry out some information about anything sexual that might have happened between Jimmy and myself.

A few nights later I was with Jimmy in the Speedster and he said Jack was driving him crazy. He said he thought Jack would take sleeping pills or cut his wrists. He told me Jack had said some things about me, even though Jimmy had claimed that he wasn't interested in the subject.

This was the night I saw Bill Smith on La Cienega at Melrose. Bill's sister had been an actress, and Bill was doggedly chasing a career of his own—years later he'd star with Clint Eastwood in *Any Which Way You Can*. I introduced Bill to Jimmy, who did not get out but reached across the passenger side to shake Bill's hand. Jimmy said, "Nice to meet you," then giggled a little and made some sort of face about Bill's forceful grip. I got out and Bill said, "I love this car." I went into a liquor store for cigarettes while Jimmy waited at the curb. When I came out, Jimmy had the hood open and they were standing at the rear of the car looking at the engine. I remember Jimmy nodding and Bill saying something about having worked on a Volkswagen engine, but never having seen a Porsche's. We got back in and Bill bent down by my side of the car, saying he was glad to have met Jimmy. When we drove off, Jimmy chuckled and asked, "Is that the guy you told me about, with the hard-on?"

I said yeah, to which Jimmy said, "What if he showed it to you now? What would you do now?" I said I didn't think he'd do that.

"That wasn't what I asked you," Jimmy said. "I said what would you do?"

"Nothing," I said.

Jimmy said, "We both know what Jack would do . . ." I said he wouldn't wait until Bill showed it to him, but I was sure Jack wouldn't survive to blab about the attempt. Jimmy laughed. He took my hand and put it on his crotch and said, "What if he did this?" He said he'd bet Bill wouldn't do something like that. He imagined Bill was all muscle without a whole lot "sparking between his ears." If Bill jacked off with the same strength he'd shown in shaking Jimmy's hand, he said, his cock was probably carried around in a sling. Jimmy had his hand around my left wrist, holding my hand on his crotch as he drove, moving both our hands to the shifter when he put in the clutch, guiding us into gear and saying, "Hey, I'm teaching you to drive, man."

A girl who had lost a leg in a motorcycle accident had been coming into Googie's, and said she really wanted to meet James Dean. She knew he liked talented and unusual people, and that he wasn't a phony like so many other movie and television assholes she claimed to know. I was sitting in a booth alongside Jimmy one night when he nudged me with his elbow and pointed across the aisle. The girl was sitting at the counter, looking right at him and smiling. He said, "You see that girl? She's a nice girl. She's only got one leg." He told me her name was Terry, though that wasn't her name. This girl, who also sang in clubs on the Strip, would later write an autobiography in which she described Jimmy coming to her apartment and asking her to take off her clothes, and when she did, telling her how beautiful she was and kissing her stump.

One night, we rode to a party at the home of Samson De Brier, a Hollywood "character" and actor rumored to have been the homosexual lover of André Gide, author of *The Immoralist*. Samson's house was a museum of pirated movie relics and antique set decorations. He usually held what was called an "open house," a kind of revolving door party. Kenneth Anger's film *Inauguration of the Pleasure Dome*—featuring De Brier, Anaïs Nin, and experimental filmmaker Curtis Harrington—had been filmed in the house. Jimmy was eager to meet and talk to Samson.

Among the people there that night was another young and struggling actor I'd seen around town, a nice guy named Jack Nicholson from New Jersey. He was all smiles when he saw Jimmy and asked me to introduce him. I said to Jimmy, "This is Jack Nicholson," and Jack reached out his hand, but Jimmy mumbled something and turned around to talk with Samson. The snub had nothing to do with Jack personally, it was something Jimmy did, but Jack was embarrassed and I made up some excuse, telling him it was the wind and the bikes that did something to Jimmy's eyes and ears.

Jack nodded and turned to a cute girl. He never let on that he'd been bothered by Jimmy's snubbing, though in the instant it had happened I could see him caving in right in front of me.

I'd met Dick Clayton, Jimmy's agent, at Famous Artists while he was handling Tab Hunter, following Tab's flight from Henry Willson. Dick was also handling a kid actress named Tuesday Weld and living in a single apartment with a Murphy bed, on Norton just north of Santa Monica Boulevard. There was no connection between Tab and Jimmy as friends, or even acquaintances. In fact, Jimmy rarely socialized with other actors, especially members of the *Rebel* cast—not even Natalie Wood. He was not friendly or on talking terms with other Warner contract players like Sal

Mineo or Dennis Hopper. In time, Sal would be one of the few people to publicly state his distance from Jimmy—while still desiring to have been closer in any way possible. Following Jimmy's death—others like Dennis and Nick Adams—would not be able to resist fabricating personal friendships with Jimmy that had little to do with real life.

During the filming of *Rebel*, Jack Simmons stayed close at hand. He was excluded from Jimmy's celebrity hobnobbing, though Jimmy only put in the occasional, obligatory "flash in the pan" appearance. His real, vital private life was being played out no differently than in his night wanderings through New York. Sammy Davis, Jr., for one, was always tickled by the bad-boy stories circulating around Jimmy, and openly fawned over the "hottest actor in town."

Jimmy's Hollywood career spanned only eighteen months and three motion pictures, two not yet released at the time of his death. In that brief time, everyone wanted to meet him or get close to him, but Jimmy shied off into the shadows of his own notoriety.

"I only have this one life to live," he said, "and there's too many things I don't know yet . . ."

Though he'd signed on to play Billy the Kid in *The Left Handed Gun* and Rocky Graziano in the prizefighter's life story, and to star in *Somebody Up There Likes Me* alongside Pier Angeli, Jimmy's "movie star" abode was a cramped furnished apartment above the Sunset Strip. It had one room, and a kitchen littered with paper cups and takeouts from Googie's or Hamburger Hamlet, plus stacks of papers and spools of reel-to-reel tapes. His clothes were thrown into the closet—he'd scoop up some shirts and pants from a chair, open the little closet with a partitioned door like a folding screen, and throw the clothes in on top of whatever else was there. "Hollywood is not my home," he said. He still kept a small apartment in New York, but claimed that that was not his home either. He'd been back again to Fairmount, Indiana with photographer Dennis Stock, who took those prophetic pictures of Jimmy sitting in a coffin, but neither was Indiana his home, he said. And neither was Santa Monica, where his estranged father still lived, remarried to another woman that Jimmy stayed away from.

One time he wanted to ride to Tijuana and had me race up to his place. He was leaning against the sink in the small kitchen, eating sardines from a

can and looking sick. He'd been cut during the filming of a knife fight for
Rebel, and he'd also been accidentally tapped on the cheekbone by Mushy
Callahan, an old prize fighter who was showing Jimmy the ropes for the
Graziano story. I asked him if the slight stab had hurt, and he told me that
the pain was good, because it "clarified direction." He said, "Any pain is like
misdirected energy." He said it was important to read Gerald Heard's *Pain,
Sex and Time*. "You know, *atado*, Strasberg in New York and these fuckers
at the studio are afraid of pain," he said. "But without pain, no discoveries
would be made. It was the fear of the pain of death," he continued, "and
not death itself that kept the fat numb people from making discoveries."

The discoveries Jimmy wanted to make were in some unknown terri-
tory a good distance from the conventions accepted by someone like Pier
Angeli. While making *Eden*, Jimmy was having sex with Pier in the dressing room he occupied during most of the filming on his first picture. He
said she'd been a little "tight," but tasted "good like a pizza."

When the picture was finished, he didn't want to leave the studio and
stayed holed up in his dressing room. Loaning out Jimmy to star in *Somebody Up There Likes Me* would give Warners the chance to further play up
the romance between Jimmy and Pier. Any connection between the two
short of marriage meant additional box office for Warners. But no one
anticipated Jimmy's volatile mood swings or the depth of the personal confusion that was being kindled by his sudden success like a heat ray through
a magnifying glass. Though the studio drummed-up the studio romance
between Pier and Jimmy, no one could have anticipated the peculiar chem-
istry that passed between them in that short, intense time.

Pier later said, in characteristically dramatic fashion, "I brought out in
Jimmy the small boy that he kept locked in his heart, or in his mind. This
small boy was a very troubled one. He wanted me to love him uncondi-
tionally, but Jimmy was not able to love someone else in return, that is,
with any deep feeling for that other person. He wanted to be loved. It was
the troubled boy that wanted to be loved very badly. I loved Jimmy as I
have loved no one else in my life, but I could not give him the enormous
amount of love that he needed. It emptied me. Loving Jimmy was something that could empty a person. There was no other way to be with Jimmy
except to love him and be emptied of yourself . . ."

Jimmy never had it seriously in mind to marry Pier. To people he
thought the idea would please, he suggested the "possibility of matrimony."
But on the practical side, he was more concerned about the horse he'd
bought and what it ate and where it was stabled.

When Pier rushed into a sudden marriage to her ex-boyfriend, singer
Vic Damone, the head-hanging attitude adopted by Jimmy drew sympathy
from those he wanted to feel sorry for him. But to others he said of Pier
and Damone, "Fuck them both—who the fuck needs them? People who
nobody needs, they find each other."

There were the rumors of a few brief "romances," rumors that have
been drastically exaggerated over the years, elaborated in the fantasies put
forth as fact by those claiming to have been "involved" with Jimmy. What
relationships he had following Pier's marriage to Damone, Jimmy handled
as carelessly as he did the sports cars he raced, with the same recklessness
as he rode his motorcycle. Back in New York, he'd used my bike a couple
of times, but he wasn't good at handling it. In Hollywood, he traded in his
Triumph and bought another one with a bigger engine. He was impulsive,
taking more chances than he had two years earlier, yet he still rode a motorcycle like a farmer. There wasn't really anything copacetic between Jimmy
and a machine, like there was with Steve McQueen. Though I'd never like
McQueen or get along with him, I had to salute his handling of cars and
bikes. Steve knew machines.

Jimmy didn't. He wanted to, but even if there had been more time it
would have remained another thing Jimmy claimed he had to do, had to
know. He would have lacked the discipline and focus to follow through.
When he entered his Speedster in races, he wasn't there to race, but to win.
Winning with Jimmy was more important than the race.

His one-month relationship with the young actress Ursula Andress was
going nowhere. Jimmy told me her mouth reminded him of Miriam's in
New York, "but Ursula and me can't get an intelligent situation going, and
her perfume chokes me," he said. "But we're getting our pictures taken and
it's hotsy-totsy time in Hollywood! We're all going to the moon!" he sang.

Some publicists claimed Jimmy rode his bike to the church where Pier
was marrying Damone, and that he sat across the street and then gunned
the engine and took off dramatically. In truth, Jimmy described himself

as an "existential pencil" who felt nothing about Pier marrying Damone. There was no sense of loss, he said, though he'd act the "poor injured soul" to the hilt for those who'd understand the "conventional approach" and readily applaud Jimmy's performance of "Woe is me, oh, woe is me!"

The pain that Jimmy felt could not be understood by others. Kazan had eyeballed it instantly and tagged it as "a crazy streak in the person who's always jumping around without any provocation from the outside." And then there were the discoveries Jimmy had to make. "Discoveries can be inside the person," Jimmy said. The thing about making them was that you had to pit yourself against the outside, and the only way to get inside yourself was by putting yourself in situations that were risky, that you couldn't back out of once you got into them.

The religious shadows hanging over Pier's life seemed to bind Jimmy up in contradictory feelings. He played out a kind of "I've been converted" role for some of those close to Pier, but was far more clearly intrigued by "those destructive influences of beliefs based on torture and blood and crucifixion." Later he said, "I believe in freedom, not God. If you want to call freedom God, then you can say I believe in God, but I say I believe in freedom." He claimed he had "a lot to discover," and that maybe others would prove that he was wrong.

He said riding bikes and driving race cars, sex, photography, bullfighting, and people like the one-legged girl were the real "avenues of discovery." Ursula Andress, he said, while she was cute and sexy, seemed to question nothing about the role Hollywood had stamped onto her. In fact, she'd bypassed Jimmy in favor of an actor of "shallow talents," John Derek. The only good thing about Derek, said Jimmy, was the line he'd delivered in the Bogart movie *Knock on Any Door*, "Live fast, die young, and have a good-looking corpse." With that, Jimmy gave a little two-fingered salute and stepped off into infinity.

11

I Almost Married Jimmy Dean

BEVERLY WILLS AS TOLD TO HELEN WELLER

Beverly Wills met James Dean through his college roommate Bill Bast sometime before April 1951. The seventeen-year-old Wills was attending high school and acting in the radio show *Junior Miss*, produced at CBS's radio and TV studio in Hollywood, when she began dating Bast, who worked there part-time as an usher. Dean replaced Bast in her affections not long after they were introduced.

Beverly was the daughter of Si Wills and Joan Davis, a comedienne who had carved out a successful career in vaudeville, movies, and television. Davis, proud of her Emmy awards and material success—she had a large closet in her Beverly Hills home filled with just her furs—was determined to make her daughter a star in her own image. She got Beverly small roles in movies and planted publicity pieces designed to give the impression she was destined to follow in her mother's footsteps: "Observers say Beverly is a dead ringer for her mother, with the same cracked features, blonde hair and expressions."

Wills's relationships with Bast and Dean were two of her attempts to escape her mother's gilded cage by finding a marriageable man. When Dean left for New York, she resumed dating Bast. Bast, a closeted gay man, was relieved when she broke their engagement after an argument with her mother, who insisted Beverly postpone marriage until she graduated from UCLA.

Though Davis worked hard to promote her daughter, even hiring her to play her younger sister in her sitcom *I Married Joan* (1952–1955), Wills's career never clicked. She appeared in episodes of several TV series and had small roles in a few movies, including *Some Like It Hot* (1959), in which she played one of the members of the all-girl band that Tony Curtis and Jack Lemmon join in drag.

There would be no happy ending for Beverly Wills. An alcoholic, she spent the evening of October 23, 1963, celebrating winning a role in the pilot for a sitcom that would have made her a series regular if it was picked up by a network. She fell asleep after midnight with a cigarette in her hand, setting fire to the Palm Springs home where her mother had died two years before of a heart attack at age fifty-three. Wills was consumed in the fire. Her grandmother, Nina Davis, and her two sons from the second of her three marriages died from smoke inhalation. Wills was twenty-nine years old.

Wills's article recalling her relationship with James Dean was published in the March 1957 issue of *Modern Screen*. —Ed.

I WAS JIMMY DEAN'S GIRLFRIEND. We went steady for seven months, and at one time we talked about getting married. I loved Jimmy at that time and I understood him as few people did.

We met on a blind date about five years ago. He was a bashful boy behind big horn-rimmed glasses and his hair looked as though it hadn't been combed in weeks. When we were introduced he merely said, "Hi," and stared at the floor.

Finally we got into his car and drove to a shore picnic—and he hardly said a word. He was a little self-conscious about his car, not because it was beat-up looking, but because he couldn't whip any speed out of it. "Good old Elsie," he said with a wry kind of smile, stroking the wheel. "I call her Elsie because she's slow as a cow. I hate anything slow. I wish I could trade this in for a fast job." After that little speech, he clammed up and didn't say another word.

I thought he was pretty much of a creep until we got to the picnic, and then all of a sudden he came to life. We began to talk about acting and Jimmy lit up. He told me how interested he was in the Stanislavsky method, where you not only act out people, but things too.

"Look," said Jimmy, "I'm a palm tree in a storm." He held his arms out and waved wildly. To feel more free, he impatiently tossed off his cheap, tight blue jacket. He looked better as soon as he did, because you could see his broad shoulders and powerful build. Then he got wilder and pretended he was a monkey. He climbed a big tree and swung from a high branch. Dropping from the branch he landed on his hands like a little kid who was suddenly turned loose. He even laughed like a little boy, chuckling uproariously at every little thing. Once in the spotlight, he ate it up and had us all in stitches all afternoon. The "creep" turned into the hit of the picnic.

I learned that it was nothing for Jimmy to run through a whole alphabet of emotions in one evening, alternating sharply from low to high and back again, and no one could ever tell what mood would hit him. A couple of nights later, we went to a movie and during the picture Jimmy sat hunched forward, his chin cupped in his hands, looking something like that statue of the thinker. When I tried to whisper something to him, he shushed me up. He was so completely absorbed in the performance on the screen!

Jimmy was still in this somber mood when we left, and when we got into his car he didn't say a word. Suddenly he said, "I feel like some music." He started to sing "Row, Row, Row Your Boat."

I was beginning to see Jimmy every day now and I noticed that he always wore the same clothes, a blue jacket and gray slacks. Either that or a pair of jeans. That was all he owned.

Once he spilled coffee on himself and it left a stain on the slacks. He jumped up and was so mad at himself. I couldn't understand it, because Jimmy didn't seem to give a hoot about clothes.

"It's only a pair of pants," I said, "send it to the cleaners."

"That's just it," he said. "I can't even pay the cleaners, and I wanted to go to the studio tomorrow and see about a job."

Jimmy wanted more than anything else in the world to become an actor. But he couldn't get a job. It would almost kill him when he'd go out to see the casting directors and return with nothing. He never lost confidence in himself, but he was angry because no one else shared that confidence. He would come by and see me after a fruitless interview, and he'd be in a black mood. "The director said I was too short," he once mumbled savagely. "How can you measure acting in inches? They're crazy!"

They also told him he wasn't good-looking enough, and always that he wasn't the type. Usually, when the casting heads told him this, Jimmy would get so mad he'd insult the men right back!

A Charmer as Well

I was doing a part in the radio version of *Junior Miss*, and Jimmy would sit in on the rehearsals and watch. One day, they needed a young man for one of the roles and Hank Garson, the director, asked me if my boyfriend could handle it. "Of course," I said happily.

I introduced Jimmy to Mr. Garson. "Have you ever done anything in radio?" asked the director. Any other actor, faced with such an opportunity, would have said *yes*, but not Jimmy. I think he was a little angry at the director for having let him sit around for so many weeks before offering him a job, and he wanted to show off. Anyway, Jimmy looked defiantly at Mr. Garson and said, "No." "Sorry," said the director, and walked away.

I ran after Jimmy. "Why did you say that?" I asked. "Why didn't you tell him you could do it? If you'd only been nice he'd have given you a chance."

Jimmy was still stubborn. "I don't have to lie to get a job in radio. Either he can give me a chance because he thinks I can act, or he can take his old job."

But although he used to rub many people—unfortunately, important people—the wrong way because of his hurts and resentment, he could charm the birds off the trees when he wanted to.

My mother didn't share my enthusiasm for Jimmy, nor was my mother to blame. Jimmy had the knack of putting his worst foot forward when he was in the mood.

Morose and Moody

I think it was the rebel in him. My mother—she's Joan Davis—was a success; he wasn't. Inside, Jimmy felt a little antagonistic toward many of the people who had achieved success in a profession where he couldn't stick his foot in the door.

He'd walk into our living room and promptly slump down in my mother's favorite arm chair, his foot dangling over the side, and sit like that for hours without saying a word. The only action we'd see out of him was when he'd reach out for the fruit bowl and eat one piece of fruit after another until the bowl was empty. When my mother would walk in, Jimmy never stood up, never said *hello*. He just remained slouched in the chair, munching on the fruit and staring moodily into space.

At the dinner table, his behavior was usually the same. Jimmy was always hungry. He loved pot roast, so I tried to have it for him whenever he was over. He'd wolf down two helpings of the meat with that same morose expression on his face, and mother would squirm.

It was more than his manners that disturbed my mother. She was afraid we were becoming serious. By this time I was wearing Jimmy's gold football on a chain around my neck. We were going steady and my mother couldn't think of any boy who had a more uncertain future than Jimmy! She thought he was too wild and would never settle down.

"Mom Was Flabbergasted"

My high school senior prom was coming up and, of course, I was going to take Jimmy. He was working as an usher at the time, and although he was in debt, he managed to put aside a few dollars every week so that he could rent a tuxedo. He asked me to go with him to the place where you rent these things, and when he saw all the dinner suits on racks he acted like a little boy in a candy store. He tried on one after another, and finally settled on a white jacket, black pants, dress shirt and bow tie. The rental on the whole works amounted to five dollars, and I don't think I ever saw Jimmy look happier.

"Imagine me in one of these things," he crowed, posing in front of a long mirror.

Although we sat out most of the dances—Jimmy didn't rhumba or jitterbug—he was in wonderful spirits the night of the prom. Some of the kids at school joined us and he laughed a lot and told funny stories. My mother stopped by with some friends for a few minutes, and even she was fascinated by Jimmy's personality that night. He jumped out of his chair when she came to our table and even helped her off with her stole. "Good heavens, I've never seen him like this before," said mother, flabbergasted but charmed.

The only other times I saw Jimmy that happy was when he was racing his motorcycle furiously. No matter how depressed he was, if Jimmy had a chance to get behind something that had terrific speed, he would laugh and come alive again.

When Jimmy learned that I had a little boat with an outboard motor, he was eager to try it out. Jimmy drove it around the cove, the salt spray making his face and his glasses glisten. I thought he enjoyed it, but he was disappointed because he couldn't get my little boat with its ten horse-power motor to whip up any great amount of speed. After that little ride, which I thought would turn out to be such fun, Jimmy was in the dumps again.

We Wanted to Get Married

I soon discovered that his moods of happiness were now far outweighed by his moods of deep despair. He was almost constantly in a blue funk. He still couldn't get an acting job and he was growing increasingly bitter. I hated to see Jimmy become so blue. When he was happy, there was no one more loveable. When he was depressed, he wanted to die.

These low moods became so violent that he began to tell me that he was having strange nightmares in which he dreamed he was dying. The nightmares began to give him a certain phobia about death.

"If only I could accomplish something before I die," he once said despairingly.

Like a lot of kids who go steady, we began to talk about getting married. I was not yet eighteen and we both knew my parents would never give their consent, so we planned to wait until my eighteenth birthday, which was a couple of months off, and elope. I had saved some money from my radio work, and we thought we would go to New York where we hoped Jimmy could get a break in the theatre.

But the dream didn't last long. A couple of months later, I had moved to Paradise Cove, a beautiful spot way out at the beach, where I was to spend six months with my father—my parents are divorced. The first week Jimmy drove out the long distance he began to gripe. "It's such a long drive, I'm running out of gasoline. Why can't you meet me in Hollywood?"

But I felt at home at the beach. I was with a lot of happy kids whom I'd grown up with every summer, and we were having lots of fun. Somehow, in this happy-go-lucky atmosphere, surrounded by boys and girls who didn't seem to have a care in the world, Jimmy stuck out like a sore thumb. He wore the same blue jacket and gray pants, only they seemed even shabbier next to the tailored slacks and sports shirts the other fellows wore. The whole crowd was very cliquey, and when Jimmy came by they looked at him as though he didn't belong.

Deeper into the Shell

Jimmy was very sensitive and it hurt him very much to be looked down on. He sensed their patronizing attitude and withdrew deeper and deeper into a shell. I think he wanted to hurt them back, too. I've often wondered if he recalled this period in his life when he portrayed the sensitive feelings of the rejected youth in *Rebel Without a Cause*.

One afternoon, the fellows were playing football on the beach. Jimmy joined them. Jimmy used to be very intense about everything he did, particularly if he wanted to show off. The other fellows were playing casually, since they weren't wearing protective football gear, but Jimmy plunged into the game like a tiger. He was out for blood. He was very strong, anyway, and he tackled one of the fellows with such ferocity that the boy yelled out in pain and the rest of the fellows ran over to pull Jimmy off him. After that, the fellows labeled Jimmy a bum sport and wouldn't talk to him.

Jimmy was miserable. He felt like an outsider in his work; he felt like an outsider with this crowd. The resentment made him sink all the more into rebellious moods that even I couldn't understand.

At a dance at the Cove one night, Jimmy remained in this strange mood. When one of the boys cut in and tried to dance off with me, Jimmy saw red. He grabbed the fellow by the collar and threatened to blacken both his eyes. I should have realized that this was his way of paying back a member of the crowd who had hurt him. But I was embarrassed. I ran out to the beach, and Jimmy walked after me, scuffing angrily at the sand, complete misery on his face. We had an argument and I pulled his gold football off the chain.

An Air of Bravado

A few days later, Jimmy called and told me that a friend was driving to New York and would give him a free ride. I was glad he called. I had been thinking of Jimmy ever since we broke off, and I realized more and more that this was a hurt and misunderstood boy. I wanted to remain his friend. I wished him luck.

A few months later my mother took me on a trip to New York. I had Jimmy's address. He was staying at the Y and I called him up. We met in

Central Park and my heart went out when I saw Jimmy walk up in the same blue jacket and gray slacks. That meant that he still hadn't gotten a job.

There was an air of bravado about Jimmy which soon crumpled when he told me that he hadn't been able to land a part in a show. He was so depressed, and he was hungry, too. I insisted that I buy us both a spaghetti dinner and he took me up on it. I think it was the first square meal he had had since he left Hollywood to come to New York.

I told him I was engaged to be married, and he told me about a girl he had met in New York who was a lady bullfighter. I could see that he was fascinated by this colorful girl. He showed me a tiny matador sword which he wore in his lapel, and he had gone overboard on the subject of bullfighting.

Later, he walked me back to my hotel. Just before he left he said, "I'm trying out for a part in a play tomorrow. It's a good, gutsy part. If I get it, I think this will be the break I've been waiting for. Maybe even Hollywood will sit up and take notice. I'll show them. If I don't get it," he paused, fingered the little sword in his lapel, and the familiar little smile played over his lips, "well, then I'll go to Mexico and become a bullfighter."

I kissed him on the cheek and wished him well, and then watched him walk down the street. He kicked at some stones like a little boy scuffing down the street, and he stopped under a lamppost to light a cigarette.

Then he squared his shoulders, turned the corner and was gone.

He never did go to Mexico.

END

Jimmy Dean can currently be seen in George Stevens' production of Giant, *a Warner Bros. release.*

12

James Dean at UCLA

James Bellah interviewed by Ronald Martinetti

Ronald Martinetti's interview with James Bellah, James Dean's fellow pledge at UCLA, was originally published at the website American Legends. —Ed.

AFTER SPENDING HIS FRESHMAN YEAR at Santa Monica Junior College, James Dean transferred to the University of California at Los Angeles in the fall of 1950. At UCLA, he took a cross section of academic courses and enrolled in an ROTC program as an air cadet. Jimmy also joined the Sigma Nu fraternity, where one of his pledge brothers was James Bellah, whose father, James Warner Bellah, had written the story that director John Ford's film *Fort Apache* (1948) was based on. Later, Bellah himself became a successful writer whose novels include *The Avenger Tapes* (with Robert G. Stimson) and *Imperial Express*. Here in an exclusive interview with American Legends, James Bellah recalls his fellow pledge brother—and budding non-conformist—James Dean.

American Legends: What was the UCLA campus like back in 1950?

James Bellah: Fraternities and sororities dominated undergraduate life. If you weren't in a fraternity, you were considered "non-org"—a non-organization person. The political climate was all-American.

AL: And into this scene came James Dean.

JB: We were in the same pledge class at Sigma Nu. I remember I walked in the house. He was vacuuming the carpet. He said, "My name is Dean," and showed me around.

AL: According to one story, Dean got into a fight with another pledge and was asked to leave.

JB: I wasn't at the meeting when he was expelled, so I don't know what really happened. But he didn't fit into that environment. He was an eccentric. Hollywood is full of born actors.

AL: You got him his first agent, Isabel Draesemer.

JB: I guess that's my claim to fame. We did a Pepsi commercial. There were a lot of young kids dancing around a jukebox. I was supposed to be the star. But Dean was a natural. He grabbed one of the girls and started jitterbugging—tossing her over his shoulder.

AL: You also appeared with Dean in an Easter special—"Hill Number One"—which had a religious theme.

JB: I played a Roman soldier. Dean had a speaking role as one of the Apostles. He had the flu, and his voice was husky. Some high school girls thought he was sexy and started a fan club. Even then, Dean could go through a lens.

AL: Another student in the Theater Arts Department was named Bill Bast. Later, he wrote a memoir that became a cult classic. (*James Dean: A Biography*. New York: Ballantine Books, 1956.)

JB: I could never finish the book. He made James Dean sound like the sweetest boy he ever knew.

AL: You also met Rogers Brackett, the radio director James Dean lived with in Hollywood and New York. Only one Dean biographer ever talked to him. What was Brackett like?

JB: He was an elegant, Clifton Webb type homosexual. There's no question he was a swish.

AL: Did James Dean ever talk about his relationship with Brackett or others?

JB: Dean was a user. I don't think he was homosexual. But if he could get something by performing an act . . . Once, when I ran into him in New York City at an agent's office, Dean told me that he had spent the summer as a "professional house guest" on Fire Island—which was a big gay hangout. Dean said this in a loud voice—he wanted people to hear. He was crazy.

AL: Someone once said that Neal Cassady, the hero of *On the Road*, had to act out every impulse. He was totally uninhibited. Maybe James Dean was the same way.

JB: Dean had an ego. He knew what he wanted and how to get it. Like all actors, he was to some extent playing himself, using a different aspect of himself to project in a role. In *Rebel Without a Cause*, that's Dean: the outsider, the lost soul . . .

AL: After James Dean's death, you and his other friends at UCLA were sought out by the media. Now, forty-five years later, you are still being asked about him.

JB: Dean captured a rebellious spirit that has always been part of our national character. He also fulfilled a need. As human beings, we need icons to bow down to. And James Dean has become a perennial hero to nonconformists.

13

---◆---

James Dean, The Hungry Matador

Peter L. Winkler

This article, which includes memories from Elizabeth Taylor, Neyle Morrow, and Budd Boetticher, was first published in *Filmfax* #135 (fall 2013). —Ed.

JAMES DEAN'S FASCINATION WITH BULLFIGHTING is central to the lore of his short life. Photos taken of Dean with his matador's cape hanging on the wall of his New York apartment or of him making dramatic *verónicas* (passes) against imaginary bulls with his cape have been fixtures of just about every biography and documentary of the actor's life. For the first time, here is the real story of how Dean acquired his matador's cape, filling in some of the gaps in our knowledge of his life before stardom beckoned.

When James Dean's mother died after a battle with uterine cancer when he was nine years old, Winton Dean, burdened with medical debts, sent his son to live with Jimmy's aunt and uncle, Ortense and Marcus Winslow, on their farm in Fairmount, Indiana.

One of Dean's significant influences was Fairmount's local minister, James DeWeerd. Fifteen years James Dean's senior, DeWeerd was the pastor of Fairmount's Wesleyan church and was a colorful but respected local figure. Born in 1916, DeWeerd completed his postgraduate studies at Cambridge University and served as a chaplain in the U.S. Army in France, where he was decorated for wounds received in battle. Well-read and widely traveled, DeWeerd was cosmopolitan, at least by Fairmount's standards.

DeWeerd drove powerful convertibles and would often have a crowd of teenage boys riding along with him. He would drive them twenty miles to the YMCA, where they would all disrobe and go swimming. Then they returned to DeWeerd's house, where he made them Sloppy Joes and called their parents to let them know where their children were.

Although DeWeerd's affinity for the company of teenage boys and his personality made him the subject of whispered rumors that he was "queer," no man has ever come forth to accuse DeWeerd of having molested him as a child or engaging with him in consensual sex as an adult.

In 1997, celebrity journalist Kevin Sessums interviewed Elizabeth Taylor for *POZ* magazine. When Sessums asked her about James Dean, she made the following admission:

> I loved Jimmy. I'm going to tell you something, but it's off the record until I die.* OK? When Jimmy was 11 and his mother passed away, he began to be molested by his minister. I think that haunted him the rest of his life. In fact, I know it did. We talked about it a lot. During *Giant* we'd stay up nights and talk and talk, and that was one of the things he confessed to me.

James Dean gravitated toward DeWeerd because, like Dean, he was an outsider in Fairmount and an empathetic authority figure. DeWeerd took Dean to the Indianapolis 500, taught him how to drive a car, and got Dean fascinated with bullfighting when he showed him the amateur movies he had taken of bullfights in Mexico.

Dean wouldn't get to know more about bullfighting until he graduated from high school and returned to Los Angeles to pursue acting. Although bullfights held in nearby Tijuana were then a popular weekend event for Angelenos, they might as well have been on the moon for Dean, who couldn't afford gas for the old Chevy his father had presented him with as an inducement to attend Santa Monica Junior College and UCLA.

---

* Sessums revealed Taylor's confession in an article containing outtakes from his 1997 interview with her, which *The Daily Beast* published on March 23, 2011, the day she died. —Ed.

Emboldened by his success in getting featured in a two-day Pepsi commercial filmed in December 1950 and shortly thereafter, playing John the Apostle in "Hill Number One," an episode of the TV series *Family Theater* broadcast on March 25, 1951 (Easter Sunday), Dean dropped out of UCLA after being rejected for two major roles in plays put on by the school's Theater Arts department. But more professional acting employment was slow in coming. Never flush with money, Dean was content to depend on his dutiful college roommate, Bill Bast, to keep both their heads above water. After a violent falling out with Bast, Dean found himself in dire straits, as recalled by Neyle (pronounced Neelee) Morrow, who met Dean when they both acted in director Sam Fuller's film *Fixed Bayonets!* (1951).

"I'll tell you what I know about James Dean," Morrow recalled. "A short experience I had, but a very friendly episode. Sam Fuller is the dearest friend I had in the film business. I did all but three of his pictures. I had done two pictures for him, *The Steel Helmet* [1951] and *Park Row* [1952]. He liked my work, so he offered me the part of the senior medic in *Fixed Bayonets!* It was a showy part and also, I worked for about five weeks out of the maybe eight or nine weeks of the filming.

"We were soldiers stationed in Korea for quite a while. As most of us got killed off, they would bring in new recruits. James Dean was the last of the new recruits, there were about three, I think, three or four. There were several of us who used to go outside for a smoke or a talk or whatever during the breaks because they kept the sound stage extremely cold to maintain the snow on the mountain. I was with two or three of the friends I had made on the picture who were very conversant with me and vice versa. We were talking and some of us carried lunches. Because of the shortness of the break, we would rest and relax, because we had these very heavy packs on our backs. They weighed fifty pounds. Running up and down the hills, fake hills, but even so, was tiring and we thought it was better to relax than go into the cafe or whatever. A couple of days toward the very end of the filming, I saw this young man kind of off to himself. The second day I saw him, he looked down and I asked him if there was anything wrong. He said he was sure glad he got the job, he hoped he would do it well because he needed the money to go to New York. He wanted to go back there, hopefully to meet someone like Elia Kazan and get in a play.

"And so I noticed he didn't have anything to eat. I asked him if he was hungry. He said as a matter of fact he was.* So I said, 'Well, why don't you eat?' And he explained that he didn't have any funds. And I said, 'Good Heavens, Sam Fuller would be mortified to think that any of us happened to be hungry.' I said, 'What can I get you?' And he said, 'The thing I like most is a good hamburger and I hear there's a hamburger stand on the lot.' He was so grateful, he said, 'What's your name?' and he wrote it down on a match cover and I knew of course he'd never keep it [laughs] because he said, 'I'm coming back here to Hollywood and I'm going to be a success and I'm going to get in touch with you.' I said, 'Wonderful, wonderful, wonderful, I hope you're a great success.'

"I never saw him again in person. He was very personable, he was very good looking and he had a few lines in the very end of the picture. He was very charming. He certainly had the appearance even then, he had a lot of charisma, a lot of personality and determination. I felt really that I would probably never hear from him again personally, but I would hear about him. The last I saw him, he was munching away on the hamburger when I was called back to work."

Shortly after finishing his brief role in *Fixed Bayonets!*, Dean's fortunes improved when he began living with his gay mentor, advertising executive and radio director Rogers Brackett. Dean and Brackett, sometimes accompanied by some of Brackett's Hollywood friends like David Wayne and his wife, drove to nearby Tijuana to attend the bullfights held there.

Dean was then in the habit of bragging to Bill Bast about his exploits with Brackett and his newfound immersion in the Hollywood social scene. "He returned to L.A. on a high from a weekend in Mexicali where he and Rogers had visited a bull-breeding ranch outside of town," Bast wrote in his biography of Dean. "He told me that Rogers' friend, film director-cum-bullfighter Budd Boetticher, had arranged for him to practice his *verónicas* on a two-year-old bull, which he was, of course, not meant to kill, but merely taunt. He had come back with a practice cape of his own,

---

* Sam Fuller's production secretary was shocked by Dean's emaciated appearance when he appeared at their office in July 1951. —Ed.

Imagining himself a matador fighting a bull, James Dean flourishes the bullfighter's cape he borrowed from film director Budd Boetticher. *Editor's collection*

made of red felt in this case, and a practice pair of real bull's horns, gifts from Boetticher for his impressive 'initiation.'

"From that day on, Jimmy was never without those damn props. They adorned the walls of every place we lived together, and later, those he inhabited alone. At every possible opportunity, he would whip them down to practice his *verónicas*, enlisting the help of any unfortunate friend or acquaintance who happened to be on hand at the time to handle the horns and play toro to his matador. Each time I saw Jimmy reach for his gear and hand me those inevitable horns, I would silently curse the name of Budd Boetticher."

When I read Boetticher those passages from Bast's book and another from Ronald Martinetti's biography of Dean, where he writes that Dean's cape once belonged to matador Sidney Franklin, his reaction was succinct: "Bullshit!"

"Sidney Franklin was a, for God's sakes, Sidney Franklin wasn't a famous bullfighter in the first place, he was an American in from New York in Spain," Boetticher said. "He was gone before Jimmy Dean ever showed up. He [Dean] never met Sidney Franklin. I've seen pictures of it [the cape] hanging on the wall and it sure as Hell wasn't Sidney Franklin's. The cape was my cape. When people [Dean] have a personality like that the truth will usually suffice. Well, I'll tell you the true story and it's better than the one you heard.

"The true story is, I walked in my office one day at Universal,"* Boetticher recalled. "There was a young man sitting there with a letter from Anthony Quinn, who's a dear friend of mine, and the letter said that they were working together at the Actor's Lab in New York† and this young man was a great aficionado of the bulls and he was Jimmy somebody, and I didn't pay any attention to his name, would I be nice to him. He also was training to be an actor. Tony's letter said that Jimmy was a young friend of his and if I would teach him he would deeply appreciate it.

"Tony and I are friends since *Blood and Sand*‡ [1941], we've made so many pictures together. So naturally I'm going to be nice to him. If he was a terrible person I would have taken him home to lunch. So I took him home to lunch, we had a great lunch. And we went out in back and

---

* Universal-International Pictures. —Ed.

† The Actor's Laboratory, the theater workshop where Marilyn Monroe first seriously studied acting, was located in Los Angeles. Dean didn't set foot in New York for the first time until shortly after he visited Boetticher. —Ed.

‡ Boetticher served as an uncredited technical adviser and directed the "El Torero" dance number in *Blood and Sand*, in which Anthony Quinn played a prominent supporting role. —Ed.

I showed him how to hold a cape and the difference between a cape and a muleta* and why and took the cape and the sword back to the studio.

"We spent about two hours together and we went back to the studio and talked for a few minutes, and as Jimmy got up he walked to the door, he turned around and did a Glenn Ford impersonation, kicking the rug. We always kidded my good friend Glenn Ford about dirt kicking, because when he was on screen, when he wanted something, he never looked anybody in the eye. He kicked a little dirt or rug or whatever. Jimmy did this as well as Ford. He went to the door, he didn't pick up the cape. He was a very good actor and he stopped at the door and he said 'Mr. Boetticher,' and I said 'I've been telling you to call me Budd,' and he said, 'Budd, you're probably going to turn me down and I don't blame you, but I've never held a real fighting cape before. Can I take it home tonight? I'll bring it back first thing in the morning.' And I said, 'Sure, Jim, go ahead.'

"So two and a half years go by, I never saw the cape again, and my ex-wife and I were at the theater, we'd gotten in late to see *East of Eden* [1955], and all of a sudden a young man came out of a shower and walked into a close-up and I just instinctively said out loud, 'Son of a bitch, that's Jimmy Dean!'

"So I called him next morning at Warner Bros. and they know him pretty well there and they got him on the phone and he was really concerned. He said, 'Before you say anything, let me tell you something and you'll understand. Budd, I slept under that cape for two years.' I said, 'That's alright, it's nice to have found you,' and he said, 'I owe you one,' and I said 'You sure do,' and right after that he was killed and I never saw him again. He was great. He was just a kid that was Jimmy Dean. But of course he never fought a bull. He was a good kid, he was very intrigued, he saw a lot of pictures in my house and he wanted to fight bulls. I really don't think he ever got around to it. Then I never saw him again, or my cape."

---

* A short red cape attached to a stick that a matador uses instead of the full cape in the final stages of a bullfight. —Ed.

OUTTAKE

The Matador of Madison Avenue

"Jimmy and I did William Inge's first teleplay, which was 'Glory in the Flower.' Hume Cronyn, Jessica Tandy, Jimmy and myself. And we walked home from doing that show. That's when I had that experience with him when I was—we were walking along, in those days Madison Avenue was a, you know, just [a] one-way street downtown and there were no stores in those days. It was just kind of buildings for people . . .

"Yes, and we're walking along and he's talking to me about bullfighting. And . . . he's talking about bullfighting and we're walking and suddenly the buses—you know the buses would travel at 40 miles an hour down Madison Avenue because there was nobody to pick up on Sunday and suddenly he whipped off his jacket and jumped in the road and did a pass, like a bullfighter with the bus. The bus absolutely just barely touched his shirt. I leapt back, like any sensible Jewish boy. You know, I was shocked because I said to myself, this guy is going to kill himself and it was a year before he died."

—Actor and director Mark Rydell on
Larry King Live, December 3, 2005

14

Life with Rogers: James Dean's Gay Mentor Tells All

Ronald Martinetti

By the summer of 1951, James Dean was scraping bottom. He had dropped out of UCLA, had a falling out with his friend and roommate Bill Bast, and was frustrated by his acting career, which was going nowhere after a promising start. Dean's salvation came in the person of Rogers Brackett, whom he met while parking cars for a dollar an hour at Ted's Auto Park, located next to the CBS studios in Hollywood. Brackett was an account executive at a major advertising agency who directed a radio show at CBS sponsored by one of his agency's clients. Brackett, a witty, well-read man, had connections in show business on both coasts. Fortuitously for Dean, Brackett was gay and found him very attractive. Small talk led to coffee, which soon led to an invitation for Dean to share Brackett's comfortable poolside apartment above Sunset Boulevard.

Although Dean later went to great pains to conceal Brackett's role in his success to Hollywood columnists like Hedda Hopper, Brackett was a pivotal figure in his life. "Rogers Brackett was the key to Dean's career," Val Holley wrote in his insightful biography of James Dean. "He took him in when almost no one else believed in him; fed, clothed, and employed him; and planned and financed his move to New York. Eventually he introduced Dean to the producer who would put him on Broadway for the first time. Although his talent and photogenic face ensured that he would have been discovered eventually, it was Rogers Brackett who delivered him from the obscurity of Ted's Auto Park."

James Dean biographer Ronald Martinetti scored a real coup when he interviewed and corresponded with Brackett in the mid-'70s, the only journalist to do so. What follows are excerpts from his biography, *The James Dean Story*, containing Brackett's revelations about his one-time protégé. I have bridged the gaps in Martinetti's narrative left after excerpting his material with my editorial insertions, printed in italics. —Ed.

Through Ted Avery, another disgruntled former usher at CBS, he [Dean] found a job parking cars on a lot adjacent to the studio. The lot was a haven for out-of-work actors, run by a sympathetic man who allowed his young attendants to take off whenever they needed to go on an interview. The arrangement was ideal for Dean: the CBS executives who used the lot tipped well, bringing his salary almost to that of a full-time job. The hours were good, the work easy, and there was the ever-present chance that a producer or director might discover him.

Then one Saturday morning he parked a car for a man named Rogers Brackett. When Dean learned that Brackett directed a weekly CBS program, "Alias Jane Doe," starring Lurene Tuttle, he didn't waste any time confessing he was an actor. Over coffee, the two talked and Brackett casually promised to keep Dean in mind when casting future shows.

True to his word, he soon called Dean in to read for a small part. Dean's reading was melodramatic and his gestures overly theatrical for a radio studio, but Brackett awarded him the role. It was the first of six shows he did for Brackett. It was also the start of a long and invaluable friendship for Dean, but one that was not without its stormy moments. "I have often thought," Rogers later said, "I should have left 'Hamlet' in the parking lot."

A tall, curly-haired bachelor with good looks and an elegant manner, Brackett was some fifteen years Dean's senior. He was the son of Robert Brackett, an early Hollywood film producer who was once in partnership with Lewis J. Selznick. Born in Culver City, Brackett had literally been raised in Hollywood, and his connections in the film industry were numerous. He himself had served an apprenticeship with David O. Selznick, Lewis' son, and had worked at the Walt Disney Studio. He had left the film business to accept a high-paying position with the advertising firm of Foote, Cone, & Belding as account supervisor. One of his accounts sponsored "Alias Jane Doe," and Brackett doubled as the show's director, an arrangement that was not uncommon.

At this time Brackett was living at the Sunset Plaza, a fashionable apartment house above the Sunset Strip.

When Ted Avery's wife returned to Hollywood, Dean was suddenly forced to find another place to live, and he accepted Brackett's invitation to stay with him.

For Dean the Sunset Plaza proved a great improvement over Avery's modest quarters. Built on a hill, it afforded a majestic view of the Valley; Brackett had a comfortable garden apartment which he was subletting from William Goetz, a Universal-International executive. The apartment was adjacent to the swimming pool.

Once again Jimmy had struck it rich—at a friend's expense.

Through Rogers, too, Dean met a large number of people, and there was now glamour and excitement in his life. Rogers took him to private studio screenings, and they would dine at La Rue, a chic restaurant, where Dean liked the Vichyssoise, always pronouncing it "swishy-swashy."

Rogers gave him books to read by writers like Saint-Exupéry and Camus, and Dean absorbed them excitedly, asking for more. "He sapped the minds of his friends," [Bill] Bast once noted, "like a bloodsucker saps the strength of an unsuspecting man."

But Dean's intelligence was largely intuitive, Brackett felt. Once Dean surprised him by making a mobile, using wire and some chicken bones that had been left over from dinner the night before. When Rogers told him how much he liked the mobile, Dean answered, "What's a mobile?"

Soon Rogers was pretty hung up on his young friend, and they drifted into an affair. "My primary interest in Jimmy was as an actor—his talent was so obvious," Brackett said. "Secondarily, I loved him, and Jimmy loved me. If it was a father-son relationship, it was also somewhat incestuous."

One afternoon Jim Bellah dropped by to see Dean. He was taken aback by his fraternity brother's new living arrangements. Brackett was polished, droll, clever. Bellah found him "terribly precious." It was definitely not his scene. When Rogers left the room, Bellah turned to Jimmy and said, "This guy's a fairy." Dean replied: "Yeah, I know."

Was this merely a convenient relationship for Dean? After all, the casting couch was as much a part of Hollywood as the tall palms and wide boulevards. Jimmy would not be the first to use or to be used. Other legends have their little secrets.

Rogers himself sometimes wondered about the depths of Dean's emotions. Long after their friendship ended, he vividly recalled coming home one evening and finding Jimmy sitting in their bedroom crying. When he asked what was the matter, Dean said cryptically, "I can't love and I can't be loved." But Rogers maintained their sex life was not one-sided. In an interview in the 1970s, he said he believed their physical relationship had been mutually satisfying.

A brilliant stage director, Brackett had had the first Equity company in California, and he began to coach Dean in plays and readings. They rehearsed *Hamlet* on the grand staircase of the Sunset Plaza, overlooking the pool. "Elsinore with room service," Rogers quipped. Then, for contrast, Dean would recite some poems by James Whitcomb Riley he had learned as a boy. "'Little Orphant Annie' was quite one of his favorites," Brackett remembers. "It was very funny and very touching . . ."

As the war in Korea heated up and Uncle Sam needed soldiers, Dean was called for induction. "Deploring that and any other war," Brackett advised Dean to get out of the draft. "Better the funeral pyre in his Porsche than Korea," Brackett later said. "With his quasi-jock predilections he'd never have made it back . . . I feel."

Through a doctor friend, Brackett set up an appointment with a psychiatrist for Dean. After a viable number of sessions, the shrink came up with a document "that cooled the draft board." Years later, in 1974, Rogers wrote frankly in a letter: "As Jimmy was living with me, there was no question that his unsuitability for military service was valid, or so they were led to believe. It's one thing in the relationship he never regretted." When Dean saw Bellah and broke the news of his deferment, he told him, "I kissed the doctor."

Dean's contact with his family had been minimal since leaving UCLA. When he and Rogers visited them in their home in the Valley to pick up some clothes, Dean discovered that to earn extra cash his father was raising chinchillas in a spare bedroom.* Rogers thought the scene was something out of *The Day of the Locust*. Conversation was strained all the way around. Along with David Wayne, the actor, and his wife, Dean and Rogers went to Tijuana for a weekend to see a bullfight, first staying overnight in Laguna. Another time he traveled with Rogers to Mexicali where they saw the matador Arruza in the ring. In Mexicali Dean met Budd Boetticher, a movie

---

* James Dean's father and stepmother lived in Santa Monica, not in the San Fernando Valley. —Ed.

director and bullfight aficionado who had served as technical adviser for the film *Blood and Sand*. Boetticher gave Dean a blood-stained cape that had once belonged to Sidney Franklin, the Brooklyn-bred matador who had achieved fame in the rings of Spain and about whom Hemingway had written.*

The cape became Dean's prize possession and thereafter wherever he traveled the cape traveled with him.

Because of Rogers' many friends in the movie business, Jimmy easily found work as an extra.† He made his film debut in Paramount's *Sailor Beware*, a Dean Martin-Jerry Lewis comedy. In a boxing sequence Dean acted as a second for Jerry Lewis' opponent. A white towel draped around his neck, Dean spoke his first words on the Silver Screen: "That guy's a professional."

He next appeared in a Korean war movie, *Fixed Bayonets!*, starring Richard Basehart, and directed by Samuel Fuller, a friend of Brackett's. Again, Dean had one line of dialogue: "It could be the rear guard coming back." "What a part," he later said.

At Universal-International he had two days' work, playing a teenager in another comedy, *Has Anybody Seen My Gal?*, starring Rock Hudson and Piper Laurie. In the film Dean comes into an ice cream parlor and orders an elaborate ice cream sundae. The counterman, played by Charles Coburn, asks him to come back the next day for a fitting. Dean described the film as "family-type" entertainment.

It was not until years later when the film was shown on television that Piper Laurie learned she had once made a movie with James Dean.

Not all of Brackett's friends liked Dean, however, or were anxious to advance his career. A meeting Rogers arranged with Leonard Spiegelgass, a story editor at MGM and an important man in the studio hierarchy, ended in disaster when Spiegelgass ordered Dean from his house. "His manners were terrible," Spiegelgass said. "He flicked ashes on the rug and behaved

---

* See chapter 13, "James Dean, The Hungry Matador," to read the real story of how Dean acquired his bullfighter's cape. —Ed.

† Dean's agent, Isabel Draesemer, claimed to have gotten him the roles he played in *Fixed Bayonets!*, *Sailor Beware*, and *Has Anybody Seen My Gal? —Ed.*

like an animal. The boy was absolute poison." Spiegelgass warned Brackett that he was "ruining his reputation" by pushing Dean so hard, but Brackett paid no attention.

At the Zuma Beach home of George Bradshaw, the short story writer, Dean accidently set fire to one of Bradshaw's favorite armchairs and Brackett had to pay for its repair.

"Jimmy was like a child," Rogers said. "He behaved badly just to get attention." But he added, "He was a kid I loved—sometimes parentally, sometimes not parentally."

Like a child, too, Dean seemed to be forever testing the affection of those closest to him. "The only way he could be sure you really loved him," another friend, Stewart Stern, later said, "was if you loved him when he was truly at his worst."

By the fall, Dean was becoming slightly bored with the life he was leading. He sought out his old friend Bast, whom he had hardly seen since the penthouse fiasco in mid-summer. Bast was now working as a pageboy on several shows at CBS and preparing to start his senior year at UCLA.

"You know," Dean confided to him "it gets sickening. The other day we were sitting at the pool and I made a bet with Rogers that the names of La Rue or the Mocambo would be dropped at least fifteen times within the next hour. We kept count and I won. What a pile of . . ."

As always, whatever the state of his personal life, Dean's career was foremost in his mind, and he again was worried about his future as an actor. "A guy could go on knocking his brains out, getting nothing but bit parts for years," he told Bast over a bowl of chili at Barney's Beanery. "There's got to be more."

To another struggling actor Dean confessed the same fear. "They'll never give me a real chance out here," he said. "I'm not the bobby-sox type, and I'm not the romantic leading-man type either. Can you imagine me making love to Lana Turner?"

Although he was attending James Whitmore's class less regularly, his respect for the actor remained as great as ever. When Whitmore took him aside after class one evening and spoke to him sharply, Dean listened. "Stop dissipating your energy and talent," Whitmore urged. He told him to "quit just hanging around Hollywood" and go to New York where he would be able to study and master his craft. "Learn to be an actor. It doesn't take anything if all you want to be is just another ham."

Later, in press interviews with Hedda Hopper and others, Dean would credit Whitmore with stimulating his interest in serious acting and encouraging him to go to New York. Although Whitmore no doubt did influence him, Dean never publicly mentioned his real mentor, Rogers Brackett, or acknowledged the help he had generously given. But if Dean had any lingering doubts about leaving, they were dispelled when Rogers was called to Chicago, the home office of Foote, Cone & Belding, on an important assignment. Eventually, Brackett hoped to be transferred to New York, but he had no idea how many months he might have to remain in Chicago. For the third time in three short months Dean was about to literally lose the roof over his head. It proved to be too much.

"I can't stomach this dung home any more," he told Bast with finality after a late-night talk session.

Several days later, when Bast returned to his apartment after work, he found a message the landlady had left: "Mr. Dean called. Gone to New York."

Before arriving in New York Jimmy first stopped off in Chicago to see Rogers Brackett, who was staying at the Ambassador East. Brackett remembers Dean made quite a stir striding through the lobby of the expensive hotel dressed in blue jeans and carrying his bullfighter's cape slung over his shoulder. After about a week in the Windy City, Dean visited the Reverend DeWeerd for a few days at his new home in Indianapolis and paid a visit to the farm to see his aunt and uncle. Then he proceeded on his journey.

Shortly after his arrival in New York in October 1951, Dean rented a room at the Iroquois Hotel on West 44th Street, several blocks from Times Square. As his funds dwindled, he took a small room at the YMCA on West 63rd Street, a short block away from Central Park. Sometime later, after meeting and beginning an intimate relationship with dancer Elizabeth "Dizzy" Sheridan, they rented a tiny, dilapidated room at the Hargrave Hotel at 112 West 72nd Street, just off Columbus Avenue.—Ed.

In late March their funds ran out again, and they were forced to move out of their hotel. Dizzy found a tiny room on Eighth Avenue, and Dean went to live with Rogers Brackett, who had come to New York several months earlier. In fact, he and Jimmy had spent Christmas together at an inn in Garrison, New York. Rogers later remembered it as an "old fashioned country Christmas." Still working for Foote, Cone & Belding, Brackett was now with their Madison Avenue office and had a loft apartment on West 38th Street, just off Fifth Avenue.

As in the past, Brackett was only too glad to help his young protégé. One of the accounts he handled was the Hallmark Company, which sponsored the *Hallmark Hall of Fame*, and by pulling a few strings he got them to hire Dean.

For his paycheck each week Dean was required to do little more than show up at the studio; the only actual duty he had was to stand at a blackboard and list the show's credits as the program went off the air. This was done live and in close-up, showing only Dean's hand on camera. But even to this Jimmy was able to bring a flair that was all his own: invariably as he got to the final words "devised and directed by Albert McCleery" he would either break the chalk or scrape it in such a way as to make an unpleasant noise.

Albert McCleery was never sure whether this was accidental or not, but because of Brackett he was forced to put up with Dean anyway.

For Dean, life now seemed curiously happy. He and Dizzy were still together much of the time, but there were again gay times with Rogers too: evenings spent at the ballet or dining in expensive restaurants. One night, Rogers remembered, he and Jimmy saw William Faulkner hanging around the Algonquin lobby. But, for a change, Jimmy was too tongue-tied to introduce himself to the great author.

Dizzy knew of Dean's relationship with Brackett and it caused her great pain. Over twenty years later, she was reluctant to talk about it out of loyalty to her dead friend. In a way, Dizzy rationalized Brackett's presence by believing Jimmy's claim that he had originally come to New York "to get away from Brackett," but that the director had "pursued" him. On one occasion she met Brackett and was noticeably cold, if not outright rude, to him. Later, Jimmy gave her a hug and thanked her for "standing up to Rogers."

On Sunday nights, after the Hallmark telecast, Sarah Churchill, the show's hostess, held open house for the cast at her penthouse on Central Park South, and Dean and Brackett always went. To entertain her guests

Miss Churchill did imitations of her father, Sir Winston, and told amusing stories of what it had been like being the Prime Minister's daughter.

Dean seemed almost star-struck by these gatherings, and was fond of Miss Churchill, who would take him aside and lecture him good-naturedly about his behavior, especially the tricks he played on Albert McCleery.

In early May 1952, Bill Bast arrived in New York and reconnected with Dean. Shortly thereafter, Dean and Bast were again sharing quarters.—Ed.

In August, as summer reached its peak and the city turned into a drab desert of concrete, another opportunity shimmered on the horizon, like an oasis, and with that strange combination of luck and guile that had propelled him through life thus far, Dean was quick to reach for it.

He was offered a job as a deckhand aboard a yacht chartered by Lemuel Ayers, a friend of Rogers Brackett's. A charming and talented Princeton graduate, Ayers was a well-known set designer and had coproduced Cole Porter's *Kiss Me Kate*. He was then preparing a new play for Broadway, *See the Jaguar*, by N. Richard Nash.

Although Ayers was part of the homosexual circle that swirled around Brackett and his friends, the producer lived with his wife and two children in an old Victorian house near Nyack, New York, in Rockland County. Brackett and Dean sometimes spent weekends there, where Jimmy enjoyed himself entertaining Ayers' young children, Sarah and Jonathan.

Although Brackett had already suggested Dean for a part in Ayers' new play, the producer felt he lacked experience. But the job as deckhand was open.

Dean joined the crew and the sloop sailed for Martha's Vineyard. Aboard were Ayers, his wife Shirley, and several guests. The trip lasted almost two weeks; the first day out the weather was bad and the sea turned rough. When the sloop reached New London, several people, including Alec Wilder, decided to get off and return by train. But Dean stayed, enjoying himself, quickly learning about lines and spars, sheets and shrouds—a farm boy turned deckhand. A young Gatsby in the making.

By the time the sloop returned to port, Ayers had been impressed enough by Dean to reconsider his earlier decision. He promised that when *See the Jaguar* was cast, Dean would be given a reading. But whether he got the part would depend on how well he did.

One afternoon, on an impulse, Dean suggested to Bill Bast and Dizzy Sheridan that they escape the heat of summer in the city and hitchhike the eight hundred miles to his aunt and uncle's farm in Indiana. They were there when Dean was called back to New York by a phone call from Lemuel Ayers's office. See the Jaguar was going into production and they wanted him to audition. Dean's first reading went badly because he had broken his glasses. Rogers Brackett and Alec Wilder worked on Lem Ayers and persuaded him to give Dean a second chance. This time, Dean gave a fantastic reading and won the role.

See the Jaguar opened on December 3, 1952, and ran only five performances. Reviews of the play were bad, but Dean's performance received praise.

There was another important change in Dean's life as 1953 arrived. He relegated Rogers Brackett to the past, replacing him with a new group of friends.

Dean saw Brackett for the last time when he visited New York and Fairmount in January 1955, accompanied by photographer Dennis Stock, who was documenting him for a Life *magazine feature. While visiting his old haunts in New York, Dean had what would prove to be his final encounter with Rogers Brackett.—Ed.*

In New York Dean met another old friend whom he had not seen for some time, but their reunion was less pleasant. Rogers Brackett, who had lost his job at Foote, Cone & Belding as a result of a cutback at the agency, saw Dean and over a drink asked him to loan him some money until things got better. Dean refused, saying, "Sorry, Pops." He also told Brackett that he felt he had "outgrown" him and Alec Wilder and no longer wished to be friends. To this Brackett replied, "You might outgrow me, but I don't think you can ever outgrow Alec Wilder."

When Wilder learned that Dean had rebuffed Brackett, he tracked him down. "I read him the riot act," Wilder wrote in his unpublished memoir, "about his dreadful behavior toward Rogers. For nowhere in all his publicity had Rogers's name been mentioned. I told him he was morally bound to write Rogers a letter of apology. He claimed that he couldn't do it, so I wrote a letter as Jimmy might have. Then I forced him to rewrite it so that it could be mailed in his handwriting. Thank God, that did a little to mend the cracks. For the following evening Rogers came by, and the three of us had a very pleasant, giddy evening. But the damage had been done, and, as far as I know, they never met again."

While Wilder was lambasting Dean, he said that Brackett should sue him to recover the cost of his past assistance to him. "I didn't know it was the whore who paid; I thought it was the other way around," Dean said.—Ed.

When Brackett learned that in the 1970s Dean's autograph had sold for more than one of Lincoln's, he noted wryly, "I wish I had saved J.D.'s love/hate letter and poetry and drawings—I'd take a world cruise on the proceeds." The letter he referred to was one that Dean had written after they said their good-bye. A few years after Dean's death, Rogers threw it out, along with other Dean artifacts.

Brackett was always discreet, and after Dean's death, regularly refused press interviews. However, Dean's agent arranged for the studio to pay Brackett a "finders fee" to allay any bad feeling towards his protégé and safeguard the company's property. After he disappeared from Dean's life, Brackett went on to hold several important advertising positions. Later, he devoted himself to travel, a wealthy, reclusive man who died of throat cancer in 1979.

15

In Memory of Jimmy

Elizabeth Sheridan

Liz Sheridan is best known today for playing Jerry Seinfeld's mother on the hit '90s sitcom *Seinfeld*. In January 1952, the twenty-three-year-old dancer and singer met James Dean (who had recently left Los Angeles for New York) and became his girlfriend. Dean, often moody and depressed when acting jobs were scarce, hung on to the free-spirited Sheridan, nicknamed Dizzy for her childhood penchant for spinning around until she became dizzy. She "kept him laughing and smiling and civilized," Bill Bast, their mutual friend, told *People* magazine for a 1996 article they ran about her passionate "first love" affair with Dean. Dean and Sheridan's relationship ended after his Broadway debut in *See the Jaguar* in December 1952. He received accolades for his performance as a backwoods teenager during the play's brief run. They hardly saw each other after that. "He was being hauled away into this career, and I couldn't follow him," she told *People*. Sheridan was living in Puerto Rico when she heard the news that Dean had been killed in an auto accident. "I was numb," she later recalled. "I didn't believe it. I still don't—I keep thinking he's going to call."

Dizzy & Jimmy, Sheridan's memoir of her affair with Dean, was published in 2000. Her article appeared in the October 1957 issue of *Photoplay*. —Ed.

> *She was a struggling dancer. He was a lonely actor. Together in the cold, hard city of New York they loved, and laughed and dreamed. This is Elizabeth Sheridan's own story:*

THE FIRST TIME I EVER KNEW THAT JIMMY DEAN EXISTED was one after-noon at the Rehearsal Club* in New York. It was raining. He was sit-ting in the living room, and I heard him ask a lot of other girls if he could borrow an umbrella, and nobody seemed particularly interested in whether he got wet or not. So I loaned him mine and he was overly grateful. A cou-ple of days later, he came back and returned it. One of the biggest interests that he had at the time was bullfighting. He caught my interest because I was also interested in bullfighting. That, I think, was the important reason we got together at the very beginning.

Then, I was dancing in a trio, two boys and me, and we were rehears-ing about two or three blocks away, and one night these two guys came to the Rehearsal Club for a rehearsal that we were going to have, and Jimmy asked if he could come along and watch. So he did, and he was very much impressed by the whole thing. We had a habit of stopping in this place—a little neighborhood joint—to have something to eat before we went home, and Jimmy came along with us.

I remember it was a very funny incident. We liked a certain kind of beer that was out at the time called Champale. It seemed it was somebody's birthday, but I can't remember whose it was, and Jimmy was, more or less, my date. The waiter, when I ordered Champale, thought I said *champagne*, and he came back and he brought a bottle of champagne and Jimmy's eyes almost popped out, because at that time he was living at the "Y" [YMCA] and he didn't have a cent, and he was borrowing from everyone in town and, instead of saying, "You made a mistake of some kind," he said, "Oh no, I can pay for it." He made a big thing about that. It was funny.

My two dancing partners and Sue Hight† were there, too, I think. Everybody used to meet at this place. Jimmy didn't impress me one bit when I first met him. I thought he was a little straggly kid that somebody had brought in—actually that's more or less what happened. One of the

---

* The Rehearsal Club was a women's boardinghouse for aspiring thespians and artists, situated in two adjacent brownstones at 45–47 West 53rd Street in New York City. Men were not allowed in their girlfriends' rooms, but could visit them in the club's downstairs parlor. —Ed.

† Sue Hight, an actress and singer who had performed in several Broadway shows, was Elizabeth Sheridan's best friend at the time she met James Dean. —Ed.

girls took a liking to him at a TV rehearsal and brought him there to give him a good meal because he looked hungry, he looked lonely, he looked like he needed a friend. Actually, years later, I found out that he always looked that way. And up until the rehearsal night, he didn't one way or the other impress me.

A couple of nights later, I remember, I was sitting in the living room of the Rehearsal Club and Jimmy was there, too. Boys were allowed to visit the girls up until 11:00 or 12:00 P.M. I forget what time it was and there were two couches, one facing the other. I was sitting in one and Jimmy was sitting in the other. And I was reading a magazine and he was reading a magazine, too. I quoted something out of the one I was reading and his answer was a quote out of the magazine that he was reading and we carried on a conversation like this for about fifteen minutes—you know, real fun— and we both got a kick out of it. Suddenly he said, "I have an idea. Would you like to go up to Tony's, the place that they have this Champale?" And I said, "All right. What the heck!"

So we went around there and we sat down in a booth and a couple of kids that both of us knew were in the next booth and we got into a conversation and his ideas and my ideas sort of jelled and he became interested and so did I.

Then we started drawing pictures on a napkin, I remember, and I was very much impressed about the way he could draw. Jimmy was sort of self-taught in almost everything he did. He was a very good artist, so I started to draw the only thing I knew how to draw—a tree. And he remarked how good it was and we just seemed to be getting to know one another closer and closer all the time. I think he was more impressed than I was at first.

A couple of nights later I had a costume fitting somewhere up in the Bronx, and Jimmy said he would meet me at a little place around the corner. He was just sitting around the Rehearsal Club and I didn't take him too seriously. When I finished this costume-fitting and I was going by this place—Tony's—instead of going straight home, I went in just to see if Jimmy was there. And he was and it turned out to be his birthday and he started saying all sorts of things about that was the best birthday he had had in years.

When I first met him he drank beer, but after I got to know him very well, he really didn't take to drinking much.

Then we started going around together quite steadily. He used to call me at night or in the daytime—any time he happened to feel like it. He'd play records for me over the telephone. We would sit and talk for hours and hours and it was a desperate kind of feeling he had towards seeing me any time that he had a spare moment and talking to me any time he had a spare moment, almost like he didn't have anybody else, either. He just sort of hung on and, I guess, I must have been particularly lonely at the time, too, because we got to be inseparable.

One thing that was quite remarkable about him was that he never for one instant thought that he really couldn't make it. I mean he always knew that he would one day be a star, and there was no question in his mind about it at all. He was interested in the stage. Well, actually he was just interested in acting.

He got a couple of television parts during the first year that we were together in New York. In one of the first ones he played a soldier that was up for court-martial and, I think, hanging or something like that.* He was supposed to die and he was called in to see the President and it was a very dramatic scene. He didn't have too big a part, though. He always insisted that I come to his rehearsals, and he always wanted me to come to his performance and sit in the back and wait for him until he got finished, and then he would always want to hear my criticism on how he did. He seemed so sort of insecure in his acting and yet he must have thought he was good because he had no doubts about getting to the top.

Well, after this went on for a month he would call me and I would see him almost every night. We would either go around the corner for a beer, or just sit in the Rehearsal Club and talk, or meet on the street, or I would go and watch one of his shows, or we would sit in an automat until late at night talking about scripts or trees or grass or bugs or anything.

---

* In the *Studio One* episode "Abraham Lincoln," James Dean plays a Union army soldier who falls asleep on guard duty, is sentenced to be shot, and is then pardoned by Abraham Lincoln. The dramatized biography of Lincoln aired on May 26, 1952, on the CBS network. —Ed.

He told me he did a lot of sketches and stuff and put them up on the wall at his place. He spent a lot of time teaching me how to draw. He got about one or two television shows and I, in the meantime, was working on Mitch Miller to do something about my singing which was lousy. Jimmy was very firm about my singing. He never really thought that it was too good. He wanted me to continue dancing, although the auditions didn't turn out very well.

Then we went through a period where he couldn't get work and I couldn't get work, so I went to American Photograph Corporation and started working there as a retoucher. We used to eat together. We ate Shredded Wheat. We bought a lot of sugar and a lot of milk and we ate Shredded Wheat, sugar, and milk for dinner at my place lots of times. I had this little card table that we would set up with candlelight and make a big thing about our dinner of Shredded Wheat, sugar and milk.

We both lived near Central Park so we used to walk there in the evenings a lot and sit on the rocks in the park and talk and during the day, if he had it free and if I had it free, we used to practice bullfighting. I would be the bull and he had a cape which was given to him by Sidney Franklin.* It still had some blood on it. I remember him talking about it.

Then I made a record for Columbia with Mitch and I remember the day Jimmy and I went all over town looking for a place where we could play it. We found this record store and we went in and we listened to my record a couple of times and we criticized it to the end and he said, "I think you should dance."

Then we really got in pretty bad condition because neither one of us had any money and I remember I quit American Photograph and he came over that night and we had fights about that and I said well all my time was going to American Photograph and I didn't have any time to spend on following any sort of a career. He got mad and walked out.

Fifteen minutes later the telephone rang and I went downstairs and it was Jimmy and he said couldn't we please go around together again. He was so unhappy and I was, too, and we made a date to meet in Columbus

---

* James Dean was given his bullfighter's cape by film director Budd Boetticher. See chapter 13, "James Dean, The Hungry Matador." —Ed.

Circle under the pigeons and we were going to go to a movie. I went up to meet him and he was sitting there. He looked as if he'd been there for hours waiting and it seemed like our first date. We were both so miserable about being poor and not getting anywhere that it was most exciting and one of the best dates that I had with Jimmy.

We went to a movie on Forty-second Street and held hands the entire time and then instead of going back to the "Y" he came over for a while. I lived in a tiny little place off Eighth Avenue and if there were two people in it it was crowded. And Jimmy and I figured out how we were going to give a party together. We wanted to give a big party, inviting all sorts of commentators and theater critics and stars.

Then I got a job with my girlfriend Sue's boyfriend to start as assistant choreographer and it was in New Jersey (Ocean City), so I went down there. Jimmy was living in the Iroquois Hotel with his friend Bill Bast, and I was down there about a month, I guess, and he came down. I went up to New York for a visit to see him and talked him into coming back down with me for two or three days. He came down and he seemed pretty unhappy.

He was around a lot of stock people. He was around the theater and everything, but he wasn't doing anything and I think he was kind of depressed and in a hurry to get back to work. He went back to the city and after that I heard that he was going to go on a cruise with his producer, who was doing the play "See the Jaguar."

With the end of the summer, I went back to New York and I didn't have any place to stay. Jimmy had made arrangements for me to stay with this friend of mine, Anne Chisholm. In the meantime, he was out sailing somewhere off the Cape. For some strange reason or other I was on a bus one night. I didn't know when he was due back in the city, and I was just passing on the bus the place that we first had a couple of drinks, the place that was right around the corner from the Rehearsal Club. All of a sudden I saw him walking down the street going towards Tony's Bar. I leaped off the bus and I saw him turn into this bar and I went in after him. When I got there he was in a telephone booth trying to locate me, and I rapped on the door of the telephone booth, and I had never seen him more shocked. We had a great big mad love scene right in the middle of the floor.

Then I got a job working in the Paris Theater as an usherette. That was when we decided to take this trip to Indiana. We were going to hitchhike all the way. To me it seemed like a wonderful escapade, so we induced Bill Bast to come with us and we started out of the city. I remember we went to New Jersey by bus through the tunnel, got off at the other side, and started thumbing on the highway there.

We got a ride through half a state, I think, and we made Indiana in three rides. The last ride we got was with a very, very famous baseball player. He was catcher for the Pittsburgh Pirates, but since then he has been sold, and I don't remember what club he has been sold to. He was very worried about the three of us. He didn't know exactly what we were doing on the road hitchhiking, and he knew we didn't have much money.

I remember he had a Nash Rambler. It was very comfortable and most of the time Bill sat in the front seat and Jimmy and I huddled in the back because it was freezing cold. We would sing songs and then we would ask him all about baseball players and what they were like, and Jimmy didn't say too much all the way out. We all seemed to be having very much fun.

He left us in Indiana at a crossroads where we could telephone Marcus, who was Jimmy's uncle. And just before we left, this baseball player took Bill aside (we found out later) and offered him some money for us, to take care of the three of us, and Bill refused and he said if ever we were all in New York some time we could get together. I think it was the next season we were supposed to meet him at the Roosevelt Hotel, where the ball players stayed, and he was going to take us out on the town and treat us to a time.

And then we called Jimmy's family and Uncle Marcus came and called for us, and we spent a perfectly glorious week on his farm in Indiana. We were up about seven or eight o'clock in the morning. We were out shooting things. We would throw tin cans up in the air and practice shooting, and we went horseback riding and we visited Jimmy's school, his old teachers, and we sat in on the rehearsal of a high school play and Jimmy coached.

We visited Jim's grandmother and grandfather. We met his father, who came all the way from California. He is a wonderful man, a dental technician and while he was out there, he gave Jimmy two new front teeth—they were coming loose because he had his teeth knocked out in football when he was a kid.

Then just about the end of the week Jimmy got a telephone call from New York saying that he got the part in "See the Jaguar," so we had to hurry back. We started out on the highway again going back to New York and we got a ride all the way back to New York with this man who owns oil in Texas. A very rich guy. He had ulcers. He said he couldn't eat anything and every time we would stop and get something to eat, he would go out and get violently ill by the car and then we would start off again.

On the ride back into New York, all of us were very, very depressed, as I remember, especially going into New York through the tunnel, because we didn't want to get back into the city. Even Jimmy didn't want to get back into the city, because we were having so much fun in Indiana and it was the freshest air the three of us had smelled in a long time.

Then it all started. He got swept up in the theater. He went out on the road, I think to Boston with "See the Jaguar."* I didn't hear from him for about a month. Then one night he called and said he was back in the city, and that they were opening in two nights and he came down to see me at the Paris Theater where I got my old job back as an usherette.

One night I was working at the Paris Theater and he came with his friend Bill Bast and Bill's friend Tony. We all went out and celebrated because he got the part in "See the Jaguar." That was one of the last fun times that I ever had with Jimmy because after he got into the play, I didn't see much of him. As a matter of fact, he sort of disappeared after opening night. He seemed completely different once he got involved with "See the Jaguar" and Arthur Kennedy.

We sat in a neighborhood joint the night that he came back, after I had finished work, and he seemed to have something really bothering him, and I asked him what it was. The way he talked it was so hard and his gestures and everything were hard and sort of I-don't-give-a-damn kind of thing. He wasn't warm at all the way he used to be when we first went around.

But he wasn't always this way. I remember one time he went out for groceries or something and while in the grocery store he called me on the telephone. I don't know what had happened from the time he left until the time he got to the grocery store, but when he called he said he didn't have

---

* Out-of-town tryouts for *See the Jaguar* were held in Philadelphia. —Ed.

anything really to call about except that he wanted to get married, and he said, "we must get married before we get caught up in all this."

I remember him saying that, and he came back and that was one night when he seemed like he was afraid. There were lots of times when I felt that he was afraid. The way he hung on to me at the very beginning. After he got established, then I was afraid and I started to hang on to him, and he didn't seem to want the responsibility of having anybody hang on to him because he was going up too fast. That was just extra added weight.

What happened to Jimmy after that I don't know. In the first period of work in New York when he started getting up there he started getting television shows maybe once a month, which was a lot for him at the time. He had a lousy attitude about working. It seemed like he didn't care about rehearsals. He didn't care about the way he dressed. Sometimes he didn't even care about whether he was decent to people or not, as long as he was acting. He felt the *business* of show business was degrading.

The change. I wish everybody could have been with us in Indiana. The way he treated the animals. The way he treated even the dirt around the farm. Sort of the love he had for nature and everything showed me how completely simple he was. Simple in his ideals. Whether he was sure of what they were or not I am not sure, but he had them. They were growing. But it made him pretty bitter, and he seemed to relax much more when we were out in Indiana.

One of the biggest things about him that I can remember is his love for animals. The way he could get so close to them, and animals get close to him. This, to me, is quite a key to somebody's character.

After "See the Jaguar," he disappeared. I found out he moved back into the Iroquois Hotel after Boston, and it took me about two months to find him. When I did, I called him one night and I went over to see him. He was living in this little hotel room, and he seemed in even a worse condition than he was when he was so hard and bitter about New York business, and the guff that you have to take with the theater in trying to get somewhere. He was studying Greek philosophy and reading Roman history and was studying music.

Alec Wilder was an interesting person and so he took up with Alec Wilder. He would hang on to anybody. Anybody that he felt he could get something out of—not money-wise or material-wise. He felt that any knowledge he would gain from anybody was valuable. As a matter of fact his time was valuable. He seemed to be in a hurry about something. I don't know what. Maybe a feeling that he wasn't going to live very long. I don't know.

Even though many of the articles that I have read about him say that Jimmy was well educated, I don't think so. He didn't have as much schooling as he had wanted and he tried to catch up with it all the time. He taught himself how to paint. He taught himself many things.

One thing he always kept telling me all the time even in his letters to me when I was in stock is that a person must know the field that he is going into. You have to know your art. This is something that he stressed all the time.

He liked steaks. He liked good steaks. He was always talking about steaks but in the early part of our friendship we didn't do much eating, and he didn't take too much notice of what he was eating when he ordered. He made up real crazy dishes when he was living in the hotel, and I used to come and eat with him because neither of us had much money and we had to concoct things other than Shredded Wheat.

That was when we really ran out of money. Before that first part we used to buy canned meats and make hashes and stuff. Clothes Jimmy never cared about. He didn't take care of his clothes very well, either. He would send them to the cleaners and maybe sometimes he would forget about them and I would have to get them out for him. He liked blue jeans. He lived in blue jeans most of the time, as everybody knows, and T-shirts. He had an old lousy camel-hair coat that some girl had given him when I first met him and felt sorry for him. And he had a raincoat which I always had my eye on. I just adored that raincoat. It was three-quarter length. I made a deal with him that he could have my blue jeans if I could have his raincoat. And he finally gave it to me and I still have it. That and a picture are about the only two things that I can remember keeping.

Lots of times we used to walk along Fifth Avenue and look in the store windows. Mostly it was cars. He was fascinated by cars. He always wanted a Jaguar and I always wanted a Jaguar and there was a place on Broadway up around the Sixties, a great big store window that had all sorts of cars in it. We used to hang around and look in the window and dream about the Jaguar we were someday going to get. It turned out he got a Porsche or it got him.

My roommate and I had a Great Dane, a beautiful dog. I used to take him for walks in Central Park. I remember I called Jimmy one afternoon and told him that maybe he would like to see our dog that we had just acquired, and I would be in Central Park at such and such a time and at such and such a place. So I remember I was playing with the dog in this great big field and I saw Jimmy and we must have spent a good hour there just running with the dog and throwing things for him, and having him run and bring it back to us and this is one of the few times that I saw him laugh during the last days that I ever saw him.

Two years ago, after I lived in St. Thomas, Virgin Islands, I came back to New York and my first dancing partner, Fobiel, heard I was home and called me. He said he met Jimmy on the street and had a conversation with him, and told him that I was in New York and where I was. Within an hour Jimmy called me. I was over at a friend's house and we were going to have a party, and on the phone, it was the strangest feeling I got. I could almost visualize Jimmy doing flips and stuff while he was talking to me, because it seemed like I didn't know he had such a wonderful life out in Hollywood and so many things had happened to him. I thought he would be so terribly happy but he didn't seem to like it at all.

He seemed like he would rather be around his old friends, and he seemed like he was glad to hear from me and went on and on about how he missed me and how much he was thinking about me and one of the first things he said was he got a horse. He always knew that I loved horses. And this gave him a large charge. Every time he would see a horse he would go blocks out of his way to point it out to me, or pet one down around Fifth and Fifty-ninth Street, where they all park.

He wanted to know immediately where I was and if he could come up, and I said we were having a party and he said he was with Jane Deacy, his agent, and Leonard Rosenman, who had written the score for "East of Eden." They were going out to get some dinner and could they come up so I said sure. So about an hour later he called from Sardi's and said that they were eating dinner and he had forgotten the address. What was it again?

They came up and it was a wonderful homecoming, and he was happy to the point of almost hysteria. He was leaping and jumping all around like a clown, which he did very often when he was happy and I remember wherever I went at that party—if I would go into the kitchen to get food—he would follow me out there and stand and talk. Never anything about Hollywood or what he was doing but what I was doing, or how was the old gang. It seemed that he had just been away from home, and all of a sudden he found it again and he seemed jovial on top—but very unhappy underneath, somehow.

We left together. I remember he asked me what I was going to do. If I was going to go home. I said I didn't quite know, and he acted like he wanted to at least have a drink or talk a little bit more before I took the train for Larchmont, but Leonard Rosenman talked him out of it and talked him into going to another party. So the three of us took a cab together and I got off at Grand Central. I remember, just before I left, he squeezed my hand in the cab and asked me if I were happy. I told him that I would be as soon as I could get back to the islands and he said, "I know what you mean," as if more or less he wished that he had found a place to go to where he could be happy. Then he said, "Now that I am more or less established and can help you, I wish you would come out to Hollywood, and I'll see if I can get you some dancing." He was the greatest enthusiast that I had about my dancing. He thought I was the living end. And that's the last I saw of Jimmy.

When I heard about Jimmy's death, I was sitting in a movie house in Puerto Rico, where I live now, and I heard a newsboy shout out in the streets that James Dean had been killed in a sports car accident. A lot of thoughts raced through my mind, mostly what I've been telling you about. About the desperate feeling he always had in wanting to see me anytime, anywhere . . . about his fascination for cars and how he always wanted a Jaguar. But how he didn't like to drive and always made me do it.

I may forget a lot of other people, but no matter what happens, I'll never forget Jimmy Dean.

THE END

16

What Jimmy Dean Believed

JACK SHAFER

In the 1940s and '50s, Jack Shafer interviewed show business personalities on the programs *Interview With a Star* and *Radio Beam*, which were broadcast by AM radio station WMCA in New York. Shafer's article recalling James Dean's visit to his show in the first week of December 1952, when he was performing on stage in *See the Jaguar*, appeared in the October 1957 issue of *Modern Screen*. —Ed.

SEVERAL YEARS AGO, the press agent for the Broadway play *See the Jaguar* suggested I interview one of the show's young stars on a Sunday evening program I was handling for a New York radio station. "His name's Jimmy Dean," the p.a. told me.

Dean was ten minutes early for our interview. We talked about his boyhood in Indiana; how he starred in high school track, baseball, and basketball; his interest in college dramatics; and why he suddenly decided to quit UCLA and get a career going the hard way—by way of a coach ticket to New York with only a couple of hundred dollars in his pocket.

But long after the program was over, I kept remembering the serious minded, friendly, handsome young kid—and the one thing that had made a very deep impression on me: he had brought a book along with him—about the Aztec Indians!

Now, theatrical crackpots might carry a book on anything from *Mah Jong* to *Life on Jupiter*, just to attract attention. But Dean impressed me as a level-headed youngster and I told him frankly that I was curious about his choice in literature.

"Well," he somewhat reluctantly explained, "I've always been fascinated by the Aztec Indians. They were a very fatalistic people, and I sometimes share that feeling. They had such a weird sense of doom that when the warlike Spaniards arrived in Mexico a lot of the Aztecs just gave up, fatalistically, to an event they believed couldn't be avoided."

"Like the Arab philosophy of Kismet?" I asked, "*what is written, is written?*"

"And for them, the arrival of the Spaniards *was* written!" Dean went on, his enthusiasm bubbling to the surface. "They had a legend that their god Quetzalcoatl had predicted they would be conquered by strange visitors from another land!"

"Well, no wonder they were fatalistic about it then," I said. "But what's this about *your* being fatalistic, too?"

"In a certain sense I am," Dean admitted. "I don't exactly know how to explain it, but I have a hunch there are some things in life we just can't avoid. They'll happen to us, probably because we're built that way—we simply attract our own fate . . . make our own destiny."

"Doesn't that sort of thinking bother you? Don't you find it depressing?"

"Not a bit!" Dean insisted. "I think I'm like the Aztecs in that respect, too. With their sense of doom, they tried to get the most out of life while life was good; and I go along with them on that philosophy. I don't mean the *eat, drink, and be merry for tomorrow we die* idea, but something a lot deeper and more valuable. I want to live as intensely as I can. Be as useful and helpful to others as possible, for one thing. But live for myself as well. I want to feel things and experiences right down to their roots . . . enjoy the good in life while it is good.

"That's how those Aztecs felt.

"They were a happy people," he went on. "Very hospitable, generous to one another, and extremely fond of beauty and music. They simply tried to enjoy every minute of life when it was good—feeling that it would change soon enough."

When Jimmy Dean died, in the same California hills where archaeologists tell us the Aztecs originated, I got to thinking of the day we talked about the love of beauty and the sense of fatalism that he shared with his beloved Aztecs.

Jimmy can now be seen in Warner Bros.' THE JAMES DEAN STORY.

17

The Little Prince

Frank Corsaro

Frank Corsaro first met James Dean during the brief run of the play *See the Jaguar*, in which Dean played Wally Wilkins, an illiterate backwoods teenager whose deranged mother kept him locked in an icehouse to protect him from the cruelty of the world outside. At the Actors Studio, Corsaro—who became a noted theater and opera director and artistic director of the Studio—became a friend and cultural mentor to Dean. Nevertheless, Corsaro offers a fairly harsh assessment of him in this excerpt from his 1978 autobiography, *Maverick: A Director's Personal Experience in Opera and Theater.* —Ed.

IN MANY WAYS, COMBING THE WORD ILLITERATE down several hairs, the role [Wally Wilkins] was a quick-sketch portrayal of Dean himself. Dean has become such a cult figure that, knowing him as I did, I still marvel how such things come to be. Not that he didn't work his mysterious ends. He saw himself as Saint-Exupéry's Little Prince—a self-appointed aristocrat condemned to wander the earth forever homeless. His talent was instinctual; his technique: zero. He admired Montgomery Clift and adored Brando inordinately. Once, cornered with the then already legendary Brando at a party, Dean had to be pried off the famous man's back. In all the years at the Studio he performed once or twice for the aggregate and retired thereafter in abject terror of the Studio's sophisticated and high-standard judgments. He would never submit to Lee's [Lee Strasberg] supremacy as a guide. Verging on thirty, he was still twelve years old emotionally. He could be a warm and cuddly beast of the field, but he demanded the world protect him in return. For all the supernal light he radiated on screen, he had a perverse cruel streak in him which negated that image in life. Rebellious, secretive, and calculating, he opted for acceptance via the route of stardom. He was practically a male Judy Garland—without a song. Sensitive and violent by turns, both the boy and the girl next door, he projected the ambivalent sexuality and chastity of the classic ideal—if in spirit he was perhaps more Icarus than Apollo.

Brando and Clift, before Dean, had at one time or another been members of the Studio, and while the Studio was not directly responsible for the growth of their talents, it grooved on their prototype. Its insistence on the actor's individuality and freedom of expression jibed with the needs of the time—and inadvertently the Studio became eponymous in the public eye with the Brando-Clift acting style. These stars were not just actors, they were Actors Studio actors—a special distinction, and "The Method" their special cross. It is still difficult for the man with the girl's eyes to find happiness in male chauvinist America. Yet for a time (and who knows? perhaps forever) America doted on them—entered into a secret confraternity with their ambivalence, and accorded them riches and fame. Dean's ascendancy to the holy grail of stardom left him more of a self-conscious wreck than ever. Given dangerous toys to play with, and more powerful expensive racing cars, his downhill ride went alarmingly out of control. He was basically a young and highly gifted adolescent in desperate need of help, yet distrustful of almost everyone who could help him. I learned of his death one morning on arrival at rehearsals for the Broadway-bound *Hatful of Rain*.* [Ben] Gazzara was sitting just inside the stage entrance when I came in. "Guess who died last night," he said. "Your pal, Dean." My immediate response was, "How did he do it?"

---

* *A Hatful of Rain*, a drama about the travails of a Korean War veteran addicted to morphine, opened at the Lyceum Theater in New York on November 9, 1955, and ran for 390 performances. The play starred Ben Gazzara and was directed by Frank Corsaro.

OUTTAKE

James Dean Craved Attention

"To this day, I can sometimes hear his [Dean's] comments and imagine his reactions and I often think of one evening in particular. We had just finished a meal and were smoking while coffee brewed. I studied my pipe and he stared ahead as streams of thin blue smoke rose from the cigarette in his mouth over his eyes and around his head, mixing with my pipe smoke and finally drifting upward. I watched a smile grow on his lips; the angle of his cigarette barely changing. It moved to his eyes, but he crinkled his eyelids into slits almost obscuring the dark blue behind them. He then asked me why my pipe was caked with crud and I told him it made the smoke taste sweeter. I asked why he had a cigarette resting over his left ear and he explained that he would light it 'as soon as I'm [*sic*] finished this one, man. But it's really there for you to ask about.' We both smiled."

—*James Dean: A Portrait* by Roy Schatt
(New York: Delilah Books, 1982)

18

Bottle, Bottle, Who's Got the Bottle?

HUME CRONYN

On Sunday, October 4, 1953, CBS television broadcast a live ninety-minute production of playwright William Inge's original teleplay *Glory in the Flower* on their anthology series, *Omnibus*. The cast included a rising young actor, James Dean, who played a self-pitying teenage delinquent named Bronco. Out on bail for possession of marijuana, he bedevils the owner of a roadside diner (played by veteran character actor Hume Cronyn) when he spikes his Coke with liquor from a clandestine bottle.

In the early days of television, shows were broadcast live as they were performed, with no opportunities for retakes or editing. Rehearsals and broadcasts were run on the clock, carefully timed to make sure the action didn't come up short, leaving dead air, or continue past an allotted time slot. "There is room for experimentation and improvisation during rehearsals," Cronyn explains in his 1991 memoir, *A Terrible Liar*, "but once the action, interpretations and the camera moves are set, woe betide you if some member of the company takes off and does his own thing. The brilliant last-minute inspiration of an actor who decides to change the blocking, to take a series of long, indulgent pauses or, conversely, to race through a passage or try an arbitrary cut can throw his fellow actors into panic and drive directors and camera crews to madness."

In this excerpt from his memoir, Cronyn recalls how Dean exasperated him during rehearsals for *Glory in the Flower*. —Ed.

JESSICA [TANDY] PLAYED THE CENTRAL ROLE, and for once escaped being my wife. My own role was that of the owner of a shabby bar and diner, boasting a jukebox and tiny dance floor. It catered for the most part to truck drivers and teenagers. It was a hangout. As a proprietor anxious not to jeopardize his liquor license, I had to police the joint and make sure there was no underage drinking on the premises. In one scene, having become aware that four rowdy teenagers were passing a pint bottle among them, I had to confront these kids and demand surrender of the bottle. The bottle was not forthcoming. I had to search for it. All this had been rehearsed and I was supposed to find the bottle in the hip pocket of the young man nearest to me. At the final technical rehearsal, it wasn't there. I fumbled about, looking under the table, behind the seat cushions of the booth, under napkins, among the plastic flowers on the table, and then gave up. The camera stopped rolling.

"Where is it, Jimmy?"

The young man said, "Why don't you just find it?"

His tone was a challenge; it implied: "You're supposed to hunt, so hunt—let's make it *real.*"

I tried to be agreeable. "Is it worth it? I think I can *act* hunting for it."

The director appeared from the control booth and asked for the bottle. It was produced from the actor's jeans, stuffed down behind his fly. The director stuck it back in the actor's hip pocket and told us to proceed. Time was running out and we still had to do a dress.

The actor involved was one I'd noticed on our very first reading of the script. He was blond, thin, handsome and had a very definite presence. He was also infinitely "laid back": not rude, not quite arrogant but with a manner that said "I'm here—pay attention—and I don't give a damn what you think." I'd never seen him before and couldn't remember his last name any more than I could those of the other dozen kids. I was lucky if I remembered their first names.

We finished the technical rehearsal and it was obvious that we had to plunge into the dress rehearsal with barely time to get into our costumes. I hate these last-minute rushes. They leave no time to check the props and none in which to compose oneself. That clock keeps ticking. You pray that nothing will go wrong and that you may get a breather before air time. I remember Jess saying, "Calm down, Calm down!"

We got three quarters of the way through the dress without anything going drastically wrong, and reached a climactic scene on the small, packed dance floor. A fight broke out and I was supposed to wade into the melee and separate the two principal combatants. One of these was my cool friend of the bottle incident. The scene had been very carefully choreographed by the director so that the camera could follow the main action and not be blocked by writhing, closely packed bodies. There was also the danger that, if the fight was not executed precisely, someone might end up with a bloody nose.

My cue came and I waded into the heaving sea of humanity and was immediately lost. I couldn't find the bottle boy with whom I was to have the next exchange of dialogue; he simply wasn't where he was supposed to be. Where the hell had he gone? I looked wildly around, pushed people aside, crouched down, stood on tiptoe, but not a sign of him. Suddenly, a laconic voice from somewhere behind me said, "I'm here." He may bloody well have been there, but if I crossed to him we would both be out of camera range as well as the light. I heard a voice from the booth say, "Cut! Hold it! I'm coming down." And I lost my temper.

Actors rarely know their reputations with crews and casts. I've known some who consider themselves angels of light, but who are spoken of less than kindly by their fellows. God forgive me, I may be one of those, but I hope not. At any rate, I seized the young actor by the arm, whirled him around and pointed to the studio wall clock.

"See that? It says twenty-two minutes to air time, and we haven't yet finished the dress. I don't know about you, but I'd at least like to have time to take a pee before we do this for real. *For Christ's sake be where you're supposed to be!*"

Everyone went into shock. The young actor tore his arm loose and started to remonstrate. "I was trying something new. I wanted to confuse you. . . . You *should* be confused."

"I was! I am! But I can *act* confused. Keep that experimental shit for rehearsal or your dressing room! You're not alone out here!"

At which point the director arrived and said, "Cool it, cool it both of you! Jimmy, get your ass over here where you belong, and let's get on with it, *NOW*!"

In the few minutes' break between dress and showtime, coming out of the men's room, I ran into Jimmy in the hall. He said quietly, "Mr. Cronyn,

I respect your work and you should respect mine. You shouldn't talk to me like that."

"You're right Jimmy, I shouldn't, and I apologize. But it isn't *your* work or mine. It's *ours*. We are all dependent on one another."

The show went on without incident, and some weeks later I ran into Jimmy on the street. In a very uncharacteristic manner he embraced me, and before I'd had a chance to say much of anything, he said, "I forgive you—you were nervous." To say that I was dumbfounded puts it mildly. However, we parted, smiling and the best of friends. I don't believe I ever saw him again—in person.

Later that year, [Elia] Kazan and I were again on a boat together, and Gadge* gave me a copy of his next film to read. It was a good script with a wonderful part for a young man.

"Who's going to play that?" I asked.

"A new kid, very talented," and he gave me the name. I suppose my expression or my silence must have betrayed me.

"What's wrong?"

"You're going to need all your patience"—and I told him the story of my experience in *Glory in the Flower*. It would have been kinder of me to keep my mouth shut, but that's not the way it works between friends. "He's still very talented," said Gadge, "and we've hired him." For those of you who haven't already guessed as much, the actor's name was James Dean and the film in question was *East of Eden*. It was later, I think, that Jimmy appeared in *Rebel Without a Cause*, and it was that very quality of "I'm here—pay attention—and I don't give a damn what you think" that served him and both films so well. Indeed, "rebel without a cause" says it all.

---

* "Gadge," short for "Gadget," was the nickname Elia Kazan had been given while a student at Williams College because of his mechanical aptitude. "I was small, compact and handy to have around," he said, an "ever-compliant little cuss."

19

◆

Drawing Blood

SHELLEY WINTERS

In her autobiography, *Shelley, Also Known as Shirley* (1980), two-time Academy Award–winning actress Shelley Winters recalls her first encounter with James Dean, which took place at the Actors Studio. Frequently cast as brassy gun molls in B movies by Universal-International Pictures, she was in New York for four days to publicize the film *Larceny* (1948) for the studio and recalls meeting Dean on her final afternoon in the city. Her account places him at the Actors Studio in April 1949. (She attended the second performance of the musical *South Pacific* during her junket, which opened on Broadway on April 7, 1949.) Dean, however, never set foot in New York until October 1951, and wasn't accepted to the Actors Studio until May 1952. One can forgive Winters for conflating memories from different times; she led a very eventful life. (During her four days in New York she was run over by theater owner J. J. Shubert's limousine, seduced by Burt Lancaster, and conducted a press interview while in the shower.) As actor Hume Cronyn put it, memory is "a terrible liar" (the title of his memoir). —Ed.

LEE STRASBERG, WHOSE PRIVATE CLASSES I also attended at the Malin Studios when I could, was moderating that day at the Actors Studio. A young actor by the name of James Dean was doing an exercise called a Private Moment, which is an activity you do at home when no one else is around, and in it must be the germ of something you need for a scene you're working on. For me in those days it was dancing around the house and fantasizing while listening to records.

The Actors Studio had by now bought an old Greek church on West Forty-fourth Street near Tenth Avenue. I sat down stiffly and carefully in my observer's seat on the side in the front row, almost behind a pole. Jimmy Dean came in wearing an immense old overcoat over a white T-shirt and from the way he moved we knew he was very alone in an imaginary crowd. Then he stepped to stage right, where he shrugged off the coat, and took out a switchblade. Leaning on the pole next to me, he began to weep. I looked at Strasberg, who was watching Jimmy in an intellectual and dispassionate manner. Jimmy began playing with the unopened knife. He was smiling, but the tears were flowing down his face. I was terrified for him and kept looking at Strasberg, hoping he would stop the exercise. I thought I noticed a thin line of blood on Jimmy's wrist which Strasberg could not see from where he was sitting. I automatically reached out and grabbed Jimmy's hand. We struggled for the knife, and he started laughing.

For the next few minutes I didn't know if I was in a Method Exercise or in Real Life. As we struggled, I noticed a white scar on Jimmy's right wrist, and when I grabbed his other hand, I saw that his left wrist also had a white scar on it.* He was quite strong for such a slight boy, and all I could think of to say was: "Stop, Jimmy! I've got a back brace on. I've been in an automobile accident!"

Instantly the Private Moment exercise became an improvisation. His attention changed like an infant's, and he forgot the knife and let me take it. He carefully sat me down on a bench in front of the class and then began a serious improvisatory discussion about *my accident*. I found myself weeping, too, and the sum total of the scene became: Why had the chocolate milk shake in the goblet tasted like hemlock; why had *I* tried to commit suicide?† I told Jimmy what had happened but didn't mention any names. He put his arm around me and kissed me consolingly, his wrist bleeding

---

* None of James Dean's friends or lovers recall seeing scars on his wrists, but his friend, composer David Diamond, told Peter Manso, a biographer of Marlon Brando: "Jimmy was terribly self-destructive, like cracking a bottle and threatening to cut his wrists. There were several suicide attempts. Marlon was aware of this." —Ed.

† Burt Lancaster brought a chocolate shake to Winters's hotel room when she was recovering from a back injury—she had been knocked down by J. J. Shubert's limousine while she was crossing the street. Winters felt guilty about having an affair with Lancaster, who was married. —Ed.

slightly on my sables. Then, pulling on his coat, he turned to Lee and said, "Okay, that's it," as if the whole thing had been a rehearsed scene.

Lee asked Jimmy what he was working for, and although he was rather inarticulate, he managed to explain that he was trying to fight his feelings of alienation because he felt everybody else wasn't real. When Lee asked me what I was working for, I didn't want to tell him I'd interrupted a scene; after all, I was still an observer. I made up some cockamamie exercise off the top of my head about a movie starlet's attempt to interfere with fate. To this day I don't know whether Strasberg believed either one of us. In retrospect, I think he was teaching us how to use anything that happens accidentally onstage that isn't planned. From this comes the famous Method expression "Use it."

At the break I was so shaken I went downstairs to have a cup of coffee. Jimmy followed me. There's a terrible Chinese proverb that if you save someone's life, then you're responsible for him for the rest of his existence. I don't believe it, but Jimmy immediately attached himself to me. He tried to clean the blood off my sables with hot coffee, and I got some iodine from the first-aid kit and put a Band-Aid on the very little cut on his wrist.

I decided I felt too shaken up to stay for the second scene, and as I went out to my waiting limousine, Jimmy followed me like a puppy. He was very impressed with the limousine but wouldn't show it, and he got right in with me, clutching an old airline bag. "Shelley," he said, "I'm very hungry." We had time, so I had the car stop at Downey's and bought him a huge breakfast. I didn't want him to feel self-conscious, so I had one, too. He also had three double Irish coffees.

For the next few hours I kept trying to get rid of him, but he obviously had no place to go. He wanted to drive out to the airport with me, so I let him. He told me that he had some place to stay in the Village, and I said he could use the limousine to take him there afterward.

His existence seemed so pointless and haphazard, and no matter how I questioned him, I couldn't get a straight answer. He was obviously very beautiful and a gifted actor, but he didn't seem to want anything. In some weird way he reminded me of Peter Pan, but without the joy, as if he had sprung from never-never land and would disappear back into it. What I didn't realize was that I was with a forerunner of the Beat Generation. He seemed to be clinging to me in some emotional way, but I didn't understand it. Besides, I was so mixed up myself I couldn't have done anything about it if I had.

When we got to La Guardia, I wouldn't let him get out of the car because I was sure he would manage by hook or crook to get on the plane to California with me. I gave him my phone number in L.A. and put $20 in his breast pocket. He smiled as if he were doing me a favor by taking it. I somehow felt he was. I told him to go to the YMCA, and when he drove away, he was smiling, but there were tears in his eyes.

When I entered the terminal, I felt terribly guilty, as if I had failed his whole generation. He wasn't much younger than I, but he looked absolutely defenseless. I thanked God for the tough Brooklyn neighborhood I had been raised in because it had made me strong. I guess that's what it does if it doesn't kill you.

20

———◆———

A Serpent in Eden

Elia Kazan

Turkish-born Elia Kazan rebelled against his father, a successful rug merchant, when he decided to become an actor. He graduated from Williams College, studied drama at Yale, and joined the leftist Group Theatre in 1934. Kazan also joined a Communist cell that year (which he broke with in 1936), a decision that would later come back to haunt him when he identified former Communist Party members in a closed session before the House Un-American Activities Committee in 1952. Nicknamed "Gadge," Kazan began his career as an actor but achieved his greatest success as a film and theater director. He established his reputation with his direction of the critically acclaimed plays *A Streetcar Named Desire* (1947) and *Death of a Salesman* (1948). He received his first Academy Award for directing his fourth film, *Gentleman's Agreement* (1947).

In 1947, Kazan founded the Actors Studio with Cheryl Crawford and Robert Lewis, the home of Method acting, which employs techniques derived from the work of Konstantin Stanislavsky. Kazan's direction of Marlon Brando, James Dean, and Montgomery Clift on film was instrumental in popularizing the Method. "Kazan was gold," actor Bill Gunn said. "If Brando was the God, then Kazan was the Godfather."

Elia Kazan directed James Dean in the role of Cal Trask, the wayward son of Adam Trask (Raymond Massey) in *East of Eden*, Dean's first starring role in a motion picture. Kazan recalls his experiences working with Dean in this excerpt from his 1988 autobiography, *Elia Kazan: A Life.* —Ed.

Paul Osborn, who was writing the screenplay, said I should have a look at the young man playing the bit part of an Arab in a play [*The*

Immoralist] at the John Golden Theatre. I wasn't impressed with James Dean—I'd begun to think about Brando again—but to please Osborn I called Jimmy into Warners' New York offices, for a closer look. When I walked in he was slouched at the end of a leather sofa in the waiting room, a heap of twisted legs and denim rags, looking resentful for no particular reason. I didn't like the expression on his face, so I kept him waiting. I also wanted to see how he'd react to that. It seemed that I'd outtoughed him, because when I called him into my office, he'd dropped the belligerent pose. We tried to talk, but conversation was not his gift, so we sat looking at each other. He asked me if I wanted to ride on the back of his motorbike; I didn't enjoy the ride. He was showing off—a country boy not impressed with big-city traffic. When I got back to the office, I called Paul and told him this kid actually *was* Cal in *East of Eden*; no sense looking further or "reading" him. I sent Dean to see Steinbeck, who was living near me, on Seventy-second Street. John thought Dean a snotty kid. I said that was irrelevant; wasn't he Cal? John said he sure as hell was, and that was it.

Now I was into studying Dean, so I decided to take him to California and make some screen tests disguised as wardrobe tests. I was being pampered with a long black limo in New York; after it picked me up to take me to the airport, I had it drive to the obscure address where Dean was holed up. He came out—believe it or not—carrying two packages wrapped in paper and tied with lengths of string. He looked like an immigrant sitting in the back of that luxury limo. He told me he'd never been in an airplane before. Airborne, he sat with his nose pressed to the window, looking at the beautiful country below. Warners' transportation had the limo's California cousin waiting for me in the airport. When Jimmy asked if we could pause on the way into town at the place where his father, a sort of lab technician, worked, I was delighted. Dean dashed into one of those very temporary-looking buildings that flank highways there, and came out with a man he said was his father. The man had no definition and made no impression except that he had no definition. Obviously there was a strong tension between the two, and it was not friendly. I sensed the father disliked his son. They stood side by side, but talk soon collapsed, and we drove on.

I believe the encounter shocked Dean. I saw that the story of the movie was his story—just as it was, in a way, my own. My father used to complain to his assistant at George Kazan, Oriental Rugs and Carpets, about me. "That boy never be man," he'd say. "What am I going to do with him?" Jimmy's father didn't seem to think his son's future very promising either.

When I shot Jimmy's tests—it was his first time before a movie camera, though he'd been on TV—he wasn't nervous.* He seemed to take to it. The crew—directors always watch the reaction of a crew to a newcomer—were not impressed. They thought Jimmy was the stand-in, that the real star was still to appear. When I told them Jimmy was it, they thought I was nuts. Warner† must have seen Jimmy's tests, but he said nothing. I don't know what he thought; he was used to Errol Flynn, Jimmy Cagney, and Gary Cooper. Now comes this twisted, fidgety kid from New York. But my magic held; Warner said nothing. I was still on my own.

What has always fascinated me is the response of newcomers to success. I watch for it and don't expect it to be honorable. A couple of weeks before the end of our shooting schedule, it was getting around that the kid on the *East of Eden* set was going to make it big. Jimmy heard the news too, and the first thing I noticed was that he was being rude to our little wardrobe man. I stopped that quickly. Then he began to complain that he couldn't do a certain scene that had to be played standing on a slanting roof outside a second-story window. He was right; he did the scene poorly; but it was an important scene, so I took him and Julie Harris, the "love interest," to an Italian restaurant and loaded Jimmy up with Chianti. That did it—it's a technique I've used on occasion to supersede Stanislavsky.

Ray Massey, the old-timer who'd played Lincoln enough times to establish a franchise and was now playing Jimmy's father, anticipated that Jimmy would quickly spoil rotten. He simply couldn't stand the sight of the kid, dreaded every day he worked with him. "You never know what he's going to say or do!" Ray said. "Make him read the lines the way they're written." Jimmy knew that Ray was scornful of him, and he responded with a sullenness he didn't cover. This was an antagonism I didn't try to heal; I aggravated it. I'm ashamed to say—well, not ashamed; everything goes

---

* James Dean had already played bit parts in three movies before starring in *East of Eden*. —Ed.
† Jack Warner, president of Warner Bros. Pictures. —Ed.

in directing movies—I didn't conceal from Jimmy or from Ray what they thought of each other, made it plain to each of them. The screen was alive with precisely what I wanted; they detested each other. Casting should tell the story of a film without words; this casting did. It was a problem that went on to the end, and I made use of it to the end.

The first thing Jimmy did with his suddenly augmented flow of money was to buy a palomino. Raised on an Indiana farm, he'd always wanted a horse of his own, and a palomino is the most beautiful of animals. For a time I arranged for him to keep the beast on the lot, but the corral was far from the sound stage where we were shooting, and Jimmy was always running off to feed or curry or just look at his gorgeous animal. I finally had the horse exiled to a farm in the San Fernando Valley. Then Jimmy bought a motorbike, but I stopped that too. I told him I didn't want to chance an accident, and that he absolutely couldn't ride the bike until the film was over. Next Jimmy bought himself an expensive camera, and he was flaunting it everywhere, taking rolls of pictures that he had the studio lab develop for him. I wasn't crazy about this either, so I told him not to bring it on the stage where we were shooting anymore. That made him sullen for a day.

I noticed that a couple of mornings he came to work late, looking pooped; whatever he'd been doing the night before seemed to have worn him out. Well, I thought, isn't it natural for a kid that age to get laid once in a while? Nevertheless it didn't help his performance, nor did whatever else he was doing at night—was he drinking or fighting? I didn't know. I began to worry that something would happen to him and delay my work or make him less able to carry out what I wanted, so I moved myself into one of those great star dressing rooms on the lot and Jimmy into the one across from me. My front door opened to his front door, and I could hear what went on in his quarters through the walls. What went on was Pier Angeli. But clearly that didn't go well for Dean either; I could hear them boffing but more often arguing through the walls. I was glad when she "found" Vic Damone. Now I had Jimmy as I wanted him, alone and miserable. All he had was his camera. Narcissism took over. He used to stand in front of the mirror in his room and take roll after roll of close-up photographs of his face, with only the slightest variation of expression. He'd show me the goddamn contact sheets and ask which one I liked best. I thought they

From left: Elia Kazan, Marlon Brando, Julie Harris, and James Dean on the set of *East of Eden*. *Warner Bros./Photofest © Warner Bros.*

were all the same picture, but I said nothing. As a hobby they were better than his unsuccessful devotion to Pier Angeli, so I encouraged them.

Brando was Dean's hero; everyone knew that, because he dropped his voice to a cathedral hush when he talked about Marlon. I invited Brando to come to the set and enjoy some hero worship. Marlon did and was very gracious to Jimmy, who was so adoring that he seemed shrunken and twisted in misery. People were to compare them, but they weren't alike. Marlon, well trained by Stella Adler, had excellent technique. He was proficient in every aspect of acting, including characterization and makeup. He was also a great mimic. Dean had no technique to speak of. When he tried to play an older man in the last reels of *Giant*, he looked like what he was: a beginner. On my film, Jimmy would either get the scene right immediately, without any detailed direction—that was ninety-five percent of the time—or he couldn't get it at all. Then I had to use some extraordinary means—the Chianti, for instance.

I was totally unprepared for his success. We had a first preview at a theatre in the Los Angeles area, and the instant he appeared on the screen, hundreds of girls began to scream. They'd been waiting for him, it seemed—how come or why, I don't know. The response of the balcony reminded me of what we'd got from the balcony when we played *Waiting for Lefty* for the first time—Niagara Falls spilling over.* The goddamn kid became a legend overnight and the legend grew more intense with every showing. When my friend Nick Ray cast him in *Rebel Without a Cause*, he intensified Dean's spell over the youth of the nation. It was a legend I didn't approve of. Its essence was that all parents were insensitive idiots, who didn't understand or appreciate their kids and weren't able to help them. Parents were the enemy. I didn't like the way Nick Ray showed the parents in *Rebel Without a Cause*, but I'd contributed by the way Ray Massey was shown in my film. In contrast to these parent figures, all youngsters were supposed to be sensitive and full of "soul." This didn't seem true to me. I thought them—Dean, "Cal," and the kid he played in Nick Ray's film—self-pitying, self-dramatizing, and good-for-nothing. I became very impatient with the Dean legend, especially when I received letter after letter thanking me for what I'd done for him and asking me to be a sponsor of a nationwide network of Jimmy Dean clubs. I didn't respond to those letters.

I doubt that Jimmy would ever have got through *East of Eden* except for an angel on our set. Her name was Julie Harris, and she was goodness itself with Dean, kind and patient and everlastingly sympathetic. She would adjust her performance to whatever the new kid did. Despite the fact that it had early on been made clear to me that Warner, when he saw her first wardrobe test, wished I'd taken a "prettier" girl, I thought Julie beautiful; as a performer she found in each moment what was dearest and most moving. She also had the most affecting voice I've ever heard in an actress; it conveyed tenderness and humor simultaneously. She helped Jimmy more than I did with any direction I gave him. The breakup of a film company when the schedule concludes is often a sad event; none was sadder for me than when I saw this young woman for the last time.

---

* Elia Kazan starred in *Waiting for Lefty*, Clifford Odets's 1935 play about a taxi drivers' strike, which was produced by the Group Theatre in New York, of which Kazan was a member. —Ed.

OUTTAKE

"What price is gold?"

"On *East of Eden*, Kazan had the whole crew and cast line up outside the soundstage. And Kazan said, 'You're gonna meet a boy and he's gonna be very strange to you and he's gonna be different, but no matter what you see or what you think of him, when you see him on the screen he's gonna be pure gold.' Then he said, 'I want you to meet James Dean' and they opened the soundstage door and James Dean came out and went [while giving the finger to everyone] 'Fuck you! Fuck you! Fuck you! Fuck you! Fuck you!' And Raymond Massey was standing there, a very religious man who doesn't like any kind of cussing on the set, he turned to Kazan and he said, 'What price is gold?'"

—Dennis Hopper in the documentary *James Dean: The First American Teenager* (1975), directed by Ray Connolly

21

Just Lousy with Rapport

RAYMOND MASSEY

Raymond Massey was bitten by the theater bug while stationed with the Canadian Expeditionary Forces in Vladivostok in 1918, where he mounted several theatrical productions while in charge of entertainment for the troops. Massey came from a prominent, wealthy Canadian family who opposed his desire to enter the theater until he promised his father, a devout Methodist, that he wouldn't perform on the Sabbath. He briefly attended Balliol College, Oxford, before returning to Canada to take a stab at working in his family's farm equipment business. He later returned to England, where he spent nearly ten years acting in dozens of plays before making his American debut in a revival of *Hamlet*. The imposing six-foot-three actor received plaudits from critics and audiences for his portrayal of Abraham Lincoln in Robert Sherwood's Pulitzer Prize–winning play *Abe Lincoln in Illinois* (1938), which he'd written for Massey. Lincoln became Massey's signature role, earning him an Academy Award nomination for his performance in the 1940 film adaptation of Sherwood's play. By the time he made *East of Eden*, the fifty-seven-year-old Massey had appeared in forty films. His recollections of working with James Dean are excerpted from his 1979 autobiography *A Hundred Different Lives*. —Ed.

IN 1954, TWO YEARS AFTER THE WARNER CONTRACT had come to an end, I returned to the Burbank lot to act one of the best parts I ever had in the movies. It was the role of Adam Trask in the Warner Bros. film of John Steinbeck's novel *East of Eden*. It was one of the few three-dimensional characters I ever played in the movies.

The character of Cal, the "bad" son, was an early example of the anti-hero. Gadge [Elia Kazan's nickname] had wanted Marlon Brando for this

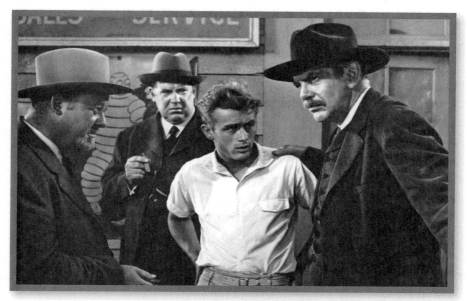

James Dean played Cal Trask, Adam Trask's (Raymond Massey) wayward
son, in *East of Eden*. From left: Burl Ives, unidentified actor, James Dean,
and Raymond Massey. *Warner Bros./Photofest © Warner Bros.*

role and when he proved unavailable, had chosen a young actor, James
Dean. Regardless of his inexperience, James Dean was a good choice. In
every respect he was the Cal of Steinbeck's novel. He was to become a sort
of cult with the young.

Jimmy had only to act himself. But that is a difficult role even for an
experienced actor to play. A rebel at heart, he approached everything with
a chip on his shoulder. The Method had encouraged this truculent spirit.*
Jimmy never knew his lines before he walked on the set, rarely had com-
mand of them when the camera rolled and even if he had was often inau-
dible. Simple technicalities, such as moving on cue and finding his marks,
were beneath his consideration.

---

* Raymond Massey disdained Method acting, a set of techniques derived from the
writings of Russian theater director Konstantin Stanislavsky, which he considered
"verbose," "often ambiguous," and "nothing particularly novel." —Ed.

Equally annoying was his insistence on going away alone once a scene was rehearsed and everything ready for a take. He would disappear and leave the rest of us to cool off in our chairs while he communed with himself somewhere out of sight. When he was ready we would hear the whistle Gadge Kazan had given him and he would reappear. We would assemble to our appointed spots and the camera would roll.

Gadge did nothing to dissuade Dean from these antics. Most directors would not have tolerated such conduct, myself included, but Gadge knew his boy and he must have figured that his only course was to pamper him and winnow the grain from the chaff as we went along. After all, he had drawn great performances from Marlon Brando, and Dean was of the same breed.

So Gadge endured the slouchings, the eye-poppings, the mutterings and all the willful eccentricities. He said to me one morning as I waited near my camera marks for that damn whistle to blow, "Bear with me, Ray, I'm getting solid gold!"

I remember a scene at a big ice house which had been built on the Warner back lot. The key moment of the scene was Jimmy in a rage pushing the huge blocks of ice from the cool storage loft down a long chute to melt quickly in the sweltering California sun. This was Cal's senseless attempt to destroy the refrigeration experiment. The action was simple. Jimmy just had to push the blocks down the chute as Burl Ives and I looked up at him. It was a set-up favoring us in the foreground, Jimmy being up on a platform and not in clear focus.

Everything was ready for the take. But nothing happened. Jimmy just continued to pace up and down glaring at the blocks of ice.

"What the hell goes on?" I said.

Burl Ives looked at his watch. "Jimmy's got to get to hate the ice," he muttered. "It takes time."

It was nearly five minutes before Dean signaled his readiness to perform. When his close-up was shot a half-hour later he was much quicker. It seems his hatred of the ice had lasted although the ice hadn't.

There was only one time when I lost my cool and, as always, I much regretted it. There was a big scene between Cal and his father in which the boy is rebuked for his misdeeds and is made to read a passage from the

Bible as an admonition. The reading is not to the father's satisfaction and he demands that Cal read it again with proper reverence.

It was a long scene and Gadge had covered it lavishly from every angle. He finally got to my close-up when Jimmy read the passage off screen for my reaction. I was astounded to hear the Bible being read, revised by Jimmy, with profanity and obscenity injected. I did not wait. I shouted "Cut!"—an insult to a director on his own set—and walked over to Gadge, saying, "I'll be in my dressing room when this young man is ready to apologize."

I sat in my portable [dressing room] for a few minutes repenting my action when there was a knock on the door. I opened it and there were about fifteen or twenty of the crew standing there. The head grip was in the center. "Ray," he said, "we just wanted to thank you for what you just did." There was a murmur of assent and as they turned to go, Kazan came through the group. We went into my dressing room together. He shut the door and we sat down.

Not a word was spoken until Kazan said, "I put Jimmy up to that. I thought it would get the reaction from you that I wanted."

There was a pause.

"Gadge, you're too smart a director to think that a kid's trick like Jimmy pulled could get anything from me that you could print. It just shamed me into a burst of temper which I regret. You know and we all know that Jimmy's got it. He's good. But there are rules to go by in our profession and he'd better abide by them. One is to stick to the script."

Within five minutes Jimmy had made a gracious apology, not for any breach of good taste, though I think that was implied, but for spoiling a take of my close-up! He was quite professional and I reciprocated by expressing my regrets at my own behavior.

Gadge shot the picture almost in continuity.* After the Bible scene we were in the final sequences in which Cal seeks a reconciliation with his father. In this phase of the story Jimmy revealed a sensitivity and a tenderness which was quite unexpected to us all. The whistle was no longer heard or needed, for the solitary "conferences" had been abandoned.

---

* A film is shot in continuity when each scene in the movie is shot in the order in which it takes place in the screenplay. —Ed.

Jimmy was openly antagonistic in our early scenes, as called for by the
script. All indicated a lack of understanding between father and son. At the
end of shooting a sequence in which a reconciliation has been initiated, as
Jimmy and I left the set he linked his arm in mine and said with a chuckle,
"You know, we were just lousy with rapport in that one."

"Lousy" had, in Jimmy's personal lexicon, no derogatory or entomolog-
ical connotation. You might say it meant "suffused." The remark impressed
me as it seemed to indicate a sense of surprise and satisfaction in Jimmy
at what he, or rather we, had accomplished in the scene just played. I had
a notion that he didn't know or care whether it was Cal or himself he had
just talked about. All along, I think, Jimmy had been following the Method
theory of the actor identifying himself with the character he is portraying.

22

Demon Dean

SIDNEY SKOLSKY

Sidney Skolsky was one of Hollywood's most prominent gossip columnists in the 1950s. His article appeared in the July 1955 issue of *Photoplay.* —Ed.

Out of the corner of his eyes he's daring Hollywood to change him. And telling the world in his bebop lingo, he means to act, not charm!

SCENE: EARLY IN THE MORNING AT GOOGIE'S. A low-priced restaurant. The young crowd gathers here after Schwab's (next door) closes at midnight. I am sitting with a group in the booth in the rear. Between coffee and hot cakes and hot chocolate, I listen to talk about acting. Then a young fellow approaches. He is wearing a black leather jacket, a pair of old-fashioned steel-framed glasses. Jimmy Dean. I can tell by the way they greet him that they respect him. The talk continues. Jimmy slumps in the booth, seldom opens his mouth. When he does join in, all listen, and he says something like this: "All neurotic people have the necessity to express themselves. For me, acting is the most logical."

The discussion continued until about three in the morning. Jimmy interrupted the debate (discussions between actors always turn into debates), asking: "Any you cats know where I can play the drums? (bongo) I got the urge." A young actress said she lived up in the hills; it should be safe there. "Wait till I go to the house and get the drums," said Jimmy. "I won't be long. I've got my motorcycle outside."

I couldn't resist saying: "What's he doing? Playing Marlon Brando?"

This was six months before Jimmy clicked in "East of Eden." Since then, a lot of people have compared him with Brando. "Is Dean deliberately doing a Brando" is good for discussion-to-debate at Schwab's and Googie's with the young set anytime. They believe an actor's popularity is definitely related to the social complexion of an era. As Binky Doyle put it one night at Googie's: "Shakespeare said actors 'are the abstract and brief chronicles of the time.' Get it?"

Well, what I got from all this talk is that Dean resembles Brando because they both represent today. That's why so many actors today work like Brando. As Brad Jackson, one of the gang, said: "If all actors who work like Marlon voted, no wonder he won the Academy Award." There's a point here. Dean represents one of a whole new hep cat school of acting.

I didn't attend the music session that night. I went home to get some much needed sleep. Now stay with me. We're going to play it again—only some months later.

Scene: Googie's. The important point is that it's months later.

Jimmy Dean had finished his first movie, "East of Eden." It had been sneak-previewed. Word was in the Hollywood air and smog that James Dean was "great," "a new star," "He'll be up for an Oscar."

Well, Dean walked in the same manner, wearing the same outfit, to the same booth. He was the same Dean. But to the customers and the waitresses he was movie star Dean.

The youngsters who sit around Googie's with Jimmy are, in the main, ambitious actors and actresses. They respect talent. They admired Dean before he hit the jackpot. These aspiring actors, and this is important, don't resent Dean's success. They don't say, as others do: "He got the break. If Kazan had his eye on me I'd be as good, maybe better."

This is a sample of the Hollywood revolution. The new style of serious young actor believes that an unknown like Dean, getting to star in a first picture, might make it easier for them. Maybe Hollywood producers will learn another lesson.

Therefore the newcomers keep studying, talking, breathing acting. They want to be ready when their big chance comes. They know it takes nights and nights of work to become an overnight sensation.

Jack Simmons and Binky Doyle and Jack Kramer and Tony Lee [Toni Lee Scott] and Maila Nurmi, who sit around Googie's, know it was this way with their boy Dean.

Look at some of those other nights quickly. The lonely nights on a Fairmount, Indiana farm. The nights at UCLA where Jimmy didn't startle the campus in any college play. The serious talks about acting with James Whitmore, who lived only a few blocks from the university. Later, the nights Jimmy left his Broadway hotel only to go to a movie, trying to throw off the bad feeling of being rejected by Broadway producers. The nights of studying at the Actors Studio under the guidance of Lee Strasberg. These were nights to stay with Jimmy Dean forever.

Jimmy, you must understand, has character and integrity. He is also undisciplined and irresponsible. Anyone who really knows him is aware that he seldom reacts the way he feels; only when bored. Then he doesn't bother with his defenses.

I'd say that the best way to describe Jimmy Dean quickly is to say he is Marlon Brando seven years ago. There's the refusal to conform to accepted patterns, right to the motorcycle. Yet, somehow, this comparison is unfair.

I'll start at the beginning. James Dean was born on February 8, 1931. He was raised on a farm by an uncle and aunt. His mother died while he was still a baby. His father was a farmer.* The farm background and the knowledge of this type of people were useful to him when playing the farm boy in "East of Eden." Jimmy could fall back on his own experiences. He could give the words and Kazan's direction a genuine and individual inter-pretation. By the way, Dean has yet to read Steinbeck's *East of Eden*. He read only Paul Osborn's screenplay. "This was all Kazan intended to put on the screen," he says.

Dean attended Fairmount High School. He is athletic and was a member of the baseball, track and basketball teams. In his senior year he won a

---

* James Dean's father was a dental technician. —Ed.

medal as the school's top athlete. He is still athletic; in fact, too much for his studio. The day before starting "Rebel Without a Cause," Jimmy went to Palm Springs for the Sunday automobile races. He entered his Porsche car in two events. He placed third in a race against veteran drivers and he won first prize in the race for novices. He couldn't understand why the studio told him he can't do this.

"It was on a Sunday," said Jimmy. "There wasn't any shooting." The studio couldn't convince him auto racing is dangerous. To him, it isn't, and they shouldn't interfere with his individuality.

Jimmy became interested in acting while at high school. I learned this during a number of coffee sessions. Binky, Brad Jackson, Maila Nurmi (Vampira) all asked each other what made them become an actor.

Dean said one of his high school teachers was a frustrated actress. Through her he entered and won a state oratorical contest, reciting something dramatic by Dickens. "Of course," continued Jimmy, "this chick only provided the incident. A neurotic person has the necessity to express himself and my neuroticism manifests itself in the dramatic." Dean and his friends were searching for the *true* reason.

Jimmy's lingo is a mixture of the bop, the analytic and the idiom of the youngsters. He is certainly in tune with the times. He uses whatever words get there first to best express his thoughts.

After graduation from high school, there came two years of pre-law followed by some TV work and the enrollment in the Actors Studio. This is acknowledged to be the finest school for young actors. Elia Kazan is in charge, but the main coaching is done by Lee Strasberg, who has great insight about talent. It's my personal belief, I haven't any proof, that Kazan spotted Dean, trained him, and had Strasberg work with him for months and months.* Almost secretly, as is done with a horse, grooming him for the big race. He wanted Dean to be ready and he wanted the right picture.

---

* Elia Kazan watched James Dean's audition for membership in the Actors Studio, but he never assigned Lee Strasberg to train Dean. After Strasberg eviscerated his first performance there, Dean rarely returned to the Studio and did almost no work there. —Ed.

Kazan waited patiently. Dean and "East of Eden" were made for each other. Kazan rode another winner.

"East of Eden" had its world premiere at the New York Paramount Theatre. It was a gala premiere. There was no doubt. It was James Dean's big night. All the hard lonely nights had now been rolled into the night of triumph. But Jimmy couldn't face his Big Night in person. Two days before, he left New York and was on his way back to Hollywood.

"This cat doesn't buy that," he explained. "I came to Hollywood to act not to charm society." Jimmy is young. He'll try to justify his conduct by saying the objective artist has always been misunderstood.

A few critics and patrons commented on the similarity of Dean to Brando. One movie reviewer hit hard and panned Jimmy for trying to act like Brando. Jimmy is sensitive. He was deeply hurt. But only a few knew this.

Dean has a unique personality, an individual quality which comes through. He has his own fine talent which shines when he allows himself to be himself.

Dean weighs 150 pounds; photographs thinner. He is 5 feet 10 inches tall, but appears slighter on the screen, because of the way he slumps. Dean represents the Montgomery Clift type; a woman wants to take care of Jimmy because he looks as if he needs help and kindness.* Brando has authority. He commands the situation and the scene.

These are some of the vital differences between Dean and Brando, according to the young performers who know actors best. However, it's a matter of record that Jimmy appeared in two plays on Broadway: "See the Jaguar" and "The Immoralist." The last named won Jimmy the Donaldson and Perry acting awards. None of the alert New York drama reviews made a single reference to the fact that James Dean reminded them of Marlon Brando. Therefore, between these plays and "East of Eden," a change took place.

---

* James Dean once defined his image to Dennis Hopper: "I know I'm gonna make it because I've got Clift in one hand saying, 'Help me,'" Dean told him, "and Brando in the other saying, 'Screw you!' And somewhere in between is Jimmy Dean." —Ed.

Dean doesn't like being compared to Brando, so those close to him confide. However, Jimmy's public comment is: "I am not disturbed by the comparison nor am I flattered."

Brando's only comment, as far as I know, was made at a party attended by both. Marlon said to Jimmy: "Don't you think you're going a little too far to attract attention?"

For his own crowd, Jimmy will give his impersonation of Brando imitating Charlie Chaplin; then he'll do Chaplin impersonating Marlon. Jimmy is a fine mimic. He is a very talented young man. He is an excellent cartoonist. He can play the bongo drums "like the living end." He is okay on the piano and on a flute-like instrument called the recorder. Jimmy is hip when it comes to true jazz. He knows the names of "obscure cats who are artists on their particular instrument." Jimmy is responsible for Leonard Rosenman writing the musical score for "East of Eden." He appreciates fine music and is sent by pure jazz.

When Jimmy first came here, he had a house at the beach.* He didn't have a phone. No one, girl or studio, could get in touch with him unless they made the trip to the beach. Later he moved into town and rented a small apartment over a garage (about a reel and a half from Googie's and Schwab's).

Jimmy is disorderly. To step into his apartment is like arriving at the scene of a hurricane. Belongings are strewn everywhere. He's frank about himself. "I'm intense. I'm so tense," he says, "I don't see how people stay in the same room with me. I wouldn't tolerate myself."

A few of his group not only tolerate but follow him. Dennis Stock, a photographer, not only believes in him but also believes they understand each other. Jack Simmons, a trying-to-make-it actor, has a prominent role in "Rebel Without a Cause," and is a good actor. Jack is always around the house and set. He gets Jimmy coffee or a sandwich or whatever Jimmy wants. Jack also runs interference for Dean when there are people Jimmy doesn't want to see. There are many people trying to contact a nobody who has just become a star.

---

* James Dean never occupied a house at the beach after he returned to Hollywood from New York to make *East of Eden*. —Ed.

Dean has a loyalty to old friends, but he also enjoys the attention or service they give him.

Recently Dean rented a house almost atop Laurel Canyon. Dean read the ad, rode his motorcycle as far up the dirt and stone road as he could, got out and spoke to the owner of the house.

"I want this place so I can play my drums late at night without complaints from the neighbors. How about it, man?"

"The only complaints you might get," said dance director Dave Gould, "is from the coyotes."

Dean was silent. Then he asked: "Could I see the inside of the house?"

Gould took Jimmy on tour. When they reached the bedroom, featuring a king-size bed, Gould said: "That's the bed Lana Turner slept in when she rented this place."

Jimmy jumped onto the bed. Then while rolling around in it, he said: "I'll take it. I'll take it."

Later, when the story of his moving plan became known, tourists began visiting the site. Jimmy promptly announced he'd look for another place to live.

This is James Dean up to and including the release of "East of Eden." It's going to be interesting keeping tabs on Jimmy Dean, watching how he responds to stardom and Hollywood. As one of the young actors trying to make it said: "It isn't too hard to become a movie star. Jimmy Dean knows it. The hard part is growing up. And don't think that cat Jimmy Dean doesn't know it."

THE END

OUTTAKES

James Dean Was Obsessed With Marlon Brando

"He was fixated on Marlon for a while. I was going to go to a get-together, and Marlon was supposed to be there and so Jimmy said, 'Do you think I could come?' And I said, 'Well, I don't know,' and he says, 'I'll tell you what. I'll go downstairs across the street to the drugstore and I'll call you and you kind of see if it's okay if I come over.' So I said, 'Well, alright,' so we went to this little get-together and we played some kind of games, I don't know, you fell on the floor and did dumb things. Anyway, the phone rang and it was Jimmy on the phone and the guy whose apartment it was said, 'No [pause] no [pause] no' and he hung up. And so I said, 'Who was that?' and he said, 'Oh, it was a kid named Jimmy Dean.' And I said, 'Oh, listen, if he calls again, let me speak to him.' So, he did, he called again and he was in a rage. He said, 'What do you mean I can't come over! What's a matter? I'm sittin' here in this goddamn phone booth!' And I said, 'Well, I don't know. Evidently he doesn't think so.' He said, 'Alright, I'll meet you back at the hotel and you tell me why' and he hung up.

"So when I got back there, he made me imitate everything that went on, what Marlon said, how he walked. 'What do you mean? Do that again, do that again. Just how did he do it? What do you mean? He did, oh, this way, that way, what way?' So there I was, trying to imitate the way he was talking, the way he was walking and then he seemed to absorb all this and then after a long pause he said, 'I don't know why I wasn't invited.'"

—James Dean's friend, actress Christine White, in the documentary *James Dean: The First American Teenager* (1975)

"I remember one story I heard. He was in a restaurant where either Hedda Hopper or Louella Parsons was and he was just eating his dinner, but when he saw that this woman was there, he got up and went to a telephone booth and called a friend to find out what Marlon Brando would have done in that case."

—Leslie Caron in *James Dean: The First American Teenager*

23

---◆---

"I Was James Dean's Black Madonna!"

VAMPIRA AS TOLD TO ROBERT REES

Finnish-born actress Maila Nurmi created a minor sensation in May 1954, when she began hosting a late-night TV program in Los Angeles as Vampira. Vampira was an outré character Nurmi originally created for a Hollywood costume ball, inspired by Charles Addams's ghoulish cartoon character that later became Morticia Addams on the TV series *The Addams Family* (1964–1966). She introduced old poverty-row horror movies on television with macabre gags and patter delivered in a blasé manner, wearing a cinch waist, low-cut black dress, a jet-black wig covering her blonde hair, and pancake makeup that give her face a deathly pallor. "Vampira played with her pet tarantula, gave gruesome recipes for vampire cocktails and bathed in a boiling caldron," Jocelyn Stewart wrote in Nurmi's obituary in 2008.

Nurmi became enthralled by James Dean's performance in the film *Has Anybody Seen My Gal?* (1952), but had no idea who he was or how she could meet him.[*] Her introduction to him two years later by a mutual friend, Jack Simmons, proved to be a singular occasion.

"He was the first and the last human being I've ever known with whom I'd felt we were of the same species," she later said. "Everybody else to me is a stranger."

Dean, Nurmi, and Simmons began hanging out together late at night, forming a trio one reporter nicknamed the "Night Watch." Simmons, chauffeuring Nurmi in his converted Cadillac hearse, would follow Dean on his motorcycle to Googie's or some other cheap eatery

---

[*] Directed by Douglas Sirk, *Has Anybody Seen My Gal?* is a 1920s period comedy starring Charles Coburn, Piper Laurie, and Rock Hudson. Dean appears briefly in the film, playing a wise guy in an argyle vest who orders a chocolate malt at a soda fountain with elaborate instructions delivered in a proto-hipster style to soda jerk Charles Coburn: "Hey, Gramps, I'll have a choc malt, heavy on the choc, plenty of milk, four spoons of malt, two scoops of vanilla ice cream, one mixed with the rest and one floating." —Ed.

that catered to night owls. There they'd occupy a booth until the wee hours, drinking coffee, chain-smoking, and regaling each other with gossip.

After Dean's death, *Whisper* magazine published an article titled "James Dean's Black Madonna," which claimed that Nurmi put a curse on her former lover after he jilted her. Nurmi, however, always maintained that her relationship with Dean was purely platonic.

"Jimmy and I were playmates," she said. "We had similar senses of humor. I was also a west coast mother figure to him."

When she first met Dean, Nurmi was the center of attention at Googie's while he was ignored. Their positions became reversed after *East of Eden* (1955) was released, and the reclusive Dean found it difficult to appear in public without being recognized. He began frequenting the Villa Capri, a restaurant co-owned by Frank Sinatra that was a haven for celebrities like Sinatra, Humphrey Bogart, and Judy Garland. He curtailed his friendship with Nurmi before his death and even disparaged her to columnist Hedda Hopper. When Jack Simmons asked him why he was cutting her out of his life, he complained, "She's too infantile."

Nurmi's celebrity vanished as quickly as it had arrived after her show was canceled on October 8, 1955, the same day that James Dean was buried in Fairmount, Indiana.

Nurmi had scoffed at low-budget movie director Ed Wood Jr.'s interest in her when she was riding high. "I always pity people who aren't very bright," she said. Scraping by on thirteen dollars a week in 1956, she reluctantly accepted his offer of $200 for one day's work in his film *Plan 9 from Outer Space*, in which she played Bela Lugosi's reanimated wife in her Vampira getup. "At the time, I thought it was horrible," she later said. "I knew immediately I'd be committing professional suicide."

Nurmi continued to face hard times. In 1962, she told the *Los Angeles Times* she was laying linoleum floors and cleaning other celebrities' homes for ninety-nine cents an hour. The resurgence of interest in James Dean in the mid-'70s and the celebration of so-bad-they're-good films like *Plan 9 from Outer Space* brought her some renewed attention and attracted a small but devoted cult following.

KHJ-TV approached her to consult on a revival of her old show in 1981, but she left the production, claiming that the producers wanted her to sign over the rights to her character. They then hired busty actress Cassandra Peterson, who hosted the new show, *Elvira's Movie Macabre*, as Elvira, Mistress of the Dark. Nurmi sued Peterson for appropriating her likeness, but she lost the case.

Nurmi was reported to be working on her autobiography *Glamour Ghoul* in 1987, but nothing more was heard of it. She appeared in the documentaries *James Dean: The First American Teenager* (1975) and *The Final Day* (2000), and eventually became the subject of documentaries about herself, but she never managed to profit from creating Vampira or from her association with James Dean and Ed Wood Jr.

Writer and James Dean specialist Robert Rees conducted this rare interview with Maila Nurmi in 1989, published in the June 1990 issue of *Sh-Boom*, with additional material from his article "Vampira and James Dean: Cult Vs. Occult" in *Screem* #5 (1994). —Ed.

Maila Nurmi reprised her character Vampira for director Ed Wood Jr.'s film *Plan 9 from Outer Space*. *Photofest*

I FIRST SAW JAMES DEAN IN A FILM CALLED *Has Anybody Seen My Gal?* and flipped for him, and yet I never realized that that young man was him until years later, after he became my good friend and then died. I first saw James Dean at the *Sabrina* premiere in 1954, but didn't get a chance to meet him. However, at the premiere I did meet a man named Jack Simmons. I met Jimmy through Jack Simmons. I first saw him in person at Googie's. It was in the summer of 1954. I was sitting inside with two friends, Jack Simmons and Jonathan Haze, when suddenly I was shocked to see him outside the window. I grabbed Jonathan, who knew him, and said, "That's the only guy in Hollywood that I want to meet!" So Jonathan went out to bring Jimmy in, but they didn't come back in. So Jack Simmons introduced us.

Jimmy had a girlfriend that nobody ever writes about. She was with Jimmy when I met him. He was with a waitress named Connie, who he was hanging out with because he was still new to Hollywood and didn't really know anybody. He wasn't in love with her, he didn't even like her, but she was one of the few people that he knew. She was just a friend of his.

In the months to follow, Jimmy and I came to know each other very well. We didn't date because I was eight years older and married at the time, but we were intimate friends.

The Jimmy Dean that you see in *East of Eden* was the Jimmy I knew. In that film alone, he was almost exactly as he was in his private life. Soon

after we met he took me to his apartment up on Sunset Plaza Drive, where
he always had a [hangman's] noose hung from the ceiling. He even put up
a noose in Jack Simmons' limousine one time. He told me, "That's the way
I'm going to die," and he wanted me to read this story by Ray Bradbury
about a boy who hung himself in the garage. Funny, that's the way he did
die. He died of a broken neck in the accident. Anyway, after that we'd meet
at Googie's. Then maybe we'd go to Barney's Beanery or Tiny Naylor's.
We'd drive around looking for adventure. We were like high school kids.
One night we climbed up on the roof of this tall apartment building on
Crescent Heights, just across from the old Garden of Allah, where they had
a big billboard with spotlights, and we ran around and acted like Jimmy
was strangling me and trying to throw me over the railing. The cars down
below started stopping, until there was a traffic jam. We acted very juvenile.

Mostly, though, we'd sit around at Googie's and talk about a new song
or what was on each other's minds—but not about each other's careers that
much. We didn't talk about serious things often. When we were at Googie's, he talked about acting twice with me. I'd have coffee and scrambled
eggs or banana cream pie, and Jimmy'd usually just have coffee. Regardless
of how much money he was making, he'd only pay for his own coffee. No
tax, no tip, no treating. He was a miser.

Most of the time, as we talked, Jimmy would draw and doodle on
paper napkins. One time he drew a picture of himself as he would look
dead, lying in state, with a candle burning. Jack Simmons saved one of
these cartoons. Now it's hard to know where they are. One time, Jimmy
drew me out of my costume as Vampira. It was quite a sight. He could get
to the core of everything. He had plenty of insight. People have asked me if
he had a death wish. I think he did. He said he wanted to die, and I asked
him why. He gave me an answer. Maybe he didn't know the real reason.
People with heavy *mortidos* who flirt with death are playing Russian roulette.* They think they want to die, but aren't sure. They want to tempt fate
and risk their lives. I asked him if he wanted to be closer to his mother. He
said no. I wondered why he wanted to die because he had such an aptitude
for life, so much zest, such a strong sense of vitality and the universe. He

---

* In Freudian psychoanalytic theory, *mortido* is the term for the instinct for death and
   self-destruction, the counterpart to the libido. —Ed.

actually was afraid of death. He didn't choose the day of his passing, but he knew he was going to die. Psychic pre-cognizance. He had a fear of death being painful and terrible. When you draw yourself dead, as he did, that suggests the death wish. He said that he wanted to die because "that's the only way I'll have any peace."

We were both painfully shy, but he said to me as he was leaving for the last time that he might have to get in touch with me to help him "light the candle."

He was heartbroken over his breakup with Pier Angeli, but he didn't talk about it because it was too hurtful for him. One afternoon, I was at Googie's and Jimmy roared in on his red motorcycle. Jack Simmons and I watched him enter. He came over to my booth and said, "I've been to a wedding." He'd gone to Pier's wedding to Vic Damone and revved his motorcycle outside. He thought he was being clever, but I thought it was childish and pathetic. I told him, "You didn't lose much, you know. She was dating Marlon Brando at the same time that she was going steady with you. I didn't think I should mention that until now." I'd seen her leave Brando's place, and I'd later been at Marlon's and remarked about all the stuffed animals in the room, and he'd let me know they'd come from Pier Angeli.

I had heard that Jimmy appeared naked on the set of *East of Eden*, and I asked him about it. He said he did. He explained that he was in his dressing room, changing clothes, when a male dresser entered. So Jimmy, in a falsetto voice, ran out on the set naked and screamed, "Ooh, ahh, there's a man in my dressing room!" But instead of seeing the offbeat humor, most people on the set branded him as an exhibitionist. A lot of people in Hollywood thought he was an obnoxious creep.

There was lots of talk about Jimmy and me being involved in black magic together, and that's not so. A lot of the gossip came from gags we'd pull on each other, that's all. Like once, during an interview with Hedda Hopper, he told her that he consulted me about black magic. Another time, he and I posed for death-oriented photos at the same time. For my [TV] studio here in L.A., I did some publicity shots at Woodlawn Cemetery in my Vampira costume. I was told to pose as if I was attending my own funeral. At the time I posed for the picture in the cemetery, we were both posing for death-oriented photos, but didn't know it. Then, I heard Jimmy was posing for Dennis Stock inside coffins in Fairmount at Hunt's

[Hunt's Funeral Home]. But when I received the contact prints on this assignment of mine, I heard about his sessions with the coffin. So, I had this photo made into a postcard and wrote on the back, "Having a wonderful time; wish you were here." I sent it to Jimmy in care of the Villa Capri. Well, Jimmy hadn't seen the postcard because Randy, a manager at the Capri, had misunderstood my point and intercepted the card. He misconstrued my message to Jimmy. So, Jimmy called me without seeing the card and his feelings were hurt. I advised him no harm was meant. But I didn't tell him the joke because I'd ruin the punch line. Anyway, he was assured I was not trying to hurt his feelings. So I said, "You'll understand when you see it." Well, this was on September 29 when we talked on the phone for the very last time. So he never actually saw the postcard, nor connected with its relevant black humor to our mutually macabre photo sessions. So *Whisper* and *Confidential* magazines wrote something else across the photo ["Darling, come and join me!"] and the whole thing was misunderstood.

One time just before that, Jimmy came to visit my place but I wasn't home, and he left me a calling card of sorts. He cut out the eyes, nose and ears of one of his 8x10 publicity stills. [Other sources say it was a full-page picture of himself from a fan magazine.] Then he climbed in my window and stuck these parts of the photo on my wall so I'd know he'd been by to see me. Well, Tony Perkins was with me at my place when the manager at the Villa Capri called to tell me that Jimmy had been killed in an accident. I told him that that wasn't a funny joke. At that moment, one of the pins that was used to hold Jimmy's partial-face photo on the wall came loose, and the photo swung pendulum-fashion back and forth. Tony pinned the photo back in place. Later I learned that I could talk to this photo, or rather the remnants of the photo, and the photo would respond by bending or wiggling its ears appropriately to various questions. Like, it would when asked, bend its ear the correct amount of time to correspond to Jimmy's favorite drumbeat. I thought this was terrible. I shouldn't treat this phenomenon like some trained seal, so I stopped talking to it. But that photo was one of the few items from Jimmy that I hung on to, at least until *Borderline* magazine borrowed it and then never gave it back to me.

Thanks to Diane Hanville, Sharon Madelien and Sylvia Bongiovanni for their help with this interview.

24

Kindred Spirits

EARTHA KITT

Dancer, singer, and actress Eartha Kitt—best remembered for her trademark renditions of the songs "Santa Baby" and "C'est Si Bon" and her performance as Catwoman in the '60s TV series *Batman*—was a friend and confidant of James Dean. She met Dean at the home of movie producer Arthur Loew Jr. in Hollywood when she was filming *New Faces* (1954), the film version of the successful Broadway musical revue *New Faces of 1952*. She was also carrying on an affair with Loew, whose identity she disguised as "Paleface" in her 1976 autobiography, *Alone With Me*, from which this excerpt is taken. Kitt and Dean, whom she called Jamie, developed a close friendship governed by his nocturnal lifestyle. —Ed.

SOMEONE ONCE DESCRIBED ME AS HAVING the hand of God on my shoulder, saying that the whole of my talent and being is larger than the sum of its parts and that, after all is analyzed, there is something about me that is elusive and indefinable. Whether this is true of me, I'll leave to more objective critics. But there were two people I had the good fortune of knowing, to whom that phrase would most definitely apply: James Dean and Marilyn Monroe. Certainly the hand of God was on their shoulders.

Jamie (as I called him) and Marilyn were remarkably alike in a number of ways. Both were loners and lonely; both were hard-driving and sure of their career goals; and both were frustrated at the exploitation, misuse, and waste of their talent. Also, both send out vibrations from the movie screen that are gripping and awesome, as though somehow the film has captured not only their sounds and images, but their unseen auras and energy fields as well.

Another thing Jamie and Marilyn had in common was their penchant for using the telephone—particularly during the wee morning hours. I was often the recipient of such calls, from Jamie more often than Marilyn, for I really didn't know her that well. And being a day person, I was always shocked and irritated to be awakened by the phone ringing at 3:00 or 4:00 A.M., fearing terrible news of some kind. But relief and pleasure would follow when I heard Marilyn's timid, soft tones or Jamie's loud voice, which was almost always accompanied by laughter.

Jamie had been moderately successful in New York but was still unknown when he went to Hollywood.* He was down on his heels, sleeping in unlocked cars and making the rounds of studios on foot. One day as he was leaving a network television station (having found no work there) and was crossing Vine Street, he caught sight of his raggedy, run-down reflection in the window of a restaurant and stood staring at himself in disbelief and frustration—just as I had stared at my own unkempt reflection on Broadway in either late December 1951, or early January 1952.

I wonder if perhaps Jamie and I were standing on opposite coasts and looking at our reflections at the exact same moment.

I don't remember when Jamie came into my life or where. I guess that we met in Hollywood in 1953, for we were each doing a movie—*East of Eden* and *New Faces*. At the time we were introduced, I didn't even know him by reputation. But it seemed as though he had always been a part of my life, or as though I had known him in a previous life. He'd make light of that last statement, I think. I can hear him now, in my mind, chuckling and saying, "Kitt, you're runnin' one of your spiritual numbers on me again."

Jamie and I were like brother and sister. He told me, in fact, that he thought of me as a sister. Our relationship was strictly platonic and spiritual; we had wonderful times together, both in New York and on the Coast. I wish I had kept a diary in those early days, but it never occurred to me to do so; we were all young, and we would never forget any of those

---

* James Dean was a struggling, unknown actor in Los Angeles from 1950 to late October 1951, when he went to New York. He had already been cast in the starring role in *East of Eden* by the time he returned to Los Angeles in early 1954. —Ed.

wonderful moments, and we would live forever. I did write poetry then—and still do—but it was epigrammatic and introspective. Nothing of Jamie there.

When we were in New York, Jamie joined a dance class I taught, but not to learn how to dance. He was a consummate artist, always striving to improve himself. He wasn't satisfied to schlepp across stage; he wanted to move, to learn body language so that his movement, too, would communicate. After class we'd stroll in Central Park for hours, eating popcorn or hot dogs, often walking for fifteen or twenty minutes in complete silence. We were so attuned to one another that there was no need to fill the silence with small talk, as strangers or casual acquaintances do because they find it awkward.

I don't even recall how we happened to be in New York at the same time. I was working—maybe it was the time of my second appearance at La Vie en Rose—and Jamie might have been visiting old friends between pictures. I remember one incident vividly. I had a date with a casual acquaintance who shared my love for dancing. Just as I was leaving my room, Jamie arrived. I told him that I was going to the Palladium ballroom—we had often gone there together to listen to the good Cuban band and to watch the dancers—and suggested that he join us there later.

I forgot all about it, and an hour or so later I was sitting at a table with my date, Mr. George Abbott, and with Marlon Brando and his date, when Jamie showed up saying, "Hi! Here I am," and plopped down at our table. George looked at the interloper with considerable disdain. I introduced them, and within minutes they were having a heated argument. I don't remember what it was about, but it soon died of natural causes. Jamie stayed, listening and watching. He loved to watch people, and since I'm a people watcher too, I understood what he was doing. We very often received the exact same vibrations from people. Jamie absorbed experience like a sponge. One could almost see him mentally cataloging and filing everything away to draw upon for some future role.

Many of those who knew Jamie describe him as a solemn, intense, and troubled young man. I rarely saw this side of him. When we were together—mostly in Hollywood—it was play time. I think we were so close because each brought out the child in the other, and we didn't have to play the adult games or put up with the adult problems.

The phone would ring, awakening me, and I'd grope in the darkness for it.

"Yes?" I'd say.

"Hi!"

"Oh, Jamie."

"Yeah, how about going for a ride?"

I'd switch on the light and squint at the clock. "Do you know it's 4:00 A.M.?"

"Un-huh."

"Okay."

"Pick you up in ten minutes."

In a child's world, 4:00 A.M. is as good a time as any to go riding. I loved it. I'd put on dungarees and a sweatshirt, grab my helmet, and be waiting when Jamie rumbled up to my place on that silly motorcycle of his. And off we'd go to cruise Sunset Boulevard. Sometimes we'd stop for coffee, or for talk at a park or bus stop. I remember one night, sitting and talking, when a drunk came weaving by. Jamie laughed and watched him closely, and when the drunk had gone from view Jamie got up and did an enormously funny imitation of him. Or sometimes he would relate conversations to me, imitating the voices perfectly. Most people don't know it, but his talents were such that he could have made his living as a stand-up comedian and impressionist.

Although we were so very close, Jamie and I had few mutual friends. John Gilmore thinks it was by Jamie's design, and perhaps he is right. In his book [*The Real James Dean*] John describes a chance meeting in the early-morning hours when I was riding on the back of Jamie's bike and John was cruising Hollywood on his. Thinking back, I have a feeling that it was Eartha Mae and the real James Dean whom John discovered that morning.* I learned from John that those small hours were what Jamie's crowd called the Night Watch. They would gather at a coffee shop, or cruise the streets on their bikes and clown around while the rest of the world slept.

I can't remember Jamie taking me to one of his haunts. Perhaps, as John suggests, Jamie blocked out that part of his life when he was with me.

---

* Eartha Kitt's birth name was Eartha Mae Keith. —Ed.

Maybe he sensed that Eartha Mae was too shy to meet groups of people. We'd often stop for hamburgers or coffee, but never where the Night Watch congregated.

I remember something from an F. Scott Fitzgerald novel to the effect that in the dark night of the soul, it is always 3 o'clock in the morning. We confront ourselves at such times. Perhaps Jamie's Night Watch served to guard against such confrontations—I don't know.

Our early-morning treks were frequent and, for me, exhausting. I often wondered when Jamie slept but never asked him. I learned only recently from John that often Jamie didn't sleep. He'd show up at the studio with deep, dark rings beneath his eyes, and the studio makeup man would skillfully cover them. If one of us was out of town, Jamie would call me in the middle of the night and we'd laugh for hours. When I was on the nightclub circuit, it would be my turn to cover dark rings.

Occasionally, Jamie would call about matters important to him, particularly when he was troubled. Sometimes he'd ask my advice about a relationship with one girl or another. At other times he'd talk about professional problems, but he never asked my advice on these; he knew what was wrong and how it could be remedied. Such calls seemed a release valve for his anguish; he would talk it out. Jamie's biggest personal trial came while filming *Giant*. He'd call almost every night, so upset with the film—and apparently so at odds with the director—that each day he dreaded going before the cameras. He vowed that when the film was completed, he'd never go to see it.

Jamie felt that he was not being allowed to develop the character he portrayed in *Giant*, particularly his change and growth during the second half of the film. He felt that he was being restrained from using his full acting potential. I had never known him to be so distraught and troubled. He felt a bit insulted, too, at being sandwiched between what he referred to as "surface actors" and "two of the weakest actors in the business": Elizabeth Taylor and Rock Hudson. Jamie said that he couldn't carry his character "under the surface" with such weak supporting actors, and his frustration erupted in arguments with the director and others. He didn't see *Giant* as just another Hollywood film. He wanted to give it his best, and it hurt me to see him suffer. It was a slick epic film, and Jamie knew it could have been much more than that. As it turned out, he never lived to see *Giant* released.

I don't recall ever dressing up to go out with Jamie. We always wore dungarees and sweatshirts or tee shirts, unless we were attending a party; even then, we never went formal. Most of them were what we called drum parties. Besides teaching Jamie the exercise and body movements of the dance, I also taught him to play drums. He loved the intricate rhythms of Cuban and Afro-Cuban drum patterns. And we often brought percussion instruments to someone's house, where we'd play records and drum to the music. Nothing stronger than wine or beer was served, and I can't recall anyone ever getting drunk. This was a far cry from the notoriously wild Hollywood one reads about, but that's the way our drum parties were.

In his very private life, Jamie was aesthetic. He wrote poetry, loved music and art, and lived to act. His wants were few and his tastes simple. He lived in a small, inexpensive apartment, which he used primarily for making phone calls and changing clothes—he seemed always to stay at someone else's house or guest house. He seemed to have no desire for creature comforts, for big houses or swimming pools or fancy clothes. He had only three passions, I think: motorcycles, sports cars, and acting. He seemed to have little regard for money—unless he had his eye on a new sports car. But the things I found most fascinating about Jamie were his childlike shyness, his wit, his extraordinary intelligence, his philosophical bent, and his uncanny psychological insight. He studied people constantly and knew more about their psychological makeup than any other layman I have ever met.

In 1955, just five days before Jamie's death in an automobile accident, I returned to Hollywood for a few days' rest between engagements. I went over to see Paleface and was surprised to find Jamie opening the door for me. As was as our custom, we hugged one another, and I felt a strange emptiness in Jamie.

"Jamie," I said. "What's happened to you? Something's wrong. You're not here."

Jamie grinned and shook his head. "Oh, Kitt, you're running one of your spiritual numbers on me again."

I had had the distinct impression that his spirit had already left him. I know that sounds weird, but it happened. As I said before and as I used to tell him, I felt as though he had always been with me. Yes, I was stunned but not surprised to hear of his death. But I never felt the loss of his presence, except for that one day when it seemed that his spirit was passing to the other side. I don't believe he has ever left me. I debated setting this part of my story down, because I'm sure that some of you will think I'm whacko. But it happened.

In his book, John Gilmore tells how James Dean entered the studio commissary one day to find a huge blow-up photograph of himself hanging on the wall. In a rage, he ripped the photograph down and screamed at the studio brass nearby that they had no right to hang his picture on the wall. That wasn't his home, and they didn't own him. His action was considered eccentric, but in light of what happened to Marilyn, one can see that Jamie's action was very rational indeed. He was fighting to keep his personal identity, to keep from being swallowed up by something commercially bigger than himself.

OUTTAKE

James Dean Was an Insomniac

"Jimmy was an insomniac—the worst I've ever met—so at odd times and in odd places he would simply pass out, for a few minutes or a few hours, then wake up and set out again. He lived like a stray animal; in fact, come to think of it, he *was* a stray animal.

"Jimmy's insomnia posed a special problem for me: *Life* had assigned me to do a possible cover of Jimmy, and I made several appointments to shoot him. Sometimes he didn't show up at all, and when he did, he'd look like utter hell—a two or three-day growth of beard, and enormous bags under his eyes. He was only twenty-four, but the effects of his lifestyle were already beginning to show.

"He was still [an] insomniac [after *East of Eden*], and night after night he would stay up driving, or drinking, with local cronies or with friends from back home who would come to visit. But no matter how late he stayed up, somehow he usually managed to make it to the set on time."

—*James Dean Revisited: Text and Photographs* by Dennis Stock
(New York: Penguin Books, 1978)

25

When James Dean Charmed the Gossip Queen

Hedda Hopper and James Brough

Hedda Hopper and Louella Parsons reigned as Hollywood's rival gossip queens for nearly three decades. Hopper, known for her trademark flamboyant hats, dished out the supposed inside scoop on the doings of stars in her syndicated newspaper column, magazine articles, radio show, and two ghostwritten autobiographies. A self-appointed guardian of morals (she once hit Jack Lemmon on the head with her heavy purse at a screening of the film *Under the Yum Yum Tree* [1963], in which he played a lascivious landlord), she often used her column to lambaste those who violated her standards. Aware of the influence she wielded with her audience and its effects on performers' careers, she nicknamed her home "The House That Fear Built."

When Hopper saw James Dean and his *East of Eden* costar Dick Davalos goofing off at the Warner Bros. commissary one afternoon, she registered her disgust with Dean in her column, vowing to boycott the film's premiere. But Clifton Webb's ecstatic praise for Dean made her reconsider her earlier dismissal of him.

Intrigued, Hopper requested a private screening of *Eden* with Elia Kazan. She sat through the film transfixed by Dean. She phoned studio chief Jack Warner to schedule an interview with Dean. At her home, he turned on his charm and soon had her eating out of the palm of his hand. She became an instant convert to the Church of Dean, becoming his biggest fan and defender. After his death, she lobbied unsuccessfully for him to be awarded a posthumous Academy Award.

What follows is an excerpt from *The Whole Truth and Nothing But*, her 1963 memoir (written with James Brough). —Ed.

IN MY BUSINESS I GET "GENIUS" DISHED OUT to me as regularly as the morning mail. To believe the press agents, every dirty-shirttail boy in blue jeans who comes over the hill from Lee Strasberg's classes is the biggest thing to hit the industry since Jack Barrymore played Don Juan. Ninety-nine times out of a hundred, the gangly lad is like a dream brought on by eating Port-Salut cheese too late at night: if you wait long enough, it goes away. There's that one in a hundred, though, when the press agent is right . . .

The chief public-relations man at Warners' was as persuasive as ever: "This one is something special. We think he's a genius, more or less. I want you to meet him." So I agreed to go over for luncheon in the commissary, and he introduced me to Jimmy Dean, brought to Hollywood to do *East of Eden* by Elia Kazan, who had been bowled over by his Broadway performance as the Arab boy in Billy Rose's production of André Gide's *The Immoralist*.

The latest genius sauntered in, dressed like a bum, and slouched down in silence at a table away from mine. He hooked another chair with his toe, dragged it close enough to put his feet up, while he watched me from the corner of his eye. Then he stood up to inspect the framed photographs of Warner stars that covered the wall by his head. He chose one of them, spat in its eye, wiped off his spittle with a handkerchief, then like a ravenous hyena, started to gulp the food that had been served him.

"Would you like to meet him?" said the studio press agent who was my escort.

"No thank you, I've seen enough. If that's your prize package, you can take him. I don't want him."

"He doesn't always behave like this," said my companion apologetically. "Why now?"

"I don't know. To be frank, he never acted this way before."

I went to my office and wrote a story describing every heartwarming detail of James Dean's behavior. "They've brought out from New York another dirty-shirttail actor. If this is the kind of talent they're importing, they can send it right back so far as I'm concerned."

When an invitation came to see the preview of *East of Eden*, nobody could have dragged me there. But I heard next day from Clifton Webb, whose judgment I respect: "Last night I saw one of the most extraordinary performances of my life. Get the studio to run that movie over for you. You'll be crazy about this boy Jimmy Dean."

"I've seen him," I said coldly.

"Forget it—I read your piece. Just watch him in this picture."

Warners' cagey answer to my call was to pretend *East of Eden* had been dismantled and was already in the cutting room for further editing. I telephoned Elia Kazan: "I'm sorry I missed the preview. I hear Jimmy Dean is electrifying as Cal Trask—"

"When would you like to see it?" Kazan said instantly.

"Today."

"Name the time, and I'll have it run for you."

In the projection room I sat spellbound. I couldn't remember ever having seen a young man with such power, so many facets of expression, so much sheer invention as this actor. I telephoned Jack Warner. "I'd like to talk with your Mr. Dean. He may not want to do an interview with me. If he doesn't, I shan't hold it against him. But I'd love to have him come over to my house."

Within minutes his reaction was passed back to me: "He'll be delighted." A day or so later he rang my doorbell, spic and span in black pants and black leather jacket, though his hair was tousled and he wore a pair of heavy boots that a deep-sea diver wouldn't have sneezed at. He carried a silver St. Genesius medal that Liz Taylor had given him, holding it while we talked.*

"You misbehaved terribly," I told him after he'd chosen the most uncomfortable chair in the living room.

"I know. I wanted to see if anybody in this town had guts enough to tell the truth." He stayed for two hours, sipping scotch and water, listening to symphonic music played on the hi-fi, pacing the floor.

We talked about everything from cabbages to kings. About George Stevens, who ultimately directed him in *Giant* and who was sizing him up at this time as a candidate to play Charles Lindbergh. "I had lunch today with him," said Jimmy, "and we were discussing Antoine de St.-Exupéry's *Le Petit Prince*—the writer's escapist attitude, his refusal to adjust

---

* James Dean had yet to meet Elizabeth Taylor when Hedda Hopper interviewed him. —Ed.

to anything earthbound. Reading Exupéry, I've got an insight into flying and into Lindbergh's feelings. I like the looks of Lindbergh. I know nothing of what he stands for politically or otherwise, but I like the way he looks."

"Do you fly?"

"I want an airplane next—don't write that. When things like that appear in print, the things you love, it makes you look like a whore."

We talked about Dietrich. Would he like to be introduced? "I don't know. She's such a figment of my imagination. I go whoop in the stomach when you just ask if I'd like to meet her. Too much woman. You look at her and think, 'I'd like to have that.'"

Grace Kelly? "To me she's the complete mother image, typifying perfect. Maybe she's the kind of person you'd like to have had for a mother."

Gable, who took up motorcycling in his middle-age? "He's a real hot shoe. When you ride, you wear a steel sole that fits over the bottom of your boot. When you round a corner, you put that foot out on the ground. When you can really ride, you're called a hot shoe. Gable rides like crazy. I've been riding since I was sixteen. I have a motorcycle now. I don't tear around on it, but intelligently motivate myself through the quagmire and entanglement of streets. I used to ride to school. I lived with my aunt and uncle in Fairmount, Indiana. I used to go out for the cows on a motorcycle. Scared the hell out of them. They'd get to running, and their udders would start swinging, and they'd lose a quart of milk."

We discussed the thin-cheeked actress who calls herself Vampira on television (and cashed in, after Jimmy died, on the publicity she got from knowing him and claimed she could talk to him "through the veil"). He said: "I had studied *The Golden Bough* and the Marquis de Sade, and I was interested in finding out if this girl was obsessed by a satanic force. She knew absolutely nothing. I found her void of any true interest except her Vampira make-up. She has no absolute."

I turned on some symphony music while he fished his official studio biography out of his pocket, glanced at it, rolled his eyes up toward heaven, and threw it away. While the record played softly, he went into Hamlet's "To be or not to be."

When it was over: "I want to do *Hamlet* soon. Only a young man can play him as he was—with the naïveté. Laurence Olivier played it safe. Something is lost when the older men play him. They anticipate his answers. You don't feel that Hamlet is thinking—just declaiming.

"Sonority of voice and technique the older men have. But this kind of Hamlet isn't the stumbling, feeling, reaching, searching boy that he really was. They compensate for the lack of youth by declamation. Between their body responses and reactions on one hand and the beauty of the words on the other, there is a void."

At that point he casually dropped his cigarette onto a rug and said: "Call the cops." He went over to the mantelpiece, raised the lid of one of my green Bristol glass boxes that stand there, and, as if speaking into a microphone, said hollowly: "Send up Mr. Dean's car."

As he left I told him: "If you get into any kind of trouble, I'd like to be your friend."

"I'd like you to be," he said.

"I'll give you my telephone number, and if you want to talk at any time, day or night, you call me."

"You mean that?"

"I don't say things I don't mean."

I learned a lot about James Byron Dean, some from him, some from his friends. He acquired his middle name in honor of the poet, Lord Byron, whom his mother idolized.* She was a little slip of a thing, a farmer's daughter, who spoiled Jimmy from the day he was born in Marion, Indiana. Five years later, in 1936, Winton Dean, a dental technician, took his wife, Mildred, and their only child to live in a furnished flat in Los Angeles.

"When I was four or five or six, my mother had me playing the violin; I was a goddam child prodigy," Jimmy reported. "My mother also had me tap dancing—not at the same time I played the violin, though. She died of cancer when I was eight, and the violin was buried, too.† I left California—hell, this story needs violin music."

---

* "I don't think she knew who Lord Byron was a'tall," Bing Traster, a Fairmount native, told James Dean biographer David Dalton. "Jimmy Dean's dad had a chum who was named George Byron Fiest and that's how he came by that name." —Ed.

† Dean was nine years old when his mother died on July 14, 1940. —Ed.

Jimmy rode aboard the same train that carried his mother's body back to Indiana, to be buried in the family plot. He was on his way to live with his aunt and uncle, Ortense and Marcus Winslow. "I was anemic. I don't know whether I went back to the farm looking for a greater source of life and expression or for blood. Anyway, I got healthy, and this can be hazardous.

"You have to assume more responsibilities when you're healthy. This was a real farm, and I worked like crazy as long as someone was watching me. Forty acres of oats made a huge stage. When the audience left, I took a nap, and nothing got plowed or harrowed. When I was in the seventh or eighth grade, they couldn't figure me out. My grades were high. I was doing like high school senior work. Then I met a friend who lived over in Marion. He taught me how to wrestle and kill cats and other things boys do behind barns. And I began to live."

"How old were you then?"

"About twelve or thirteen. Betwixt and between. I found what I was really useful for—to live. My grades fell off—"

"Living without learning," I said.

"I was confused. Why did God put all these things here for us to be interested in?"

His Aunt Ortense was active in the Women's Christian Temperance Union. When he was ten, she took him along to do dramatic readings for her ladies. "I was that tall," he said, indicating half his adult height, "and instead of doing little poems about mice, I did things like 'The Terror of Death'—the goriest! This made me strange; a little harpy in short pants."

"You must've been a worse brat than I was."

He gave me a sharp look. "I don't know about that. I had to prove myself, and I had the facility to do so. I became very proficient at wielding a paintbrush and sketching. I won the state pole-vault championship.* I was the bright star in basketball, baseball. My uncle was a tremendous athlete—he won the Indiana state track meet all by himself. I won the state dramatic-declamation contest doing Charles Dickens' 'The Madman.'

---

* James Dean was not the statewide pole-vaulting champion of Indiana. His best pole vault once got him tied for third place in a sectional meet. —Ed.

When I got through, there were broken bones lying all over the stage. If 'Medic' had been running then, I'd have been a cinch for it. But let me say this: no one helps you. You do it yourself."

"Who would you say has helped you the most?"

He gestured toward himself in answer. "When I graduated from high school, I came out to Los Angeles and went to UCLA to take pre-law. I couldn't take the [long pause] tea-sipping, moss-walled academicians, that academic bull."

"You sure as hell cleaned that phrase up," I said.

He had two years at UCLA, keeping in touch with his father, who had married again, and establishing good terms with his stepmother, Ethel. Jimmy discovered that James Whitmore, movie and stage actor, ran a theater group that met once a week. "There's always somebody in your life who opens your eyes, makes you see your mistakes and stimulates you to the point of trying to find your way. That was James Whitmore. I met him around 1949, and he encouraged me to go to New York to join Strasberg's Actors Studio. I did different things on television there and a couple of plays.

"When I came back to Warners, *Battle Cry* was being made, and Whitmore was on the lot. I wanted to thank him for his kindness and patience. He said: 'It's not necessary. Someone did something for me—Elia Kazan. You will do something for someone else.' I've tried to pass it on. I feel I've been of some benefit to young actors. It's the only way to repay Jimmy Whitmore. But you do it yourself."

I steered him onto another subject—New York. He had a contract with Warners calling for a total of nine pictures in six years. He would have had 1956 completely free to go back to Broadway. I have a feeling he'd be one of the few actors who would, in fact, return to the theater and, what's more, play *Hamlet*. He had the urge and push to do it.

"New York's a fertile, generous city if you can accept the violence and decadence," he said. "Acting is wonderful and immediately satisfying, but my talents lie in directing and beyond that my great fear is writing. That's the god. I can't apply the seat of my pants right now. I'm too youthful and silly. I must have much age. I'm in great awe of writing and fearful of it. But someday . . ."

"How old are you now?" I asked.

"Twenty-three."

"You've got a long and beautiful life ahead of you."

"I hope the second adjective is the more abundant," he said. He then had almost exactly nine more months to live.

He made *Rebel Without a Cause*—and made a friend of its director, Nick Ray.

Hollywood started to simmer with excitement over this new, young talent when *East of Eden* was released and Jimmy went into *Rebel*, causing no problems for anybody because Nick Ray could communicate with him; they got along like a house on fire. Then came *Giant*, which he should never have gone into. The part of Jett Rink, Texas wildcatter turned millionaire, was not right for him.

George Stevens is a martinet, a slow-moving hulk of a man who tried to force Jimmy to conform to George's interpretation of the role. Now Jimmy could be led but not driven; he'd bend like a young tree but not break. How poorly Stevens understood him showed in his remarks after Jimmy died: "He was just a regular kid trying to make good in Hollywood. He was determined to reach his goal of being a top-notch movie star at any price."

Tremendous trouble was brewing on the set. It reached [the] boiling point when Jimmy went on strike and boycotted *Giant* for three days. The newspaper and town gossips started picking on him, pinning all the blame on his shoulders. It was high time we had another talk.

"I've been reading some bad things about you," I said. "I understand you haven't been showing up for work."

"Right, I haven't. Stevens has been horrible. I sat there for three days, made up and ready to work at nine o'clock every morning. By six o'clock I hadn't had a scene or a rehearsal. I sat there like a bump on a log watching that big, lumpy Rock Hudson making love to Liz Taylor. I knew what Stevens was trying to do to me. I'm not going to take it anymore."

"I hold no brief for Stevens," I said, "but what you don't know is that there's a man on that set who put the whole deal together. Henry Ginsberg, Stevens, and Edna Ferber are partners. It took Henry two years to do it. This is the first time in Ferber's life she took no money, only an equal share

Elizabeth Taylor and James Dean in *Giant*. *Editor's collection* © *Warner Bros.*

of the profits as they come in. If this picture goes wrong, Stevens can walk out, and those two years of Ginsberg's life go down the drain."

"I didn't know," Jimmy said.

"Something else. Henry has a great deal of affection for you, but he can't show it or else Stevens might walk off the set."

"I'd no idea of that. I'm sorry. It won't happen again. Thanks for letting me know."

He could do anything he set his hand to. In Texas for *Giant*, he had so little to occupy him that he learned to ride and rope, until he could twirl a lariat as well as Will Rogers. He had overpowering ambition. Like John Barrymore, whom he might have equaled had he lived, Jimmy never thought of consequences. There was no risk he would not take. He was too young to know restraint, and he was marked for death.

He got even with George Stevens. I watched him play the climactic banquet scene where Jett Rink, middle-aged and defeated, is left alone to get drunk at the top table. He had some marvelous lines, but he mumbled them so you couldn't understand them. When Stevens realized what had happened, he wanted to retake the scene. Jimmy refused.

There was no time for Stevens to try again to talk him into it. On the evening of Friday, September 30, 1955, Jimmy was racing down Highway 41 in his new, 150-miles-an-hour Porsche, which he had christened "The Little Bastard." He ran into another car, and Jimmy Dean was dead.

Liz Taylor had two more days' work left on *Giant*, including a call for the next morning. She was extremely fond of Jimmy, had presented him with a Siamese cat, which he treasured. That Friday night she telephoned George Stevens: "I can't work tomorrow. I've been crying for hours. You can't photograph me."

"What's the matter with you?" said Stevens, who had heard the news just as she had.

"I loved that boy, don't you understand?"

"That's no reason. You be on that set at nine o'clock in the morning, ready to shoot."

She was there. When she started to rehearse, she went into hysterics, and an ambulance had to carry her to the hospital. She was in the hospital five days before she could finish *Giant*.

The body of Jimmy Dean was claimed by his father, who rode on the same train that took the casket back for burial in Fairmount. The only man from the *Giant* set who went back to Indiana for the funeral was Henry Ginsberg.

Only once before had anything equaled the mail that deluged my office, and that came after Rudolph Valentino died. Letters mourning Jimmy came by the thousands week after week. They came from young and old alike, some crisply typewritten, some pencil scrawls, and they kept coming three years after. He was an extraordinary boy, and people sensed the magnetism. He stood on the threshold of manhood, the adolescent yearning to grow, trying to find himself, and millions knew that feeling.

I begged the Academy to award him a special Oscar, to stand on a plain granite shaft as a headstone to his grave. The Academy declined.

OUTTAKES

James Dean Courted Hedda Hopper

"Hedda Hopper entered [Warner Bros.' executive dining room] from the street door and Jimmy leaped up to greet her. She swept in with a flourish, her flowered chiffon dress and enormous picture hat fluttering in the crosscurrent of the warm outside breeze and the cold of the air conditioning. It was a dramatic entrance that deserved recognition, but for a moment I was afraid that Jimmy was going to throw himself on his knees in front of her."
—*Baby Doll: An Autobiography* by Carroll Baker
(New York: Arbor House, 1983)

"When Rogers Brackett read the [Hedda Hopper] story, he called it 'a perfect example' of his former protégé's 'put-on technique.' 'She, too, bought the act,' he noted dryly."
—*The James Dean Story: A Myth-Shattering Biography of an Icon* by Ronald Martinetti (New York: Birch Lane Press, 1995)

OUTTAKE

"Dean kissed a lot of asses"

"The thing I resent most . . . is that Jim was never honest with himself. He put down the games that one had to play in Hollywood in order to succeed. He felt that he was above having to kiss anyone's ass in order to get a part, and whenever he saw his friends in this situation, he put them down for it, said he lost respect for them. The truth, though, is that Dean kissed a lot of asses, and he hated this about himself. That's why he took it out on others."

—William Bast, quoted in *The Advocate*, February 25, 1976

26

James Dean: Rebel with a Cause

JOE HYAMS

Joe Hyams was the *New York Herald Tribune*'s West Coast bureau chief at the time that he was introduced to James Dean by their mutual friend Lew Bracker. Bracker met Dean through his cousin Adele's marriage to Dean's friend Leonard Rosenman, who composed the scores for *East of Eden* and *Rebel Without a Cause*.

"[James Dean] liked to hang out with the brash columnist for the now-defunct *New York Herald Tribune*, reveling in the warmth of Hyams' close family life, encouraging the young father to race cars daredevil-fashion on Mulholland Drive," Jane Glenn Haas wrote in a 1993 profile of Hyams promoting the publication of *James Dean: Little Boy Lost*, his biography of Dean. "It was an even exchange. Dean soaked up nurturing. Hyams mentally shed responsibilities," she reported.

"I lived a vicarious life through James Dean, no question about it," Hyams told Haas. Hyams's recollections of James Dean are excerpted from his 1973 memoir, *Mislaid in Hollywood*. —Ed.

THE SOUND OF A MOTORCYCLE GUNNING DOWN OUR STREET set off a series of instant reactions in the house. Ellie ran to the hall mirror and began to primp, while my five-year-old son Jay started yelling, "Jimmy's coming! Jimmy's coming!"

Booted feet stamped up the front steps, and then the door burst open and James Dean entered, arms loaded with packages, which, miraculously, he had managed to carry on his Harley-Davidson while negotiating the streets full blast, that being the only speed he knew.*

---

* James Dean rode a 1955 Triumph TR5 Trophy motorcycle. —Ed.

He clumped into the kitchen with Jay tugging at his black leather jacket, and dropped the packages on the table to swing Jay up in the air. Eyes glistening behind steel-rimmed glasses, he hugged Jay close. "Vanilla ice cream for your mother, you and me, and chocolate for your dad."

Jimmy's grin was a lovely sight to behold. Not yet the idol of millions of youngsters who would see in him their own image, he was farm-fresh from Fairmount, a small town in Indiana. He was small and nearsighted and his speech was halting, but he was already starring in his second film, *Rebel Without a Cause.*

Jimmy came to our house often, because, he said, he missed Markie, a young cousin of Jay's age who had been raised with him and whom he considered a brother. Jimmy had a remarkable ability to communicate with young people. He would sit on the floor with Jay and play with his toys, listening attentively to stories about his school friends, asking the questions one youngster asks another—"Why do you like so-and-so?" . . . "Is he stronger than you are?" . . . "Are you afraid of the dark?"—and paying close attention to the answers.

Now as Jay and Jimmy happily spooned their ice cream, they kept breaking each other up, their unfinished sentences interrupted by conspiratorial giggles. Ellie watched with an indulgent smile; Jimmy was a favorite of hers, which was convenient for me because it meant that she never offered any objection to my going out in the evening with him, something I was now doing frequently.

Although I considered Bogie [Humphrey Bogart] a friend, he was of another generation and no matter how much time we spent together, it was never possible for me to relax with him; he was too public a personality and I was always too aware of his celebrity. Also, ordinary activities like shopping expeditions were out of the question. The minute he walked into a store, salespeople would fall all over themselves. And he could afford to buy whatever he fancied, no matter how costly, and I missed having a friend with whom I could browse in peace, handling the merchandise and talking it over at length with someone who, like me, would have as much fun discussing it as actually buying it.

So I was glad to meet Lew Bracker, a young insurance salesman who raced cars in his spare time. Lew, who was about my age, had grown up around Los Angeles and had a native's scorn of most film people. He also had a delightfully no-nonsense attitude toward himself and life. We quickly became friends and when one day he said he wanted me to meet an actor he knew, I was surprised and even a little jealous.

"You'll like Jimmy Dean," Lew promised. "He doesn't take any shit from anyone and even though he's an actor, he's one of us."

One afternoon I went with Lew to Warner Bros.' studio. Jimmy had just started *Rebel Without a Cause*. He sauntered over to us between takes, wearing faded jeans held up by a silver-buckled cowboy belt, scuffed cowboy boots, a short-sleeved sport shirt and red cotton twill golf jacket; this apparel, I soon discovered, was his off-screen uniform.

Jimmy gave Lew an affectionate hug. Turning to me, he shook my hand firmly, then rocked back on his heels, cocking his head to one side and squinting at me for a long moment while he sized me up, too.

I must have passed because finally he grinned. "I like you. I didn't think I was going to because you're a newspaper man."

I laughed. "I was about to say the same to you because you're an actor."

It was his turn to laugh. "That's what you think," he chuckled. "You haven't seen me act yet."

A few nights later, Lew insisted I go with him to see Jimmy's first film, *East of Eden*, which had just opened. To me it was just another picture; after all, I saw dozens each month. But after Jimmy's first few scenes I had stopped keeping my distance, found myself thoroughly involved with him on the screen, unable to take my eyes off him even when there were other people in scenes with him. As I watched Jimmy I recalled scenes from my own youth. I had never before identified with a screen personality in this way and I was amazed and a little unnerved by my response. When the film ended I was both drained and exhilarated. There was no doubt in my mind then that James Dean was going to be Hollywood's next big star.

Later, Lew and I drove into Hollywood to meet Jimmy, at the Villa Capri, an Italian restaurant which was his favorite hangout. He was sitting alone at a table, carefully building a house out of breadsticks.

"Well, what did you think of it?"

I was embarrassed to admit how impressed I had been. "Pretty good for a first film," I said lightly.

Jimmy gave a little laugh and I was immediately sorry my praise had been so faint. But before I could amend my answer, Lew spoke up. "In the car coming over here, Joe told me he thought you were the most dynamic new personality he'd seen on the screen."

"What I said was I thought you were great. Really great," I chimed in.

Apparently we'd overcompensated because at this Jimmy scrunched down in his seat and readdressed himself to his breadsticks.

"Well then," he said, "now that you've seen the picture, let's get on with the business of life."

The business of life varied with our moods, but it usually involved sitting some place and rapping about anything and everything. Frequently we went to Jimmy's house, a small garage apartment in the Hollywood Hills that he had rented from Nicco, one of the Maître Ds of the Villa.* It was the first house he considered permanent and he planned to buy it one day. It was designed like a lodge, with paneled walls and a living room with a high-pitched ceiling. A bedroom-loft reachable only by a ladder jutted out into the living room. There was a small modern kitchen and a den papered with bullfight posters. Jimmy was a bullfight aficionado and often drove to Tijuana on weekends during the season. He was on first-name terms with many of the toreros and his house featured autographed capes draped over chairs and banderillas sticking into the walls. They formed part of a clutter so extensive that visitors practically needed a compass to navigate around the belongings he had strewn about.

We sat on the floor; Jimmy and Lew sipping red wine while I drank Coke, and talking into the early hours of the morning about life and what we wanted from it. Jimmy's desires were pretty limited then: enough money to buy his home and trade in his MG on a new Porsche so he could one day be a professional racing driver. If he was serious then about his acting career, he never admitted it.

Although I sometimes thought him immature—which was in fact part of his charm—he also astounded me with the acuity of his perceptions about

---

* The log cabin–style house James Dean rented from Nicco Romanos was located at 14611 Sutton Street in the city of Sherman Oaks in the San Fernando Valley, not in Hollywood. —Ed.

himself and other people. I noticed this particularly when I watched him operate with press people. Before each interview Jimmy would research the interviewer, getting a complete rundown on him and his special interests from the film press agents. Then he would proceed to charm the interviewer by transforming himself into whatever he thought would appeal to them.

After watching him in operation with Hedda Hopper, whom I knew he didn't like, I accused him of being a phony. "If you don't like her, why do you go to such pains to win her over?" I asked.

After a long uneasy pause, Jimmy, who had had many unkind things to say about ass-kissing actors, nodded his head.

"You're right, but look at it as protective coloration. If I conform to myself, the only one I'm hurting with the press is myself. So instead I'm a nice, polite, well-raised young boy full of respect—which is what Hedda likes. Instead of being on my back, she'll be on my side and she'll defend me against the other press, the people who say I'm just an irresponsible no-good rebel. She's my friend in court." And, probably because of Jimmy's courtship, Hedda was a constant supporter of his career.

Jimmy also did something that I later realized was typical of many actors. When he was working on a film, he would live whatever role he was playing and the people he worked with became, for the period of time, his whole world. Thus during *Rebel Without a Cause* he was very much the young rebel and his best friends were the other actors in the cast—Dennis Hopper, Nick Adams (who was to commit suicide some years later), Sal Mineo and Natalie Wood. Natalie was not a genuine rebel, though. Jimmy knew this and liked to put her on, most often by taking her for hair-raising drives in his Porsche. He had a crush on her but she was only one of the many girls he was dating then.

Usually he and Lew doubled, sometimes courting the same girl simultaneously. They spent hours hashing over the various attributes of some of the girls they dated and I listened enviously to their exploits with many of the young actresses I knew professionally. One of Jimmy's more bizarre seduction techniques was to bring a girl to his home where he would demonstrate the art of bullfighting for her, using a cape and *muleta*. At the "moment of truth," he would drop the cape and his pants and plunge in for the kill.

Jimmy had gained considerable experience with women in his less than twenty-one years.* He had learned, for example, that he scored most successfully with older women and he told one story of how he had managed to get a pass mark in one of his school classes only after having an affair with the teacher.

His most reliable seduction technique—and one that he said never failed him—was to curl up with his head on a woman's lap and let her cuddle him. "All women want to mother you," he told me. "Give them a chance to and before you know it, you're home free."

Although I was sometimes tempted to get a date myself and join Jimmy and Lew, I kept such thoughts to myself and each time they asked me to go along with them I refused, using the fact that I was married as an excuse. I could, of course, have taken Ellie along, but the high cost of babysitters limited her to only occasional nights out.

Actually, I sensed that Jimmy liked me all the better for not cheating on Ellie, whom he liked. His parents had had a happy marriage until his mother died when he was eight and the aunt and uncle who raised him had apparently also had a good relationship.† Despite their promiscuity, Jimmy and Lew both claimed to be looking for the right girl to marry. "When I find her, I'll settle down myself and raise a passel of children," Jimmy said.

Sure enough by the time *Rebel Without a Cause* was in the can, it appeared that Jimmy had found that girl in Pier Angeli, a dark-eyed Italian beauty who had become a star after making seven films, including *The Story of Three Loves* and *The Silver Chalice*.‡ She and Jimmy had met at Warners and, according to Jimmy, had fallen in love over occasional lunches at the studio commissary.

Pier had been raised a strict Catholic and she lived at home with her mother and young sister, actress Marisa Pavan. Mrs. Pierangeli (the family name) watched over her two beautiful daughters carefully, and Pier was

---

* James Dean was already twenty-four years old when production began on *Rebel Without a Cause*. —Ed.

† Dean was nine years old when his mother died on July 14, 1940. —Ed.

‡ James Dean began dating Pier Angeli in mid-June 1954, early in production on *East of Eden*. Their brief affair ended at the beginning of October 1954, before production on *Rebel Without a Cause* began. —Ed.

James Dean and Pier Angeli met when both were making films at the same time at Warner Bros. *Warner Bros./Photofest © Warner Bros.*

very much a proper young lady, in contrast with Jimmy, then at the height of his young rebel days.

Even before I had met Jimmy he had begun seeing Pier in out-of-the-way places and taking her on long private rides. They traveled in a small circle of other young actors who served to camouflage the fact that they were seeing each other. Pier knew that Jimmy would never meet with her mother's approval, not only because of his hell-raising image but also because he was not Catholic.

Although there were still other girls in his life, Jimmy began to talk about Pier with increasing frequency and seriousness. It was my private opinion that much of their attraction for each other lay in the differences between them, heightened by the romantically clandestine aura of their meetings.

Lew and I were sworn to secrecy about the romance and, for the first time in my Hollywood life, I became the trusted confidant of a star. I found it a heady sensation. I liked knowing that I was privy to something which could make a big story, and it pleased me to have the lovers beholden to me. I was increasingly aware of the power I had as a columnist, but I still prided myself on my ethics. Of course, being honest, I would have to admit that there was also a practical side to my discretion, since betraying such a confidence would have destroyed our friendship and lost me many other contacts in town.

After *East of Eden*, Jimmy and Pier started dating publicly, despite her mother's objections. Many were the nights I spent with them and Lew at the Villa Capri, where Pier would spoon-feed Jimmy and he, after a few glasses of wine, would become sleepy and fall asleep with his head on her lap.

To please her Jimmy even started to wear suits occasionally. And he became more concerned than ever about his press image in terms of its possible effect on Mrs. Pierangeli. He was, I felt, on the right track. I had met Pier's mother once or twice. Small, dark and beautifully elegant like her daughters, she impressed me as the kind of woman who would fight fiercely to protect her daughter from any kind of threat.

Just how serious Jimmy was about Pier I was to learn one night after he finished work at the studio and I set off with him for a test drive in his new Porsche. He and Lew had bought almost identical white cars and they were planning to enter a road race in Palm Springs on the weekend.

As we came to a ninety-degree curve the speedometer needle flickered between sixty and sixty-five and I was certain we would never make the turn. Jimmy hit the brakes hard, shifting from fourth to second, and he went into the curve at thirty-five mph. The Porsche drifted to the edge of the road and I braced myself, but Jimmy adroitly accelerated out of the curve and into a series of S-curves on top of Mulholland Drive, a mountain-top road which separates Beverly Hills from the San Fernando Valley.

Behind us I heard the squealing of Lew's Porsche, coming up fast on the outside. By the time we got to the next curve the cars were almost abreast; quickly, Jimmy double-declutched and downshifted for just enough speed to keep him in front of Lew.

Right before we reached Marlon Brando's Japanese-style home, barely visible from the road, Jimmy abruptly turned off the road into a patch of dirt, flicked the gear-shift into neutral and, without warning, moved the steering wheel from eleven o'clock to three and grabbed the handbrake. We did a complete hundred-and-eighty-degree turn and came out of the spin almost face to face with Lew.

My stomach caught up with me as we drove back along Mulholland at a more sedate speed.

Quite suddenly, Jimmy broke the silence. "You studied psychiatry in college," he said, keeping his eyes on the road.

"A little."

"Then tell me what you think of this. Last night I dreamed of my mother again. In the dream I was a child and my mother was calling to me. We were in a desert and I tried to run to her but my feet kept plunging in the sand. With each step I took toward her she seemed to drift away so the distance between us was constant no matter how hard I ran. She was trying to say something to me—something I knew was important—but I was never able to get close enough to hear her words clearly. Then I awoke from the dream with the sensation of falling."

Jimmy put a hand on my arm just as we came into another curve. I watched nervously as he negotiated it with only one hand on the wheel. "Well, what do you think of it?" A shadow crossed his face. "Does it mean I'm going to die soon?"

"Only if you insist on driving flat out on curves like this. And I'm not ready to die yet, so take it easy."

Jimmy didn't smile. "I'm serious."

I looked at him and tried to recall what little I knew of his childhood. His mother had died of cancer when he was eight years old and his father had sent Jimmy with his mother's coffin on the train from their home in Santa Monica, California, back to Fairmount where she was buried and where Jimmy remained to be brought up by his mother's sister Ortense and her husband, Marcus Winslow. The Winslows raised Jimmy as their own son, but Jimmy never forgot his mother. A lock of her hair, snipped from her forehead while she was in the coffin, was kept always in a small envelope under his pillow.

I knew just enough about dreams to realize that any interpretation I could offer would probably be wrong, and I sensed that what he was really asking for was reassurance. So off the top of my head I told him what I thought he wanted to hear, "I think it probably means that your mother didn't have a last chance at the end to tell you she loved you and that's what she's trying to say in the dream."

Jimmy's hands relaxed a little on the steering wheel and his face became more placid. He nodded. "I know she loved me. She loved me more than anything."

Then again tightening his grip on the wheel, he downshifted, causing the car to surge forward. "I'm lonely, Joe. I want to be married. Goddamnit, I'm going to study and become baptized as a Catholic. Then I'll join the Church so we can have the wedding that Pier and her old lady want."

After this, a conversation we had some nights later at the Villa Capri came as a surprise to me. Jimmy had been sullen and moody all evening and had refused to eat his dinner.

"What's the problem?" Lew asked.

"I've got to go to New York tomorrow for a TV show."

"What about Pier?"

"I asked her to go with me and get married there, but she said it would break her mother's heart if we eloped."

"So?"

"So, it's all off. I put it to her, if she loves me and wants to marry me she comes to New York. Anyway, my agent thinks I'd be crazy to marry her now. She says if I do I'll be known as Mr. Pier Angeli. So I'm going to New York alone to think it all over."

If I was surprised at that, two days later, just after Jimmy had arrived in New York, I was dumbfounded to hear a news flash on the radio: Pier was engaged to marry singer Vic Damone. I didn't even know they knew each other. Immediately I telephoned Lew, who had also just heard the bulletin and was trying to reach Jimmy in New York. We joked that it might turn out to be a good match, if only because Damone, like Pier, was Italian and Catholic. But we were both certain that Pier was as much in love with Jimmy as he was with her, and we could not put together a reasonable explanation for what had happened.

We never really solved the mystery of Pier's sudden engagement and her marriage a few weeks later. The only theory that I came up with in view of later developments was that possibly Pier had found herself pregnant and, thinking that Jimmy was fed up and had run out on her, she had reacted in haste by getting engaged.

Jimmy told me he had tried to reach Pier by telephone from New York, but she had refused to take his calls. When he returned to Hollywood a few days later all he would say was that he had seen Pier secretly, but that the wedding was going ahead as planned within a very few days.

Jimmy wasn't invited to the wedding, but he was there, sitting slumped on the seat of his motorcycle watching from across the street as the bridal party left the church. Ironically it was the very same church in which he and Pier had planned to be married and it would also be the church where, in less than two decades, memorial services would be held for Pier after her suicide.

A few days later I dropped by Jimmy's house to see what I could do to cheer him up. The door was open and a current of air wafted the heavy scent of hyacinths through the room. It was dark and all the curtains were drawn. Gradually I made out Jimmy, huddled on the floor rocking back and forth like a mother with a child cradling Pier's picture in his hands. His eyes, though open, were unseeing and if he was aware of me he gave no sign of it. I quietly backed out of the door and drove away.

The next morning Lew called me to say that Jimmy had been asking why he hadn't seen or heard from me, so I went by his house again that afternoon.

This time Jimmy was sitting cross-legged on the floor, playing a wooden recorder he bought months earlier and listening to the discordant sounds with a rapturous look on his face.

I waited for a moment, then coughed discreetly. Jimmy looked up and smiled. There was no sign of yesterday's misery on his face and I decided against mentioning my previous visit. He put down the instrument and we talked about cars and Lew and life in general for a while until Jimmy asked me if I could do him a favor.

He had never asked me for a favor before and I was flattered. "Sure, if I can."

"It involves publicity."

"Name it and you've got it," I said expansively.

"There's this girl," Jimmy said. He picked up the recorder again and tootled a few notes. "I just met her. Her name's Ursula Andress. Do you know her?"

I knew her name, having read something about her when she signed with Paramount. But all I could remember was that she was Swiss, had done

James Dean and Ursula Andress at the Villa Capri
restaurant in Hollywood. *Photofest*

films in Italy and was being kept under wraps until she learned English. A studio press agent had told me she was being groomed as a young Marlene Dietrich and that she was not to be interviewed yet. I told Jimmy this.

Jimmy grinned. "That's the point. They'll never do anything with her unless she gets some publicity on her own, so I'll be her press agent."

"How come?"

"Because she thinks I'm a hot-shot Hollywood type, but the truth is you're the only one I know who can really get things done. Will you do it for me and make me a big man with my girl?"

"I'll see what I can do," I promised. I was curious to meet the girl who seemed to have gotten Jimmy over his depression so quickly.

Ursula lived in a small guest house on a side street in an unprepossessing neighborhood in Hollywood. It was dusk when I arrived to talk to her.

She was on the lawn waiting for me, wearing an old blue sweatshirt, several sizes too large, and faded blue jeans. Her feet were bare. She was carrying a Siamese kitten in her arms and by her side was a huge German shepherd. A miniature French poodle was waiting inside, tail wagging, as we walked through the door of her house.

Ursula put the cat down and picked up the poodle.

"The studio tol' me I shouldn't talk to nobody. You're a nice man and a friend of Jimmy so I talk with you. Jimmy a nice boy but he come by my house one hour late. I hate to wait. He come in room like animal in cage. Walk around and sniff of things like an animal. I don' like. We go hear jazz music and he leave table. Say he going play drums. He no play drums, no come back. I don' like be alone. I better go home.

"He come by here later with motorsickle. Say he sorry and ask if I want see motorsickle. We sit on walk in front of motorsickle and talk until five. He nice but only boy."

I sat down on a couch between the shepherd and the poodle and made some notes about Ursula; she had short blonde hair in a boyish cut, almond-shaped dark eyes framed by black eyebrows. Her face was oval and she had a generous, full mouth, strong, healthy teeth and a straight nose.

Physically she was in complete contrast to Pier, except that they were both European types. I thought her one of the most attractive girls I had seen for some time. It was easy for me to understand why the studio had such high hopes for her and why Jimmy was interested in her.

"Do you know anyone else in Hollywood besides Jimmy?" I asked her.

"I know Marlon Brando two-three-four year. My friends in Europe tell me I look like him, talk like him, act like him. I am female Marlon Brando, they say. They tell him about me, too. Finally we meet."

From the way she smiled, I got the impression that Marlon was one of her boyfriends and made a note on my pad to interview him about her if she were to become famous.

And after she mentioned it, I did see a resemblance between her and Marlon. Her movements had the same lack of coordination that characterized Marlon, and for expression she used her arms, not just her hands, as he did. She also had his habit of lowering her head so she looked up at the person she was talking to.

I was intrigued by Ursula. She was unlike any of the starlets I had inter-
viewed before. I was also uncomfortably aware that my press contacts at
Paramount would probably be furious if they knew I was seeing her. Well,
I thought, since I've gone this far I might as well do it right.

"How did you get discovered?" I continued.

Ursula sipped at her glass of wine and tucked her bare feet underneath
her on the couch. "Paramount chase me all over Europe and test me in
Rome. They say they have picture in Hollywood for me so I sign. Hollywood interes' me. Everything interes' me but only little while. Then I tire.
I am learning English only four months. When I talk it good they put me
in a picture. If they don', I go back to Italy.

"I am no beauty queen who not know feelings. I am actress. I act with
eyes and heart. I shouldn't talk with press because I am under wraps. What
that mean?"

"That means they don't want anyone to write a story about you," I said
as I put away my notes.

My column two days later was headlined: A Female Brando.

"The New York offices of Paramount Pictures will be unhappy to learn
that we have discovered Ursula Andress, whom the Hollywood studio is
keeping under wraps," the first sentence read.

To my surprise and pleasure the studio was delighted with my "discovery" of their new star. More important, Jimmy telephoned me to say he
thought the story was great, too.

He, meanwhile, had started working in *Giant*, and Liz Taylor and Mercedes McCambridge had now replaced the *Rebel Without a Cause* group
as his good friends. I saw him less frequently during *Giant* because the
director, George Stevens, did not like to have the press on set. But one
afternoon when Jimmy was off I brought him out to meet Bogie, who was
curious about him. I thought they would hit it off because they were both
mavericks and masters of the I-don't-give-a-damn attitude. Bogie had often
told me that when he came to Hollywood for the first time he was as much
a nonconformist as Jimmy and Marlon.

I was wrong. Although I was like a mother hen during the meeting in
Bogie's den, it was soon apparent that neither man really understood the
other. Bogie was a master at hiding whatever insecurities he suffered from,

while Jimmy's uncertainties were expressed in almost every word and gesture he made. Bogie did most of the talking while Jimmy sat, literally, at his feet, mumbling pleasantries and agreeing with everything that Bogie said. It was a surprise to me to realize that my young friend was as starstruck as any tourist and I liked him all the more for it.

On the ride home in Jimmy's car he told me that he had been awkward with Bogie because he felt they really had nothing much in common to discuss about acting. "Bogie and Cooper and Gable, they're different kinds of actors than me. No matter what the role, they're always themselves because they have such strong personalities. They adapt their roles to themselves, whereas I adapt myself to the role."

Later, Bogie told me he was still impressed with Jimmy's talent but that he didn't like him. "He's too conscious of himself every minute." Bogie was right. Jimmy was constantly trying to impress the world, to conform to nonconformity, while Bogie's rules were only for his own benefit.

During the last week of *Giant*, Jimmy talked so often about his "estate" that I later wondered if he had a premonition of death. Since Jimmy was now making good money, Lew was trying to work out an investment program for his future—one that would guarantee him an income for life even if he never worked again—starting with a good insurance policy.

Jimmy was all for it, but he was bored with the details and refused to sit down and work them out. One night in September, just before he was going to a big race in Salinas, he told Lew to make himself out as beneficiary.

Lew refused.

"All right, damn it," Jimmy said. "I'll take care of it when I come back from Salinas."

Before *Giant* started, Jimmy and Lew had gone to Palm Springs every weekend to race their Porsches. Jimmy had won several races and Lew was the Pacific Coast champion.

While Jimmy was filming *Giant*, George Stevens, the director, made Jimmy promise not to race. During the film, however, Jimmy had bought a new Porsche Spyder—a special model—and, on the first Friday after the picture ended, he planned to tow the car behind his station wagon to Salinas.

On the preceding Wednesday night I drove by his home to wish him well. As I pulled into the driveway, Pier passed me, coming out in her car. I waved and honked but she only nodded to me, and her face looked tear-stained.

Jimmy, too, looked distraught when I went in. For the second time since I had known him I felt it was best to leave him alone. Before going out I asked if there was anything I could do.

He looked down at his hands; he was balling his fingers into fists, over and over.

"It's already done," he said in a choked voice. He looked at me, and what I saw in his face shocked me.

"Pier's going to have a baby," he blurted out, finally.*

I was stunned by the news. I knew he had seen her from time to time since the wedding, and I had been hoping that somehow they might get back together again. I stood there silently, not knowing what to say.

Then Jimmy started to cry and for the first and only time in my life I took a man in my arms and rocked him the way he had rocked Pier's picture.

Two days later Jimmy was dead. His car crashed into another en route to Salinas. The police said he died on impact. His body was claimed by his father, who accompanied it on the train to Fairmount where Jimmy was buried next to his mother.

I heard the news on the radio at home and called Lew. He sobbed brokenly on the telephone. We were still talking about Jimmy in the present tense, unable to accept the reality of his death.

Months later, I came to realize the Jimmy was the first star whom I'd really known and liked as a person. It was a measure of my adjustment to the Hollywood environment that I'd been able to think of him as a friend first and good copy second.

---

* Rumors of James Dean's paternity are unfounded. Singer Vic Damone proposed marriage to Pier Angeli on October 1, 1954. Angeli and Damone wed on November 24, 1954. She gave birth to her first child, Perry Rocco Luigi Farinola Damone, on August 21, 1955. Brown-eyed, dark-haired Perry Damone, who died of lymphoma on December 9, 2014, looked very much to be the offspring of his legally recognized parents. —Ed.

OUTTAKE

Humphrey Bogart Meets James Dean, Round 2

"Dean never looked at Bogart. He said 'Hello' and stared at the floor. For a minute and a half Bogart tried to carry on a gentleman's conversation; he paid Dean a great compliment by saying he admired the young man's technique. Dean said, 'Yeah? That's okay by me.' Suddenly, Bogart grabbed Dean by the lapels, nearly yanking him off the ground. 'You little punk, when I talk to you, you look into my eyes, you understand? Who the hell do you think you are, you two-bit nothing!' Then Bogie shoved the stunned actor away and stormed off the set."

—*Merv: An Autobiography* by Merv Griffin with Peter Barsocchini
(New York: Simon and Schuster, 1980)

27

Romeo and Juliet in Burbank

Peter L. Winkler

This piece includes memories from a number of witnesses to James Dean's affair with Pier Angeli, as well as quotes from Angeli herself. —Ed.

ITALIAN-BORN ACTRESS PIER ANGELI (christened Anna Maria Pierangeli) met James Dean in June 1954, when they were both making films on adjoining sound stages at Warner Bros. He was starring in *East of Eden*. She was appearing in *The Silver Chalice* (1955), starring Paul Newman, whom Elia Kazan had screen tested for the role of Dean's brother Aron in *East of Eden*.

Angeli and Dean began a tempestuous affair they conducted furtively in his dressing room to escape the reproach of her domineering mother, Enrica Pierangeli, a strict Catholic. "Mama Pizza," as Dean called her, objected to his irreverent and disrespectful attitude, casual attire—T-shirts and leather jackets—fast cars, late dates, and to his not being a Catholic. Pier Angeli spoke wistfully of Dean to reporters, but Elia Kazan, who lived in a trailer next to Dean's at the studio, recalls a more complex situation. "I could hear them boffing, but more often arguing through the walls," he wrote in his autobiography.

There were happier times too, as evidenced by the recollections of Gene Owen, Dean's former instructor and counselor at Santa Monica Junior College. In "An Unforgettable Day with Jimmy Dean," an article in the February 1957 issue of *Movieland*, she remembered the Sunday that Dean

James Dean and Pier Angeli attend a celebrity screening of
Gone with the Wind in August 1954. *Photofest*

brought Angeli with him on one of his occasional visits to her home.
Though there will always be debate among students of Dean's life about
how serious he and Angeli were about their relationship or whether it was
just a youthful fling, Owen's recollections suggest they were planning on a
future together when they visited her.

"We were always so delighted to see him," Mrs. Owen recalled. "We never knew when to expect him. He never called. He would just appear. And always with that shy smile . . . such an appealing smile . . . and always so happy! On this particular Sunday afternoon, I had set up my tape recorder in the living room and was working on the preparation of a school play. My husband was reading. My daughter and her school chum were in the garden. It was such a beautiful, warm summer's day. Suddenly the bell rang. We opened the door and there he was with the loveliest dark-eyed girl I had ever seen. He introduced us. She was Pier Angeli. Since I had never seen her on the screen, I didn't know whether she was an actress or not . . . except for the fact that she was unusually beautiful. This was the first time Jimmy had brought a young lady to our home. We were completely charmed by her . . . and overjoyed to see Jimmy. They both looked so very young, and yet they had such a dignity . . . She was exquisite in a white blouse and pale blue slacks, the slim, tapered kind young people wear so well. Her dark hair, thick and shining, touched her shoulders. She had grace and Old World charm. Jimmy wore gray slacks, I remember, and a red sleeveless sweater over his white shirt. It was a warm day so he removed his coat when he came into our living room."

In reliving the precious moments of that afternoon . . . Mrs. Owen recalled vividly the bright snatches of conversation . . . the laughter . . . the excited plans for the future, the future of everyone in that room, and the wondrous feeling of friendliness and warmth that all of them shared.

"To us, he was always a captivating personality. He was lighthearted, warm, gay, and always in high spirits. He was always a fascinating talker on a subject that intrigued him and as I look back now, it seems we covered every subject on that afternoon. We spoke at length about Italy. My husband and I were planning a European trip the following summer. Miss Angeli told us of her life in Italy, suggested the places we should visit and told us how much we would enjoy Rome and Florence. Jimmy spoke of travel, too, and was quite elated that Miss Angeli had been able to teach him a few Italian phrases which he repeated with a fine accent."

Dean and Angeli's relationship ended abruptly after he returned from filming a TV show in New York in late September 1954. Singer Vic Damone impulsively proposed marriage to her on October 1. Two days later she informed Dean of her engagement without telling him who her suitor was. He was floored when he heard it was Damone.

"I married Vic only because my mother preferred him to James Dean for a son-in-law," Angeli later told a reporter. But she may have become frightened by one too many of Dean's temperamental outbursts. (Angeli might have also suffered from an approach-avoidance conflict with men. One day during the German occupation of Italy in WWII, two German soldiers playacted wanting to rape her. She became mute for several days after the encounter.) "Jimmy would get drunk on a couple of glasses of wine, and when he got drunk he could become very nasty," Dean's friend, Leonard Rosenman, said. "He also became violent and he had a reputation for beating up his girlfriends. He did this to Pier once too often and I think she had just had enough."

Wearing the black leather jacket that Angeli's mother hated, Dean sat astride his motorcycle across the street from St. Timothy's Roman Catholic Church in West Los Angeles on November 24, 1954, the day she wed Vic Damone. Standing behind her, Esme Chandlee, Angeli's publicist at MGM, saw Dean gun his bike and burn rubber as Angeli and Damone exited the church. Dean headed straight to Googie's. "I've just come from a wedding," he told Maila Nurmi. "Well I knew which wedding—Pier Angeli and Vic Damone," she recalled. "I revved my motorcycle and I took off outta there," Dean told her. "His heart was broken," Nurmi said. "He was deeply, deeply in a state of love with her."

Angeli's marriage to Damone went sour almost immediately. She quarreled with him over his gambling during their honeymoon, blaming his extravagant spending and extreme jealousy for the failure of their marriage, whose dissolution in December 1958 was followed by an acrimonious custody battle over their son Perry Damone. A second marriage to Italian film composer Armando Trovajoli in 1962 also ended in divorce.

By the late '60s, a drug dependent Angeli was reduced to acting in cheaply made foreign productions. She played the diva and sought men's companionship through brief affairs. In her last years she kept framed pictures of her father and James Dean on her nightstand.

She became obsessed with pathetic fantasies about the now unattainable Dean. In September 1968, the cash-strapped Angeli gave an exclusive interview to the *National Enquirer* headlined "James Dean's Ghost Wrecked My 2 Marriages, Says Pier Angeli."

Between sobs, an emotionally distraught Angeli blamed the failure of her marriages on her undying love for James Dean and turned her summer interlude with him into an idyllic romance that she claimed went on for three years.

> He is the only man I ever loved deeply as a woman should love a man. I would wake up in the night and find I had been dreaming of Jimmy. I would lie awake in the same bed with my husband, think of my love for Jimmy and wish it was Jimmy and not my husband who was next to me.
>
> We used to go together to the California coast and stay there secretly in a cottage on the beach far away from all prying eyes. We'd spend much of our time on the beach sitting there or fooling around, just like college kids. We would talk about ourselves and our problems, about the movies and acting, about life and life after death.
>
> Sometimes we would just go for a walk along the beach not actually speaking but communicating our love silently to each other. We had complete understanding of each other. We were like Romeo and Juliet, together and inseparable. When Jimmy died, I also wanted to die. I wanted to join him in death as we had been joined in life. It seemed so important to follow him and to die with him exactly

the way Juliet followed Romeo. And yet I knew I had to live for his sake.

Sometimes on the beach we loved each other so much we just wanted to walk together into the sea holding hands because we knew then that we would always be together. It wasn't that we wanted to commit suicide. We loved our life and it was just that we wanted to be that close to each other always.

We didn't have to be seen together at film premieres or nightclubs. We didn't need to be in the gossip columns or be seen at the big Hollywood parties. We were like kids together and that's the way we both liked it. We saw a great deal of each other when we weren't making films. We were young and wanted to enjoy life together and we did. Sometimes we would just drive along and stop at a hamburger stand for a meal or go to a drive-in movie. It was all so innocent and yet so emphatic.

I must now have Jimmy or a man exactly like him. Unless I find another James Dean to love, I'll always love his ghost . . . even though he has completely ruined my life.

Pier Angeli was found dead of an apparent drug overdose on September 10, 1971, at the home of a friend who she was staying with in Los Angeles. She was thirty-nine years old. Though widely reported as a suicide, her death was determined to be accidental by the medical examiner.

"I don't think any man can save me now," she wrote to a friend two months before her death. "I think it may be too late. I think I was meant to live and die alone. Love is far away, somewhere deep inside of me. My love died at the wheel of a Porsche. It's now been 17 years that I've been lonely, desperately lonely. I want to find peace and be free and finally be with my father and Jimmy again."

28

A Kind of Loving

Toni Lee Scott, edited by Curt Gentry

In 1952, ten days after her marriage, nineteen-year-old jazz singer Toni Lee Scott was riding on the back of a friend's motorcycle when they were hit from behind by a car. She eventually lost her left leg, which had been mangled in the accident, to amputation after enduring twenty months in the hospital and seemingly innumerable surgeries in an attempt to save it. It devastated her life and self-confidence. Then, in 1954, she began encountering a young man on a motorcycle in the parking lot of Googie's coffee shop in Hollywood. The young man turned out to be James Dean, whose friendship with Scott touched her deeply and inspired her to live anew. In this excerpt from her 1970 memoir, *A Kind of Loving*, Scott recalls her unusual friendship with Dean. —Ed.

On my way to work in the mornings I'd often stop at Googie's for breakfast to catch up on the previous night's happenings. It was a place to go for the "would-bes, has-beens, and the maybes" of the movie industry. Frequently I sat next to a sleepy-eyed, tousle-headed kid. Aside from mumbling "Pass the sugar" we rarely spoke.

Each morning after breakfast he'd go out, hop on his motorcycle, and blast off.

One morning I followed him out.

"You know I have only one leg?" I asked.

"Yeah," he said. "Somebody told me that."

"Want to know how I lost it?"

"How?"

"On a bike just like yours."

He looked at me quizzically.

"Sell it," I said.

"Sell it?" he asked, looking at me as if I were a little crazy.

"If you put any value on your life, or have any appreciation of yourself, sell it."

Thoughtfully, he shoved it into gear and drove away.

After that when I'd see him I'd say, "You haven't sold it," and he would reply without words, just an odd look. Obviously what I had said was bugging him.

Now that I had my leg I went out more often. I went to Arthur Murray's and learned all the new dances. And one evening I went to see a movie everyone was raving about, *East of Eden*.

The actor playing Cal looked familiar. But it was several minutes before I realized—that's my sleepy-eyed friend from Googie's!

I sat through the movie twice, entranced by his performance. He was one of the most sensitive actors I had ever seen. Watching the credits I learned that his name was James Dean.

After that I avoided Googie's for a time. Although my presumptuousness had been well meant, I was too embarrassed to face him. Then one day I dropped in.

"Hey," Dean rushed up to me. "Where have you been? I've been looking for you." He kissed me on the cheek.

"Why did you do that?" I asked.

"To remove all bad feelings."

We slipped into one of the booths. I couldn't resist playing Mother Superior. "I saw it outside so I know you haven't sold it."

"No," he immediately turned serious, "but I've been thinking about what you said."

At this point I was a little embarrassed. After all, Jimmy Dean, a motion picture star, and I had been hounding him! Grasping for another subject to let him know that I had interests besides motorcycles, I remembered the newspaper articles written about Jimmy since *East of Eden*. Many of them had mentioned his great admiration for Marlon Brando.

"There's a little shop I've passed to and from work that sells art objects. They have a marvelous bust of Marlon Brando!"

That aroused his interest immediately. "Where is it?"

"On Santa Monica Boulevard near Crescent Heights. Come on, we'll take my car."

It was late, but there was a light still on. As the man let us in he recognized Jimmy. We looked around and talked for awhile. And before leaving the man asked if he could do a bust of Jimmy. Jimmy was quite thrilled at the idea and made plans to stop in soon to discuss it further.*

All my embarrassment and searching for another topic of conversation wasn't necessary at all, but good did come from it because Jimmy and the artist became close friends.

We were sitting in Googie's drinking coffee later that night when several actors I knew came in and sat in the next booth. Since my back was to them, they didn't see me, but I recognized their voices.

They were discussing their dates for the premier of *A Star Is Born*. One, whom I had dated several times, admitted he hadn't yet decided whom to take.

"Why not take Toni?" someone asked.

Jimmy stopped talking and we both listened.

"For a premier this important do you think I want to be seen with a one-legged girl?"

I ran out.

About four the next morning the doorbell rang. I was still living on Orange Grove with Mom and Bill. Both Mom and I got up. She saw that it was Jimmy and went back to bed.

It surprised me to see him. I didn't think he knew where I lived. Later I learned he had been searching for me since I fled Googie's.

"I want you to do something for me," he said, coming in and closing the door behind him.

"Sure," I replied.

"Take off all your clothes."

---

* Sculptor and painter Kenneth Kendall (1921–2006) never saw Dean again, but was so taken with him that he spent the rest of his life creating images and busts of the actor. One of his bronze busts of Dean is mounted at the Griffith Observatory in Los Angeles, where key scenes in *Rebel Without a Cause* were filmed. —Ed.

"What?"

"You heard me. Just do it for me, will ya?"

"O.K." I trusted him. I undressed.

Kneeling on the floor in front of me, he ran his fingers over the scars on the stump. "How did you get this one?" he asked. I told him about the particular surgery. "And this?" He went over them one by one. When he finished he very gently kissed the leg.

"It's beautiful," he said, "and you're beautiful. And don't let anyone convince you otherwise. Now get dressed."

I did.

We talked for a long time that night, and on many other nights, or rather, Jimmy talked and I listened. Over and over again he told me that I was beautiful, until I almost believed him. You've got a good mind, he'd say; use it; develop your insight, so you can look behind the words and see why people say them. Learn to appreciate people; that's hard, but important. But even more important, first learn to appreciate yourself. Because you're special, very special. So don't let yourself be smothered under all this ugliness in Hollywood.

It was a rough time for me. He sensed it and worked with me, helping me get through it.

Part of it was career. I still lacked the self-confidence necessary for a steady singing job. But it was also, as Jimmy pointed out to me very gently, that I was adopting Hollywood values rather than trying to discover my own. He sensed that I was stumbling, confused, in pain.

He knew because he had his pain too.

I was living with Mom and Bill Scott at the time that Jimmy's visits frequently came at odd hours of the morning. They didn't seem to mind, and I grew accustomed to answering the door at 4 AM.

While I fixed raisin toast and hot chocolate—he loved that strange combination—he would sprawl out on the couch and tell me what was bothering him. Much was. With his sudden stardom, people were constantly using him, friends betraying him. There were few people he could really trust. And then he lost the most important.

He came to the apartment early that night, completely shattered. The one girl he really loved, Pier Angeli, was to marry Vic Damone the following day. He couldn't believe she was actually going through with it. For a long time they had dated secretly, because both the studio and her mother disapproved.

In anguish he asked, "Why is she doing this to me, when I gave her her womanhood?"

Which I thought was a very beautiful way of saying it.

I tried to convince him that if she wasn't able to stand up to her mother and the studio she wasn't the girl for him. "Yeah, but I love her," he said. "I love her."

We talked for a very long time that night.

When Jimmy moved into the valley he offered me his apartment, for the rent had been paid a year in advance. He felt that I should be on my own again. I convinced mother that it was a good idea, but after the first month I found it lonely in the Hollywood Hills, and soon moved down on Doheny, where I overcompensated, with another menagerie. In addition to the seven who lived with me, Nick Adams and Dennis Hopper were next door and Vic Morrow just down the street. Nick and I didn't get along, but Vic and Dennis were among my favorite charges. Dennis, who played the younger brother in *Giant*, worshiped Jimmy.

Jimmy arrived periodically, for raisin toast, hot chocolate, and talk. When we went out it was usually to some private party, Googie's, or [the] Villa Capri. But many nights we stayed in the apartment, Jimmy reading aloud from a script or book. His favorite book was Lord Chesterfield's *Letters to His Son*, which his mother had given him. Because his own life was so disorganized, he gave it to me for safekeeping. I'm still keeping it for him.

What he gave me was infinitely more precious. He turned me in the right direction. There was never any romance between us; there was friendship; and that, too, is a kind of loving.

I stopped by Googie's one night on my way home from work and ran into Jimmy and Dennis Stock. Jimmy said, "Let's go to a party." Since there were two cars and one motorcycle, for good and obvious reasons we decided to leave Jimmy's motorcycle at Dennis' house, which was on the way to the party. Dennis and his girl drove out of the parking lot first, followed by me, then Jimmy. The first car suddenly put on the brakes.

Instinctively I hit mine, as did Jimmy, but he was already going so fast that both he and the bike slid under my car.

I got out screaming, sure he was dead.

He crawled out from beneath the car, grinning, but not very much, just enough to let me know that he was all right, because he knew the details of my accident and knew what I was going through.

"You've got to sell it, Jimmy!" I yelled. I yelled it over and over again until I was hoarse.

The night after he finished filming his last scene in *Rebel Without a Cause* he showed up at my apartment with a very special gift, his shooting script of the movie. "Maybe," he said with a grin, "in a couple days I'll give you something else you've been wanting."

He did.

"Well, I sold it!" he said. "And bought a new Porsche!"

"I'm glad," I said, hugging him. It was a tremendous relief.

The filming of *Giant* did not go easily for Jimmy and I saw him infrequently. Once he turned up about midnight, honked his horn, then raced the motor. I opened the door and looked out. Instinctively knowing he wasn't going to come in, I closed the door quickly behind me, walked out and slipped in beside him. I said, "Hello," but he said nothing, neither then, nor during the next four hours as we raced around the Hollywood Hills at ninety miles an hour.

It was a curious thing but, because I trusted him, I never felt fear in his company. I knew he was going through something disturbing and needed to be with someone who understood. Without words.

Pulling up in front of the apartment, he leaned over and opened the door. I said, "Goodnight," he kissed me on the cheek, and drove off.

I saw him again on a Thursday night in late September, 1955. He was driving up to Salinas the following day, to race his Porsche in the road races there, and wanted to know if I'd like to come along. He and his mechanic Rolf intended to take his station wagon and tow the Porsche, so there would be plenty of room.

"I can't, Jimmy," I said. "Tomorrow's Friday, and I've got to work. It's the last day of the month and you know how hectic that is."

"Dennis?" he asked.

"I've got a date with Natalie Wood tomorrow night," Dennis said.*

"O.K. Then rather than tow it up, we'll drive it and leave the station wagon at home."

He kissed me goodbye.

---

* Dennis Hopper could not have taken Natalie Wood out on Friday, September 30, 1955, the day that James Dean was killed in an auto accident. Wood was in New York to perform in a television show the following day. While Dean sped toward Salinas under a setting sun, Wood was enjoying dinner with Dick Davalos, Nick Adams, and Sal Mineo, who had accompanied her to do prerelease publicity for *Rebel Without a Cause*. —Ed.

29

Jimmy Dean: Giant Legend, Cult Rebel

Leonard Rosenman

When James Bridges, the writer and director of the film *September 30, 1955* (1977), asked film composer Leonard Rosenman to adapt the music he wrote for *East of Eden* and *Rebel Without a Cause* to score his film, the assignment moved Rosenman to recall his friendship with James Dean in this piece published in the December 18, 1977, edition of the *Los Angeles Times.* —Ed.

SEPT. 30, 1955. I was in New York, spending an evening with my parents, when the phone rang. It was my agent, Jane Deacy, who also represented James Dean. She was calling from California and had somehow tracked me down to tell me that my friend Jimmy had just been killed in an automobile accident.

For weeks afterwards, with gradually diminishing frequency and vividness, I kept hearing her voice in my mind, telling me of my friend's death. It seems to me analogous to the brain running traumatic information over and over again, until it gradually digests it and ultimately assimilates it into one's total awareness.

As one of Jimmy's closest friends, as well as the composer of the musical scores to "East of Eden" and "Rebel Without a Cause," I suddenly found myself on the edge of what had turned into a cult phenomenon. On the strength and impact of his first film, "East of Eden" ("Rebel" and "Giant" had not yet been released), Jimmy had become a legend overnight.*

---

* James Dean was propelled to major stardom after his death by the release of *Rebel Without a Cause*, his second film. —Ed.

I met Jimmy Dean in 1953 when a mutual friend, poet-playwright Howard Sackler, introduced us. Jimmy wanted to study piano with me and became an off-and-on student. I felt he was gifted and sensitive but didn't have the patience or the rigor to practice. He never was able to figure out why he couldn't sit down and simply play the Beethoven sonatas without learning something about music.

When I asked Howard about Jimmy (Howard had known him a number of years), he replied, "A tough kid . . . sleeps on nails." Actually this wasn't true. His main attraction (and I feel this was the singularly important element in his public attractiveness) was his almost pathological vulnerability to hurt and rejection.

I have neither the desire nor the credentials to discuss the genesis of this in Jimmy. It is sufficient to say that it was there and required enormous defenses on his part to simply cover it up, even on the most superficial level. Hence the leather-garbed motorcycle rider, the tough kid having to reassure himself at every turn of the way by subjecting himself to superhuman tests of survival, the last of which he failed.

It was Jimmy who brought my work to the attention of director Elia Kazan, and thus he was responsible for my entrance into film music. Jimmy and I were on location during the shooting of both "East of Eden" and "Rebel Without a Cause" and were inseparable.

I was seven years older than he and the inner nature of our relationship was revealed to me in the following interchange one afternoon.

He asked me to come out and play ball with him. I said no, being preoccupied with something else at the time. He kept insisting and finally I shouted in exasperation: "You know I don't like sports. Why the hell is it so important that I play ball with you?"

Stammering, he replied, "It's . . . like . . . you want your father to play ball with you." It is not to my credit that I testily told him that if he wanted to play ball, to call his father and that I was not his father, etc., etc. That was the end of the discussion.

I recall another incident. I was reading some book by Kierkegaard at the time. Suddenly Jimmy was carrying around books by Kierkegaard and other philosophers, though he never did get to read them. His desire for respect as an "intellectual" was profound and, coupled with his impatience

Leonard Rosenman and James Dean fool around on the set of *East of Eden*.
Warner Bros./Photofest © Warner Bros. Photographer: Floyd McCarty

with ordinary formal learning experiences, resulted in what our friend Frank Corsaro called "a chapter-heading knowledge of things."

One important aspect of the private tragedy of Jimmy was that he had the natural intelligence and potential to become most of what he desired, to be versed in what he had only admired from afar. The public aspect of that tragedy was his hatred of the very aspects of his personality that called public attention to him; his "not-caring" attitude, his daredevil exploits on motorcycles and in racecars, his seeming independence from society.

His true friends responded to him despite these latter elements, and not because of them. Shortly before he died, at the insistence of Stanley Meyer and myself, he went into psychoanalysis. He had at least taken a positive step in his behalf towards consciousness and possible change. It was unfortunately too little and too late.

By his short presence on this earth, my friend Jimmy Dean caused more to transpire socially than many of the great rulers of history.

I don't think all of it is too good and am convinced that a great deal of the subsequent pop and attendant revolutionary culture (revolutions of the self-defeating kind) had arisen out of a misinterpretation of what Jimmy Dean was as a person. I loved Jimmy but would have preferred that society had listened to Mozart instead.

30

Chickie Run on the Sunset Strip

SHELLEY WINTERS

In *Rebel Without a Cause*, teenagers Buzz Gunderson (Corey Allen) and Jim Stark (James Dean) compete in a dangerous test of courage called a "chickie run," where they drive stolen cars fast toward the edge of a cliff. The first one who jumps from his car is a chicken (coward). When Buzz's sleeve gets caught on his car's door handle, he is trapped inside and plunges to a fiery death. Life nearly imitated art one evening when Shelley Winters and Marilyn Monroe attended a screening of *On the Waterfront* (1954), where *Rebel*'s director Nick Ray and his new protégé James Dean were also present. In the second volume of her autobiography, *Shelley II: The Middle of My Century* (1989), Winters recalled what happened after they left the screening. —Ed.

As WE DROVE UP SUNSET BOULEVARD to drop Jerry [Paris] off at his car at the Hamburger Hamlet, Jimmy Dean circled us on his motorcycle. He knew we were trying to get rid of him. He was playing chicken with us, and it was quite dangerous, both for him on the motorcycle, with no helmet, and for me and my passengers. At times it seemed as if I had a choice of hitting either Jimmy's motorcycle or another car. Thank goodness, in those days, there wasn't any traffic on Sunset that late at night.

When we got to the parking lot of Hamburger Hamlet, where Jerry got his car, Jimmy sped away up the hill on Doheny Drive. Jerry, Marilyn, and I were shaking. Jerry made sure that Jimmy was gone and then turned my car around for me. As Marilyn and I set off east on Sunset toward the Chateau Marmont, we hadn't gone more than three blocks when, somewhere around La Cienega, Jimmy came roaring down the mountain.* He started the same deadly game of circling us. I was so angry, I was ready to run him over. I kept honking at him, and he kept putting his brakes on right in front of me. He was laughing and enjoying the game. I had once seen a cyclist's head crushed like a melon in an accident on Highland near Universal Studios, and we were scared out of our wits.

When we got to the Chateau Marmont, I quickly drove into the underground garage. Jimmy followed. Marilyn was rigid with fear, and I was ready to punch him out. He stood there grinning like a little boy who had been playing a practical joke. His face was so childlike. He knew we were going up to Nick Ray's bungalow, and he couldn't imagine that we wouldn't take him along with us. I don't recall whether this was before Nick directed him in *Rebel Without a Cause* or not, but they were friends. So I relented and took Jimmy along—much to Marilyn's disgust.

Now that I think about it, I realize that Jimmy and Marilyn treated each other like resentful siblings. As we walked to Nick's bungalow (the same one where John Belushi a few decades later died of an overdose), they ignored each other, and this attitude continued throughout a long night of conversation. Jimmy was sardonic and made fun of everything, especially things about Hollywood that pained or embarrassed him.

Nick's bungalow was surrounded by night-blooming jasmine. It was sparsely furnished, and he had a big Mad Man Muntz black-and-white TV set. There was a peculiar box on top of it which I didn't pay much attention to. I guess he had taken this bungalow unfurnished (nowadays, when actors or rock musicians die there, it's very elegantly furnished). What I didn't know was that the long, thick wire leading from the TV to the dial changer was rigged with a microphone leading to this mysterious box, which was one of those newfangled tape recorders. In those days, they were reel-to-reel and as large as a complicated computer is now.

---

* The Chateau Marmont, a seven-story hotel located on Sunset Boulevard and Marmont Lane in Hollywood, originally opened its doors in 1929 as a luxury apartment house. The hotel has acquired a notorious allure over the years as a haven for celebrities behaving badly. Nicholas Ray rented a two-story poolside bungalow there, where he carried on affairs with Jayne Mansfield, Marilyn Monroe, and the then sixteen-year-old Natalie Wood during the production of *Rebel Without a Cause*. —Ed.

Nick mixed rather strong piña coladas, and we were so shaken by both *Waterfront* and Jimmy Dean's motorcycle games that Marilyn and I abandoned our earlier resolution of a nonalcoholic early night. After a couple of piña coladas, I was able to calm down enough to complain to Nick how enraged we were by Jimmy's dangerous game and to tell Jimmy that if he wanted to play Russian roulette, he should do it by himself and not involve his so-called friends.

Jimmy just said, "It's midnight. We have to turn on Vampira."

Vampira was a girl posing as a dragon lady with as much bosom exposed as the traffic would bear and a long black wig, long black nails, and three sets of eyelashes and horror makeup. She MC'd the late-night horror movies on a local L.A. station. Jimmy was currently having a mad affair with Vampira—they probably made love in her coffin, from which she introduced the TV broadcast of old horror movies.*

That night, Jimmy turned off the sound on the set and pretended to watch the movie as I harangued him about his self-destructive propensities. Around 4:00 A.M., he agreed to see Dr. Judd Marmor, a psychiatrist Marilyn and I were both seeing. It was sort of a bet. He eventually did spend an hour with Dr. Marmor and didn't say a word to the doctor. After an hour of silence, the doctor asked him why he was there.

"I lost a bet to Shelley Winters," Jimmy said.

The reason I remember is that I paid the $25 for his hour of "therapy."

---

* Vampira was a character created and played by actress Maila Nurmi. After Dean's death, Nurmi insisted that her relationship with him had been purely platonic. —Ed.

OUTTAKES

James Dean's "Murdercycle"

According to the *Hollywood Reporter*, James Dean called his motorcycle his "murdercycle."

"He [Dean] was fast and reckless. Jack [Simmons] had an antique hearse, and one night we were going up Sunset Plaza Drive, Jimmy on his motorcycle in front of us, with our spotlights on him. He held his hands over his head and his hips were swaying from side to side, so that the motorcycle was almost lying on its side. Any car coming the other way wouldn't have seen him and he would've been killed instantly. I was yelling at him to stop, but the only way to get him to stop was to pull over and turn our lights off so he no longer had the stage and audience."

—Maila Nurmi, quoted in *James Dean: The Biography*,
by Val Holley (New York: St. Martin's Press, 1995)

"James Dean, March 1955. At 7:30 AM, I was cruising west on Sunset Boulevard, heading for *Life* magazine's photo lab on the Strip. Coming down Laurel Canyon was a crazy motorcyclist who was driving through a red light. We were on a collision course. We both braked and careered through the intersection. I came close to killing him—just a few inches saved his life. I stuck my head out the window, screaming profanities, as he got up off his bike with a dopey grin on his face. It was James Dean.

"We ended up having a two-hour breakfast at Schwab's Drug Store [Schwab's Pharmacy], and I invited him over to the *Guys and Dolls* set, where I had a still gallery rigged to shoot Brando and Sinatra. Dean was fascinated by cameras, and came along."

—*Phil Stern's Hollywood: Photographs, 1940-1979*,
by Phil Stern (New York: Knopf, 1993)

31

James Dean: The Actor as a Young Man

Nicholas Ray

Nicholas Ray's classic films, such as *In a Lonely Place* (1950), *Johnny Guitar* (1954), and *Rebel Without a Cause* (1955), featured imperfect protagonists struggling with existential crises. Ray himself was one such character, his notorious life only contributing to the mystique surrounding his oeuvre. "My heroes are no more neurotic than the audience," he said about the characters in his films. "Unless you can feel that a hero is just as fucked up as you are, that you would make the same mistakes that he would make, you can have no satisfaction when he does commit an heroic act. Because then you can say, 'Hell, I could have done that too.'"

Ray was brilliant behind the camera. Away from it, he was about as fucked up as one could get: a misogynistic womanizer; an alcoholic depressive; a drug addict; a compulsive gambler. The night he wed actress Gloria Grahame—because he had impregnated her—he gambled away thousands of dollars at the gaming tables in Las Vegas to deprive her of the money. Ray's marriage to Grahame ended when he found her in bed with his thirteen-year-old son from a previous marriage, whom she later married. In his Hollywood heyday, Ray occupied a poolside bungalow at the Chateau Marmont hotel on Sunset Boulevard, where he enjoyed afternoon trysts with pliable young actresses, notably Marilyn Monroe and Natalie Wood, with whom he had an affair while directing the sixteen-year-old in *Rebel Without a Cause*.

Ray's colleague John Houseman, who produced Ray's first film, *They Live by Night* (1948), believed he was troubled by his inability to reconcile his Depression-era values with his six-figure Hollywood income and lifestyle. "Brought up in the Depression, one of a generation with a strong anti-Establishment bias, he had been taught to regard hardship and poverty as a virtue and wealth and power as evil," Houseman wrote in his autobiography.

Like his friend and mentor Elia Kazan, Ray identified former Communist Party members before the House Un-American Activities Committee. Unlike Kazan, who remained unrepentant about informing on his former colleagues, Ray's decision only added to his burden of guilt.

"He was a very dear man in many ways, very generous, very creative," recalled novelist and screenwriter Gavin Lambert, who had an affair with Ray when they worked together on his film *Bigger Than Life* (1956). "But he couldn't work out his life. He was very conflicted, very lonely." In Lambert's view, Ray suffered from sexual confusion and was torn between his conflicting desires for creative independence from the studios and access to their resources and perks. "He wanted to be put up in a five-star hotel," Lambert said. "He wanted the big stars and he wanted it all his own way. He didn't even want the studio to know what he was doing. All these conflicts led to him drinking and eventually, that got around."

Ray enjoyed such a good collaborative relationship with James Dean during the filming of *Rebel Without a Cause* that they made plans to work together on several more projects. Dean's unexpected death devastated Ray, precipitating a downward spiral of erratic behavior that rendered him unemployable in Hollywood by the mid-'60s. "When Jimmy checked out," *Rebel* cast member Frank Mazzola said, "it really took a big chunk away from Nick's dream. With Jimmy, Ray could've been the biggest thing in the world."

Two articles that Ray wrote with Lambert (a critic for the British film journal *Sight & Sound*, whom Ray met while promoting the release of *Rebel* in England)—intended to be part of a book on the making of *Rebel* that he never completed—were published on the first anniversary of the film's release in October 1956. "Story into Script," describing the evolution of *Rebel*'s screenplay, was published in the autumn 1956 issue of *Sight & Sound*. This piece, originally entitled "From *Rebel—The Life Story of a Film*," appeared in *Daily Variety* on October 31, 1956. It is essential to an understanding of James Dean. —Ed.

THE LAST TIME I SAW JAMES DEAN was when he arrived without warning at my Hollywood home, about three o'clock in the morning. That evening, we had met for dinner. We had talked for several hours of many things, of future plans, including a story called *Heroic Love* that we were going to do. When he reappeared later, he had been given a Siamese cat by Elizabeth Taylor, and he wanted to borrow a book of mine on cats before driving home.

The first time I met James Dean was in my office at Warner Bros. studio, just after I had started preparatory work on *Rebel Without a Cause*. I didn't know why he came into the office. I didn't know what he had heard.

But he was not going to take me, or anyone else, for granted. He had been in the room less than a minute when I thought: He's like a cat: maybe a Siamese; the only thing to do with a Siamese cat is to let it take its own time. It will come up to you, walk around you, smell you. If it doesn't like you, it will go away again; if it does, it will stay.

This is no more than a coincidence. Yet I like to think it is a coincidence of some meaning. A Siamese, even more than other cats, creates its own fierce laws of independence. There are times when it withdraws completely, the world seems too much to bear, and it becomes restless, morose and unassailable; there are times when it appeals, with an almost helpless docility, for sympathy and attention. Its actions suggest a creature that has never become truly domesticated, that carries atavistic memories or intuitions of a freer, less perplexing life. It is not really at ease with the world in which it has to live, sometimes it tries to reject it altogether—but it comes back, it must always come back, because there is no other.

I came to know James Dean as a friend through the film on which we worked together. Here again there is a coincidence. After seeing *Rebel Without a Cause* many people drew parallels between the character of Jimmy Dean and of Jim Stark. In the letters written to James Dean and, after his death, to me, the two are identified to an extraordinary degree. These letters . . . are not simply admiring demands for photographs and mementos. They are expressions of personal sympathy for someone who seemed to symbolize the aspirations and doubts of his generation; they are expressions of personal loss.

In these letters, Jim Stark and Jimmy Dean become one and the same person. In life they were, and were not, the same—but what allowed the actor to bring such a fine, intense perception to his role was that Jim Stark, like himself, was jealously seeking an answer, an escape from the surrounding world. Through a tragic irony, the escape that James Dean found was total and absolute. But he is mourned through the image of Jim Stark, whose escape was the one he really hoped for, constantly searched for—a full, complete realization of himself.

First, there was the revolver.

He kept a Colt .45 in his dressing room at Warners. He also lived there. When he came back to Hollywood at the age of twenty-two for *East*

From left: Natalie Wood, Nicholas Ray, James Dean, and dialogue supervisor Dennis Stock on the set of *Rebel Without a Cause*. *Warner Bros./Photofest © Warner Bros.*

of Eden, everything that Jimmy Dean did suggested he had no intention of belonging to the place.* He came to work; he would remain himself. Inside the studio, he found a sanctuary of steel and concrete, and at night he could be alone in this closed, empty kingdom. Perhaps the revolver was a symbol—of self-protection, of warning to others.

He rode a motorcycle. There were days when he did not shave. He dressed casually, untidily, which was invariably interpreted as a gesture of revolt. Not entirely true. For one thing, it saved time, and Jim detested waste. (It also saved money. This is a simple consideration, often ignored. Most young actors are poor: T-shirt and jeans for going to work, which later became a mannerism, was originally a quick and comfortable habit that cut down the laundry bill.) In the same way he would forgo shaving because there was something more important to do.

---

* James Dean was twenty-three years old when he made *East of Eden*. —Ed.

Like the revolver, these habits were also self-protective. If you ride a motorcycle, you travel by yourself. Sleeping in a studio dressing room, you have complete solitude. He could leave, but nobody could come in. He shied away from social convention, from manners, because they suggested disguise. He wanted his self to be naked. "Being a nice guy," he said once, "is detrimental to actors. When I first came to Hollywood, everyone was nice to me. Everyone thought I was a nice guy. I went to the commissary and I ate and people were friendly and I thought it was wonderful. I didn't think I would continue to be a nice guy—then people would have to respect me for what I was doing, for my work."

So the revolver guarded this world of self-respect. Then, soon after shooting on *East of Eden* was finished, he went to his dressing room and found the gun had disappeared. Without explanation, someone had taken it away. He was furious—but it was only the beginning. A few days later the studio authorities told him he could no longer sleep in the dressing room. (For one thing, it comes close to violating safety regulations, and Warners had had a couple of disastrous fires.) He refused to believe them until, that night, he was refused admittance at the gate.

There are names and number plates on the doors of the offices at Warners. Next morning Jimmy took them down, hung them from ceilings and fountains, caused general confusion. Then he rode away on his motorcycle, vowing never to make a film there again.

The episode of the revolver, and what followed, was not my first experience of him. But it was when I first realized some of his needs. His eviction from the dressing room destroyed all possibility of a climate of tolerance at the studio; catlike, he had prowled around and found his own preferred corner. Then he was forbidden it. A wound to the pride of a cat is serious.

I had first heard Jimmy's name mentioned by someone who knew him, a few weeks earlier at dinner with Elia Kazan and his wife.* Kazan had

---

* Nicholas Ray had been a member of the communal left-wing theater group the Theatre of Action in New York from 1934 to 1937 as an actor, where he was directed by fellow member Elia Kazan. Ray's first job in movies came when he served as an uncredited dialogue director on Kazan's directorial debut, *A Tree Grows in Brooklyn* (1945). —Ed.

been shooting that day, and came home late and angry. He was red in the face. When we asked what was the matter, he said something about Jimmy Dean. The boy was "impossible . . ."

Not long after this, when I had written the first outline of my film, Kazan invited me to see a rough cut of *East of Eden* in the music room at Warners. The composer, Leonard Rosenman, was there, improvising at the piano. Jimmy Dean was there, aloof and solitary; we hardly exchanged a word. It didn't occur to me then that he was the ideal actor for my film. That he had talent was obvious, but I had too much respect for Kazan's talent to draw many conclusions from it.

When I moved into an office at Warners, adjoining Kazan's, Jimmy came in and asked me what kind of story I was working on. I told him the idea, the approach; he seemed warily interested, but didn't say very much. A day or two later he came in with a tough, dark-haired young man called Perry Lopez, whom he had met in New York. He told me that Perry came from the Lexington Avenue district. "You should talk to him," he said. "You may be able to get some information from him."

After a few more incidents like that, I decided he had to play Jim Stark.

But he had to decide, too. It was not a simple question of whether or not he liked the part. After the incident at Warners, neither he nor the studio could be sure he would ever make a film there again, regardless of contract. Also, after the success of *East of Eden*, agents and well-wishers were eager to advise him. It would be foolish, they told him, to appear in any film not based on a bestseller, not adapted by a $3,000-a-week writer, not directed by Elia Kazan, George Stevens, John Huston or William Wyler. He was not a person to take this kind of advice very seriously; but, intensely self-aware as he was, he could not fail to be troubled by "success." If there were aspects of it he enjoyed, it also added to his doubts.

One evening we had a long, passionate discussion with Shelley Winters about acting and show business. "I better know how to take care of myself," he said. This attitude lay behind his choice of work. He had no hard professional shell; lack of sympathy, lack of understanding from a director or any of his staff disoriented him completely. That was why, in his brief career, he had won the reputation of being "impossible." He had a personal success on Broadway as the Arab boy in the adaptation of Gide's *The Immoralist*, but during rehearsal he had quarreled with the director and, as a way of getting even, gave his notice on opening night. He quarreled with Kazan during *East of Eden*, but retained a respect for him and would have been flattered to work for him again. He should have been. Kazan is the best actor's director of our time.

There were probably very few directors with whom Jimmy could ever have worked. To work with him meant exploring his nature, trying to understand it; without this, his powers of expression were frozen. He retreated, he sulked. He always wanted to make a film in which he could personally believe, but it was never easy for him. Between belief and action lay the obstacle of his own deep, obscure uncertainty. Disappointed, unsatisfied, he was the child who goes to his private corner and refuses to speak. Eager or hopeful, he was the child suddenly exhilarated with new pleasures, wanting more, wanting everything, and often unconsciously subtle in his pursuit of it.

Late one evening he arrived at my house. He was with "Vampira," the television personality, and Jack Simmons—at this point a young, unemployed actor, who was to become a close friend of Jim's and appear in a television play with him. (Jimmy would extend sudden affection to lonely and struggling people; he "adopted" several. Since he had few permanent relationships, his companion of the moment was most likely to be a new adoption or a new object of curiosity. He said later that he wanted to meet Vampira because he had been studying magic—was she really possessed, as her television program suggested, by satanic forces? "She knew nothing!" he exclaimed sadly.)

On entering the room he turned a back somersault, then looked keenly at me.

"Are you middle-aged?"

I admitted it.

"Did you live in a bungalow on Sunset Boulevard, by the old Clover club?"

"Yes," I said.

"Was there a fire in the middle of the night?"

"Yes."

"Did you carry a boxer puppy out of the house in your bare feet and walk across the street with it and cut your feet?"

"Yes," I said.

He seemed to approve. Vampira had told him the story; he had come to find out if it were true.

Then there were the "Sunday afternoons." I used to invite a few people round, we played music and sang and talked. Jimmy always came to these, and enjoyed them. It was, of course, exploratory on both sides. Was he going to like my friends, would he find their climate encouraging? Both of us had to know.

One afternoon he stayed late, after the others had gone. Clifford Odets came in to see me, and I introduced them. Jimmy was peculiarly silent. He stared, retreated to a corner. I went out to the kitchen to mix some drinks, and Clifford told me afterward what happened.

There was a long silence. The distance of the room lay between them. At last Jimmy said in a grave voice:

"I'm a son of a bitch."

Clifford inquired why.

"Well," he explained, "here I am. You know . . . in this room. With you. It's fantastic. Like meeting Ibsen or Shaw."

Naturally Clifford has remembered this as one of the most charming remarks ever addressed to him.

Jimmy approached all human beings with the same urgent, probing curiosity. "Here am I. Here are you." At a new presence, invisible antennae seem to reach out, grow tense, transmit a series of impressions. Sometimes he had an extraordinary, uncomfortable tenderness. Two friends arrived at my house from New York—Michael and Connie Bessie, a married couple I had known for many years. After I had introduced them to Jimmy, Connie sat down on the couch. There was a cushion beside her. With an unconscious, mechanical gesture she picked it up and cradled it in her lap.

Jimmy watched her. After a moment he asked, very intent and quiet: "Can't you have a child of your own?"

She was speechless. She left the room and I went out after her. She was almost crying, not out of self-pity but profoundly moved by this perception. She and her husband had just adopted a baby.

In December he went to New York. Just before Christmas I also went there to interview actors. I visited his apartment, for there were things I had to know, too. Jim retained this apartment after he went to Hollywood, and never lived anywhere else in New York. It was in the brownstone district, on the fifth floor of an old Sixty-eighth Street building.

There was no elevator. A fairly large, plainly furnished room with two porthole windows, a studio couch, a table, some unmatching chairs and stools; on the walls, a bullfighting poster, capes and horns; everywhere, piles of books and records, some neatly stacked, some precarious or spilling over. A door led to the kitchen and bathroom, another to a flight of stairs by which one reached the roof. It was evening. The only light came from the fireplace, scrap wood and boxes burning.

He began playing the phonograph, changing record after record, and I had an impression of crazy sounds. Where did he first hear them? I wondered—African tribal music, Afro-Cuban songs and dances, classical jazz, Jack Teagarden, Dave Brubeck; then Haydn, Berlioz . . . Many of the books were on bullfighting. I remember, on the table, *Matador* and *Death in the Afternoon*.

No doubt two things attracted Jimmy to bullfighting. There was the ritual, the matador's inescapable endurance test, the challenge of proving himself, and there was its physical grace. Jimmy had an instinctive grace of movement, and developed it by attending Katherine Dunham's classes. Already in *East of Eden*, the bitter, slouching, uncertain awkwardness of adolescence that he so exactly captured was the result of a practiced control of his body. He had an immediate response to vital rhythms; the flick of a matador's cape, the percussive insistence of an African dance, the tension of driving at high speed. He gave himself up to these experiences as if to the magic promises of another world. Each of them—bullfighting, jazz, racing—had the dominating, obsessive quality of a search. Did they, like the analyst he went to for a time, hold out hope of an answer?

In New York, I introduced Jimmy to my son Tony, wanting to know whether they would get along together, to see him through his own generation's eyes. Tony stayed in New York after I returned to Hollywood. He told me later that he saw Jimmy several times, mainly at "parties"—at the Sixty-eighth Street apartment or the rooms of one of the half-dozen young actors and actresses who were his most frequent companions. The same group was always there. Nobody ever wanted to go home. There were bongo drums, which Jimmy played; a Negro dancer did calypsos and imitations of Gene Kelly; conversation ranged from new plays and movies to (as dawn broke) Plato and Aristotle; they read stories and plays, going right through *27 Wagon Loads of Cotton* once, while people took turns to sleep.*

Jimmy also went to more orthodox parties. These were larger, given by people he knew less well. Here it was different. He didn't like crowds, they seemed to make him insecure. Ignoring the games and the talk, he would find his own melancholy corner.

He swerved easily from moodiness to elation. The depression could lift as completely and unexpectedly as it arrived. Once it was cured by going to see Jacques Tati in *The Big Day*. Unshaven, tousled, wrapped in a dyed black trench coat, glasses on the end of his nose, he was morose as he entered the theater. Within ten minutes he was laughing so wildly that nearby members of the audience complained. He ignored them—there was nothing else to do, the spell of laughter and delight grew more and more irresistible. Before the film was over he had to leave, making his departure a series of hurdles over the ashcans in the aisle. Outside, in the street, he stopped at a pastry shop. Then, down the sidewalk, an éclair in his hand, he turned into Tati's postman, with a brilliant re-creation of the elongated, slightly Grouchian walk and the inquiring, bulbous-eyed face.

Another time it was an umbrella. On a sad, gray, rainy New York day he decided to buy one. Umbrellas were everywhere in the store, rack upon rack. But which? Finally he let Tony choose one for him, an ordinary three-dollar umbrella. He seized it as if it were the umbrella he had been looking for all his life, playing with it as a child with a new toy, exploring all its movements, flapping it open and shut and twirling it above his head. In the street, suddenly exhilarated and brilliant, while the rain poured down, he became Charlie Chaplin.

His gift for mime was profound. A friend wanted to do an audition for The Actors Studio, and Jimmy offered to direct the scene. He chose a

---

* *27 Wagons Full of Cotton* is a one-act play written by Tennessee Williams in 1946 that later became the basis for Elia Kazan's controversial 1956 film *Baby Doll*. —Ed.

fairy tale, with a fight between a little prince and a fox.* Almost at once he concentrated on the fox, with a ferocious longing. It was clear he wanted desperately to play the fox.

He played it, of course—and his imagination winged. He became a human fox. No doubt many actors have studied animals, but Jimmy used his knowledge in his own way. He didn't imitate; the stealth, the beauty and the menace of the animal seemed to enter into his body. He was the fox.

Like the fox he was wary and hard to catch. In the minds of many people their relationship with Jimmy was complex, even obsessive. For him it was simple and, probably, much less important. He was still intensely determined not to love, not to be loved. He could be absorbed, fascinated, attracted—by something new or something beautiful—but he would never surrender himself.

Involvement was out of the question because—he was convinced of this at the time—it risked pain. The pain that can come out of human relationships was a risk he was not prepared to take: safer to love a fox, to be a fox, or Tati, or Chaplin. He became other people with obvious passion and relief. "If I were he," he would say. This was a great part of his magic as an actor.

When he was poor and unknown in New York, he had reason to be grateful to several people for food and companionship. Yet it seemed this was not enough to create trust. When he returned to New York after *East of Eden*, he sometimes used his success not to be vain or distant but to be cruel.

A young photographer he had known quite well in the struggling days wanted to buy a Rolleiflex camera. He asked Jimmy to go halves with him—the price was twenty-five dollars. Jimmy took the suggestion as a personal affront. "Why should I go and buy a secondhand camera with you? I can get all the new stuff I want now."

---

* The fairy tale that Dean chose was the children's book *The Little Prince*, by Antoine de Saint-Exupéry. The titular character is an alien prince who falls to earth from a tiny asteroid. A fox who encounters him expresses one of the book's central messages, telling him, "One sees clearly only with the heart. What is essential is invisible to the eyes." *The Little Prince* quickly became James Dean's touchstone after his lover, Rogers Brackett, introduced him to it. —Ed.

He accused others. "They bum meals from me," he said. One day, in a restaurant, he grew depressed. He asked: "Where are my friends?" Four of his closest ones were sitting at the table with him, but before anyone could answer he got up abruptly and walked out.

"I don't want anything seventy-thirty," he liked to say. "Fifty-fifty's always good enough for me."

The idea symbolized something for him. He came back to it often. "I don't want to have to give anybody seventy, I don't want anybody to give me seventy. I want fifty."

The drama of his life, I thought after seeing him in New York, was the drama of desiring to belong and fearing to belong. (So was Jim Stark's.) It was a conflict of violent eagerness and mistrust, created very young. It lay embedded in his own personality, with its knife-sharp awareness and inquiring spirit, and when he was a child events had intensified it. The early death of his mother, whom he deeply loved, who idolized him and Lord Byron (she gave him Byron for a middle name), involved years in which true parental contact was lacking. Very soon he learned the difficulties of hope and affection that could not be anchored anywhere, and the loneliness that follows.

Because he was not self-pitying, he looked at the same time out from, as well as into, himself. Every day he threw himself hungrily upon the world like a starving animal that suddenly finds a scrap of food. The intensity of his desires, and his fears, could make the search at times arrogant, egocentric; but behind it was such a desperate vulnerability that one was moved, even frightened. Probably, when he was cruel or faithless, he thought he was paying off an old score. The affection he rejected was the affection that had once been his and had found no answer.

It seemed that anything interested him. There was a story that he became fascinated by a parrot in a restaurant and studied its behavior for an hour. It is probably true. It is like his sudden curiosity over my boxer puppy rescued barefoot from a fire, or the woman who cradled a cushion in her arms, or the umbrella that turned him into Charlie Chaplin.

In art this kind of touch is usually called "significant detail." Jimmy's life was significant detail. The night before I went back to Hollywood, we had dinner together, as we had done each night of my visit. It was at an

James Dean ponders a chess move in his dressing room during production of *Rebel Without a Cause*. That's a bird on his shoulder. *Photofest*

Italian restaurant, and he had ordered the food with great ceremony, taking pride in his knowledge of obscure dishes. By now I felt he trusted me. I felt even that he would like to do the film—though, if he wanted to, other difficulties lay ahead—the situation with the studio and the objections from those who were beginning to hitch their wagon to a star—and, though I knew what I wanted in the story, I only had thirty pages of script.

I was thinking about this when he looked up at me, something in his expression that suggested he was about to impart a confidence. He was a little restless, not in his usual way, but as if some unaccustomed problem had come up.

"I got crabs," he said. "What do I do?"

I took him to a drugstore. Outside, in the street, we parted. He thanked me for my help, smiled, then said: "I want to do your film. But don't let them know it."

I said I was glad. Then we shook hands on it.

(The above represents a portion of a book now being written by Nicholas Ray, who directed James Dean in *Rebel Without a Cause*.)

OUTTAKE

The Real *James Dean*

Shafrazi: How did you first meet James Dean?

Hopper: I was walking down a hallway at Warner's. I was on my way back to Nick's [Nicholas Ray] office with my agent, Robert Raison. You've got to understand, Hollywood, at this time, was all suits and ties. These guys were old-school gentlemen. They smoked cigars, but they were gentlemen. Suddenly I see this guy walking toward me in a turtleneck and dirty Levi's. He looked like he had five days' growth [of beard], and his hair was all messed up. As we walked by, my agent said, "That's James Dean." And I said, "*That's James Dean?*" I'd just seen him in *East of Eden*, but I didn't even recognize him. So I had my meeting with Nick, and then I went to the drugstore across the street from Warner's, and Dean was sitting at the counter. He had a cup of coffee and sugar, and he was pouring the sugar on the spoon until it got to be heaping, and then he would watch it dissolve in the coffee, and then he'd pour another one. He was doing this over and over. He wasn't talking to anybody. Raison said, "Let me introduce you." So we went up, and he said, "Jimmy, this is Dennis Hopper. He's going to be in the movie with you." But Dean never stopped. Never looked around.

—Dennis Hopper interviewed by Tony Shafrazi and Peter M. Brant, *Interview*, August 1, 2010

32

James Dean

JIM BACKUS

Jim Backus, who secured a measure of screen immortality by playing James Dean's father in *Rebel Without a Cause*, is best known for portraying wealthy castaway Thurston Howell III on the TV series *Gilligan's Island* (1964–1967) and performing the voice of the bespectacled, bumbling cartoon character Mr. Magoo. At Dean's request, Backus taught him how to do Mr. Magoo's voice. Dean proved so adept at it that his mimicry was incorporated in *Rebel Without a Cause*. Backus was the first of Dean's colleagues to devote a chapter to him in his memoir *Rocks on the Roof* (1958), which is excerpted here. —Ed.

THREE AND A HALF YEARS AGO, a new performer caused the kind of mass hysteria we had not witnessed since the early days of Frank Sinatra. With the release of *East of Eden*, the country was swept by a new overnight sensation—the late James Dean. After his second picture, *Rebel Without a Cause*, in which I played his father, his popularity became even greater. I know, because I have literally received thousands of letters, mainly from teenagers, and they are still coming in by the sack full. These are usually three or four pages long. They are actually quite literate, and because they feel I was his "father," they pour out their hearts to me. They want to know everything about him . . . what he said . . . how we got along . . . And what he was like. Every single writer asks me to send something that belonged to Jimmy or that he even touched. They even beg for articles of clothing that I had worn in scenes with him, against which he might have brushed.

When the mail first started to arrive with all these strange requests, I complied and, for example, sent one fan club four pages from a scene Jimmy and I had done together, with scribbled notations in his handwriting. This, in a way, was a mistake, as it started an avalanche of more requests—each one more pathetic than the other. Many of the writers tell me that they have erected shrines in his memory. Others say that they are going to manage somehow to get to Hollywood and visit his grave. The pilgrimage idea got so overwhelming that the studio asked the newspapers to run a story informing his fans that Jimmy is not buried in Hollywood. He is buried in his hometown of Fairmount, Indiana.

Now, I am equipped to handle a normal amount of fan mail, but when this deluge started I became desperate and called Joe Halpern, who handled the studio's publicity on the picture, and told him my situation. He said he couldn't help me and that I was not alone, as other members of the cast were being snowed under, too. He told me that the studio was receiving literally roomfuls and roomfuls of fan mail, and that Warner Bros. was in relatively the same position.

Day by day, Jimmy's popularity keeps mounting. At this moment, he is the actor most in demand by the fan magazines. Dozens of articles are being written about him. The director of *Rebel Without a Cause*, Nick Ray, has completed a biography of Jimmy Dean called *Rebel*.* France is very "Dean conscious," and its *Cahiers du Cinéma* wants to reprint most of Ray's book. There are several other books on Dean in preparation. And next year, the Academy of Motion Picture Arts and Sciences intends to give him a posthumous Oscar.† This is pretty remarkable when you consider that Jimmy was only twenty-four years old and had had only two pictures released.

The Jimmy Dean worship by the teenagers is the current topic of conversation in Hollywood. The "professionally analyzed" set explains it as

---

* Nicholas Ray never completed *Rebel—The Life Story of a Film*, his book about the making of *Rebel Without a Cause*. Two articles derived from the unfinished book were published in 1956. —Ed.

† Although gossip columnist Hedda Hopper lobbied the Academy of Motion Picture Arts and Sciences to award James Dean a posthumous Oscar, her pleas fell on deaf ears. —Ed.

utter self-identification—a rejection of the father image and the projection of a bewildered generation seeking a symbol. They may have something there, but I think it can best be described in two words—great talent!

I first met James Dean on Thanksgiving night of 1954 before *East of Eden* had been released, and frankly at that time I'd never heard of him. Since Henny was out of town, Sharley and Keenan Wynn, knowing I would be alone, asked me to come to their home and share their turkey.* They explained that they were inviting a few other lonely bachelors. The bachelors included Rod Steiger, Ralph Meeker, Arthur Loew, Jr., and a rather small young man who didn't look a day over eighteen. He was dressed in a navy blue suit that looked like he had worn it to his Confirmation, plus a black shirt, black boots with buckles, and a pair of oversized horned-rimmed glasses.

I felt sorry for this strange kid because he seemed ill at ease. As it always is with actors, the conversation was mainly about show business, which he never entered into. The only time he spoke up was when, as it often does at the Wynns', the talk turned to racing cars and motorcycles. After the other guests had departed, I lingered on and remember saying to Keenan, "It was sweet of you and Sharley to have all of us lost souls over for dinner, but don't you think that that kid who works in a garage was uncomfortable with all of us hams?"

"Works in a garage? Are you kidding?" said Keenan. "Sharley and I saw a preview of that new picture *East of Eden*, and that kid you called a garage mechanic is so brilliant in it, he tore the theatre apart."

I remember tolerantly thinking on the way home, "What a character that Keenan is. As far as he's concerned, anyone who rides a motorcycle can do no wrong."

Four months later, I was signed to play the "garage mechanic's" father. Before we started the actual shooting of *Rebel Without a Cause*, Nick Ray got Jimmy and me together and we spent a lot of time discussing the relationship between the father and son and analyzed the motivation of each scene, rather than simply going over the dialogue. We studied the entire

---

* Born Henrietta Kaye, Henny Backus (1911–2004) was married to Jim Backus from 1943 until his death in 1989. —Ed.

script in continuity instead of the usual movie practice of learning isolated scenes as they come up in the shooting schedule. The picture was shot that way, too . . . from the beginning to the end in sequence wherever it was economically possible.

James Dean worked very closely with Nick. May I say that this is the first time in the history of motion pictures that a twenty-four-year-old boy, with only one movie to his credit, was practically the co-director. Jimmy insisted on utter realism. And looking back, I sometimes wonder how we finished so violent a picture without someone getting seriously injured. For example, in one scene where Jimmy and another young man had a fight with switchblade knives, the knives were the real McCoy. And this is one of the few films where doubles were never used.

To digress for a moment, I'm afraid the public has a misconception about the use of doubles. The fact that actors are doubled in many hazardous stunts has long been the subject of jokes. Actually, far less doubling goes on than the TV comics have led you to believe. Most actors do as many of their stunts as the studios will permit. When the production department insists on having an actor doubled, it is only because there is so much money involved. If, let us say, an actor had to do a fight scene in the middle of the picture and got a sprained ankle, or even a bruise on his face that could not be covered by make-up, this would hold up production and would cost the studio many thousands of dollars.

A great many people, including members of our craft, seem to feel that Jimmy had some sort of secret weapon or magic formula. I do not go along with this. I know that if anyone was ever dedicated to the art of acting, it was Jimmy. He had the greatest power of concentration I have ever encountered. He prepared himself so well in advance for any scene he was playing, that the lines were not simply something he had memorized—they were actually a very real part of him. Before the take of any scene, he would go off by himself for five or ten minutes and think about what he had to do, to the exclusion of everything else. He returned when he felt he was enough in character to shoot the scene.

On the stage, an actor has a chance to build and sustain a character, and through his evening performance, to finally reach a climax. Unfortunately, this cannot be done in motion pictures, and many times you have to plunge "cold" into a highly emotional scene. When this was the case, Jimmy would key himself up by vigorously jumping up and down, shadow boxing, or climbing up and down a fifty-foot ladder that ran to the top of the soundstage. In one scene in *Rebel* he was brought into Juvenile Hall on a charge of drunk and disorderly conduct. The scene called for him to have an intensely dramatic argument with the officer in charge, and end up by hysterically banging on the desk in frustration and rage. Before the actual filming of the scene, he kept the cast and crew waiting for one whole hour. Keeping an entire company waiting for an hour sent the production department into a panic. I overheard one old crew member say, "What the hell does he think he's doing? Even Garbo never got away with that."

Jimmy spent the hour preparing for his scene, sitting in his darkened dressing room with a record player blasting out the Ride of the Valkyries, and drinking a quart of cheap red wine. When he felt ready, he stormed out, strode onto the set, did the scene, which was practically a seven-minute monologue, in one take, so brilliantly that even the hard-boiled crew cheered and applauded. He played that scene so intensely that he broke two small bones in his hand when he beat on the desk, which he practically demolished.* Actually, he saved the production department money with his method of making them wait while preparing himself for his one-take perfection. As a matter of fact, on the average "A" picture, seven minutes of film is considered a pretty fine full day's work.

During the shooting of *Rebel*, Mushy Callahan, the former fighter, acted as technical advisor on the fight scenes, and also worked as Jimmy's trainer. Mushy told me that Dean was a natural, and if he'd wanted to, he could have become boxing champion of his weight. Boxing was only one of the many things this remarkable kid did well. He had studied ballet and modern dancing, and was no slouch in either. When he used to finish sparring a few rounds with Mushy, he would surprise the onlookers by doing some beautifully executed leaps, glissades and *entrechats*. Under the great Marcel Marceau, he had studied pantomime, which is the telling of a complete story by use of only the face and body. And as a result, he had the greatest control over his body of any actor I have ever known.

---

* James Dean only bruised one of his hands. —Ed.

Enraged by his father's (Jim Backus, at left) inability to "stand up" for him, Jim Stark (James Dean) drags him to his feet as his horrified mother (Ann Doran) looks on in *Rebel Without a Cause*. *Warner Bros./Photofest © Warner Bros.*

The crucial scene in *Rebel* was where Jimmy and I had a terrible argument at the top of a staircase, at the climax of which he threw me down the flight of stairs, across the living room, into a chair which went over backward, and tried to choke me to death.* There is only one way to do such a scene. I had to remain completely passive and put my trust in Jimmy. If I, for any reason, got tense, we both could have been severely injured or even possibly killed.

I was two hundred pounds of dead weight, and this boy, who could not have weighed more than 140 pounds, tossed, carried, dragged and lifted me down those stairs, across the room and into the chair over and over again all day long, while they shot their many angles.

---

* The scene was not *quite* as violent as Jim Backus remembered it. James Dean doesn't throw him down a flight of stairs. He pulls him upright by the lapels of his bathrobe from a sitting position and drags him into the living room. —Ed.

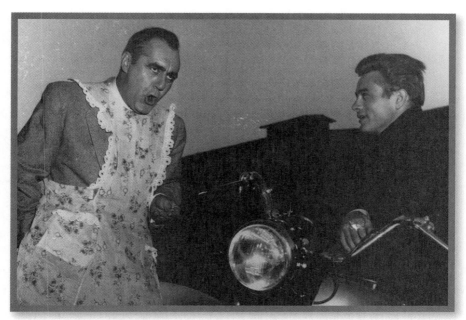

Jim Backus entertains James Dean. *Editor's Collection*

Due to the tremendous intensity with which Jimmy Dean approached his work, people got the impression that he was rude, ill-tempered and surly. At first, I must admit, I felt the same way. After I got to know him, I realized that he was very shy, although essentially a very warm person.

I was one of the few people who knew what his real ambition was. He secretly wanted to be a baggy pants comedian and was quietly working on a nightclub act. Believe me, he would have "killed" the people.

I will never forget the night when Henny and I were driving along in the car, listening to the radio, and the shock with which we heard the news flash of his untimely death. We still can't believe that the vital, talented James Dean is gone. The entertainment world has lost the greatest young actor of our time, and I have lost a friend.

33

You Haven't Heard the Half About Jimmy!

NATALIE WOOD

Natalie Wood's life during the production of *Rebel Without a Cause* proved to be as eventful as that of the character she played in the film. Only a few months shy of her seventeenth birthday when *Rebel* began shooting, she campaigned for the role, knowing it would be a game changer for an actress best known for playing the precocious tot in *Miracle on 34th Street* (1947). She showed up repeatedly at Nicholas Ray's office and was soon having an affair with the forty-three-year-old director. Wood's mother, a Russian émigré who pushed her daughter into the business, condoned the affair but complained to studio executives about her daughter's simultaneous affair with Dennis Hopper, which Natalie initiated after they were screen tested together.

Originally published in the November 1955 issue of *Photoplay*, Wood's article was the only one written about James Dean by one of his costars before his death. Although it betrays the hand of a studio publicist in places, its charming naïveté reflects the authentic voice of the wide-eyed girl whose infatuation with Dean compelled her to see *East of Eden* dozens of times. —Ed.

The writer worked with Jimmy Dean—and she's all steamed up. But we'll let her tell you why!

JAMES DEAN AND I SAT IN HIS PLUSH WHITE PORSCHE, sipping a Coke at Hamburger Hamlet on the Sunset Strip. We'd just finished a long hard day on the set of "Rebel Without a Cause" and were in that delightful state of silence that only comes when the air is slightly tangy, the company really companionable and you've had a terrific day at the studio.

"Hi, Jimmy," said a man who appeared to be a little older than either of us. Jimmy flushed slightly and said apologetically, "I'm sorry, I don't think I know your name." It was not only an apology to the man but to me, too.

The man gave Jimmy his name, and I could tell by the expression on Jimmy's face that this recalled nothing and with very good reason—he'd never met him before. Jimmy listened politely as the man explained he'd been sitting in the drive-in when we arrived and couldn't help hoping that a fellow actor, who'd succeeded, would give him a few tips on how to get his foot in a studio door.

With that quick sympathy Jimmy has for a person trying, they were soon off comparing notes. I sat and listened and, as I did, I grinned all over. I thought, What a whale of a lot of things people don't know about James Dean.

Jimmy, an oddball? Jimmy, weird? Jimmy, sullen?

The first time we met was while Jimmy was making "East of Eden" and I was working on an adjoining sound stage where he had several pals. We were introduced when he came over for a visit. He was nicely dressed in well-pressed slacks and a sport shirt, was polite and intelligently interesting. There was nothing strange about him.

Six months later, in an old abandoned theatre in Los Angeles, the two of us were working on a television script that was to be my first grown-up role. I had been cast opposite James Dean and, like everyone else in Hollywood, I had heard the stories. I was, frankly, afraid of him. During the morning absolutely nothing out of the ordinary happened. The two of us worked, took our breaks when the director called them and finally lunchtime rolled around.

It had been a long time since I'd walked in this particular neighborhood, so I made my way through the crowds, hoping I'd see a little restaurant. There was no roaring motorcycle with brakes screeching to a stop to announce the fact that James Dean was following me. He simply caught up to me and asked, "Mind sharing lunch?" We found a café and, like actors, gabbed about the script we were working on and the show. During

Natalie Wood, James Dean, and Nicholas Ray on the set of *Rebel Without a Cause*.
Editor's Collection © Warner Bros.

the four days we worked together, I brought my portable radio, tuned to the classical music Jimmy likes, and he brought hamburgers—which I like.

"Eden" made Jimmy Dean into a juvenile delinquent. I shudder to think what "Rebel Without a Cause" is going to do. In one terrific scene Jimmy, carried away by rage, knocks his father down the steps into the living room and almost kills him. Poor Jim Backus—who plays his dad—really thought he was going to finish him.

In "Rebel," both Jimmy and I play disturbed teenagers who go wrong from lack of sympathetic understanding and turn to each other for comfort. But there's no sense diagnosing Dean a delinquent and explaining his symptoms in unloved terms.

"I had a happy childhood," Jimmy will tell you. After his mother died—he was nine—his dad sent him out to live with his sister and her husband in Iowa [Indiana]. They were thoughtful, religious folks—Quakers, I believe—and owned a farm. It was a fine place to grow up, to go to school. Although Jimmy never had any aspirations for farming, the only rebelling he ever did was to skip cleaning the chicken coops once in a while. In school, he was an A student in art, an easy mixer, the class athlete.

After graduating from high school, Jimmy headed west to California and Santa Monica College for a degree in Physical Education and, he hoped, later a basketball coach's job. He'd won the Indiana State Dramatic Contest as the best high-school actor and this started him thinking. When a junior, he switched to UCLA and law. One day, he says, he finally faced facts. He quit school to tackle Hollywood. This was no cinch.

Hollywood didn't exactly welcome Jimmy Dean with open arms. He managed to get an usher's job at CBS-TV, landed a one-minute TV commercial for a soft drink (Jimmy danced around a jukebox, sang the ad—for $30). An agent helped him get a few bit parts, but that was all. In one Rock Hudson film, he had two lines. (I bet Rock was surprised when Jimmy reminded him when they met for "Giant.")

Realizing he wasn't the Hollywood matinee-idol type and lead roles were not destined to come to him fast, Jimmy pocketed his last few dollars and climbed aboard a cross-country bus for New York. Arriving in New York, he made the rounds of Broadway producers, getting nowhere in a hurry. Finally he turned to TV agencies, wangled jobs as an extra. At one time, he was a stand-in for contestants on "Beat the Bank." ["Beat the Clock"] They tested the consistency of custard pies—later to be thrown in jest at contestants—by throwing them first at Jimmy.

Jimmy says there were plenty of nights he'd walk up and down Broadway, alone and pretty despondent, sure he'd never make it. Plenty of times, too, when he didn't have the rent or food money. Temporary jobs—and a series of little miracles—helped tide him over.

His first break on Broadway came in a rather peculiar way. He was told one evening of a job opening for a crewhand on a sloop—and he needed a job. Besides, the skipper knew someone who knew someone who might arrange a tryout. What could he lose, Jimmy decided. He took the job, got the tryout, won the role—and the play, "See the Jaguar," was a flop. It did one thing for Jimmy though—it brought TV leads, gave him money for good drama coaches. With his top performance in the hit play, "The Immoralist," he received rave notices, won the David Blum award for the most promising newcomer of 1954 and caught Hollywood's eye.* Not easy? Jimmy's the last one to tell you it was. I doubt whether he'll ever forget those days or the people who had faith in him.

Believe it or not, Jimmy's a sentimentalist. I remember a hot afternoon, soon after we started shooting "Rebel." We were sitting around, killing time, while the lights were being adjusted and readied. I hardly knew Jimmy then, so I busied myself with a manicure. I think he was reading a book—on astronomy or bullfighting, I don't remember which. Neither of us said a word. There was only the constant hum of voices, directions and moving apparatus in the background. Then, quite by accident, I looked up. Jimmy was sitting with the wildest grin.

"Penny for your thoughts?" I said, curious.

"Aw, guess," he teased.

"Thinking about your new sports car," I offered.

"Nope."

"Your new stallion?" I guessed, knowing Jimmy was forever running down to Santa Barbara after work to ride and exercise Cisco.

"Nope," he answered, arching his eyebrows in that funny way he does when teasing.

"I got it," I fairly screamed, delighted because I felt I'd outwitted him. "Your new sixteen millimeter movie camera." Jimmy had bought it only yesterday. It cost two hundred dollars with special lenses and I knew he had saved up for it.

"Nope," he said quietly, in his soft-spoken way. "Remember that scroll? The one I got from the folks back in Grant County? I was just sitting and thinking how nice it was for those three thousand people to sign the scroll, to tell me they liked my acting."

Jimmy's proud to be an actor, don't ever doubt that. But it's not for the fame, the glamour, the money. It's the sense of achievement, the thrill

---

* James Dean won one of Daniel Blum's "Promising Personalities" awards for the 1953–1954 Broadway season for his performance in *The Immoralist*. The award, chosen solely by Blum, was just a piece of parchment he giddily handed to winners in his West Village apartment in New York. In 1969, the award officially became known as the Theatre World Award, named after the annual publication, cofounded by Blum in 1945, which provides a pictorial and statistical record of each year's theatrical season. —Ed.

of doing a good job. "I'm an actor not a personality," he'll complain, sometimes giving the wrong impression, getting labeled non-cooperative, ungrateful.

I had plenty of opportunity to see how grateful Jimmy Dean is to his fans. "Rebel" was shot all over Los Angeles and we had a chance to meet a lot of people. For one sequence we used the Planetarium and some high-school students.* I had a late call the first morning so I arrived at the Planetarium after Jimmy.

Rushing to makeup,

James Dean delights his fans with an impromptu autograph party on the set of *Rebel Without a Cause. Warner Bros./Photofest © Warner Bros.*

I turned the corner full speed, came to a dead stop! Sitting in a big old trash can was the star of "Rebel"—Hollywood's newest, brightest, most talented boy actor—James Dean. Crumpled up in an awkward ball, he busily signed autographs, exchanged stories—very obviously unaware that he'd been pushed there, and equally unaware of his position or dignity!

Photographers have been reported to complain that Dean is uncooperative. If so, that doesn't explain the twenty minutes I had to wait for him to go to lunch.

---

* In writing "planetarium," Natalie Wood was referring to both the Griffith Observatory, where key scenes in *Rebel Without a Cause*—including the film's climax—were shot, and the circular theater inside the observatory where the high school students in the film watch an animated presentation on astronomy projected on the domed ceiling. The Griffith Observatory is situated on the south-facing slope of Mount Hollywood in Los Angeles' Griffith Park. —Ed.

Everything was humming along smoothly and we all found ourselves working a little longer than usual one morning. When lunch was mentioned, we realized we'd have to cut it short, so I hustled my belongings together, plus Mr. Dean, and we started for the commissary. I hadn't noticed, but Jimmy, in his uncanny ability to sense people's needs and problems, did. Standing off by the camera were three women, one shyly pushed her companion toward us.

"Can I do something for you?" Jimmy asked.

"Would you mind—posing for a picture for us—" she hesitantly inquired.

"Sure," obliged Jimmy.

He hammed it up with me, stood on one foot, clowned around, posed and postured until their hearts were content. A shutterbug himself, he offered composition suggestions, pointed out camera angles and gave tips on lighting—while I starved.

When I badgered him, in a deathlike whisper, about my hunger, he looked surprised. Then, like a little boy, said, "Aw, we're having fun."

Despite stories, Jimmy Dean does have fun. Acting can be fun. In "Rebel" I play my first grown-up film role and I also get my first kiss—from Jimmy. There's no sense denying it, I was a little nervous.

"You look green," Jimmy complimented me while we waited for the signal to begin the love scene. "And you know how green photographs in color."

I managed a grin, I think. I really can't remember. I felt like a fighter before a match—let's go in and get it over with. Jimmy was saying something, but all I could think of was, "Is this the way—should I do it the way I rehearsed? Maybe that was too smooth. Maybe I should fumble a little."

"Come on," coaxed Jimmy. Suddenly I realized we were on. Complete silence. Then—"Roll," shouted the director and the camera began clicking.

It was Jimmy's move. I listened to him and felt almost inspired. He played it so gently, he brought out the best in me—under the circumstances. Then came the kiss. I heard the director call "Cut," but the cameras seemed to be grinding away. I didn't exactly know what to do, but I had no choice. Jimmy held and held and held. Might as well enjoy it, he kidded afterwards as I turned from green to red. But the nervous spell was

James Dean poses for a gag photo with Natalie Wood, his adoring costar in *Rebel Without a Cause.* *Warner Bros./Photofest © Warner Bros.*

broken. His kidding did it; I relaxed and the rest of the shooting went like a breeze!

Comes a big dramatic scene, Jimmy's the opposite. Boy, is he intense. I didn't know what he was going through the first time he prepared for an important scene.

"Hi, Jimmy, what are you doing?" I asked. He mumbled something—and completely unlike him—made it plain he wanted no conversation. He was kind of working himself into the role. Flailing his arms about, going through a bicycle-type movement with his legs. "I'm concentrating," is all he said.

"By doing that?" I asked, sure that he'd be worn out before he began the scene. Patiently, he put up with me. "It gets me in form."

I left him. By the time the cameras rolled, he was no longer Jimmy Dean. He was the confused, rebellious, unwanted *Jim* of "Rebel."

Something went wrong, lights or camera position, and the director called cut to the scene. Jimmy stood where he left off, motionless. Then—and I remember this clearly—one of the fellows went up to him and started to kid. Wow! Was Jimmy furious. He made it clear, between breaks, no talk. He has to stay in "character." This is true even when it takes a whole day to complete a scene.

Later that afternoon, Jimmy was scheduled to finish the sequence. It was hot, the cast had worked hard all day and most of us were exhausted. I had one idea—shared by the rest of the cast and crew—let's go home. "For those who aren't in the last scene, scram," came the welcome reprieve.

For some reason, we hung around for a few minutes—and I'll never forget this experience. Cameras rolled, the set quieted and Jimmy began—to go into one of the most tragic, heartbreaking scenes I've ever seen. One by one, members of the cast returned and stood, gripped by the tremendous emotional impact of the moment. We were carried away. At the end, not one of us could honestly confess there weren't tears in our eyes. It was electrifying.

Director Nick Ray asserts Jimmy is the finest actor for his age he's ever directed, also adds that, contrary to reports, he's a breeze to handle. For his fine work and cooperation, the production staff gifted Jimmy with a bicycle. As for me, I'm greatly indebted to him for his stimulation and help. There's no question, Dean's [a] great talent.

For the future, Jimmy hopes to direct. For the present, he hopes to act, to vary his roles, to grow as an individual, learn as a professional. He studies acting techniques, writing, photography and the stock market! To direct and produce, he grins slyly, you need money, too. With his new Warners contract, he'll do nine films in the next six years. He'd like to return to the stage, maybe try *Hamlet* someday. This year, he may wind up playing *Romeo* for a color featurette for Warners. Talks about doing the life of Harry Greb, the middleweight fighter of years ago, too. He and stand-in Mushy Callahan, the champion ex-fighter, were forever "getting into shape," for the role.

Jimmy's 5 foot 10 and looks short ("because I slump," he says), but he's amazingly strong. Always a good athlete, he keeps in trim by swimming, playing volleyball, sailing and deep-sea diving. Ask, "Tennis anyone—boxing, riding, baseball or basketball"—and you've got a partner. But his chief love, I think, is bullfighting. Someday he wants to get into the ring himself.

I don't mean to imply that Jimmy isn't a character. He is—but a pretty interesting one. He'll hardly say a word in a crowd until someone mentions architecture, hi-fi, sports-car racing or music. Then try and stop him. Question him about himself, he'll answer straight. Show some ulterior motive, he'll clam up even if you're a V. P. in charge of world news. He can talk about carburetors in one breath, discuss William James' pragmatic philosophy in another and be off on the subject of design two minutes later. If he has a free moment, chances are you'll find him behind a serious book or buried underneath a pile of travel folders. Mention music and he'll go mad—over native African rhythms, Beethoven's Ninth or progressive jazz. Take a drive with him, and you'll be tuned in to classical music. Jimmy studied violin as a child, has picked up his studies again with Leonard Rosenman, who was his roommate in New York and is now a Warners composer. Invite him to Sunday dinner, he'll accept. What's more, he'll win your parents over with charm and intelligence.

An oddball, did you ask? Yes, if you call talent odd. A weirdy? Maybe, if you don't like individualists. Sullen? Never! Jimmy Dean's too busy living to sulk.

THE END

34

A Tenderness Lost

George Stevens

James Dean campaigned for the role of Jett Rink in *Giant* because the film's director, George Stevens, had directed Dean's idol Montgomery Clift in *A Place in the Sun* (1951), and was considered one of Hollywood's finest directors. "Then there's George Stevens, the greatest of them all," Dean told interviewer Howard Thompson for the *New York Times*. When Alan Ladd, Stevens's first choice to play Rink, bowed out, he offered it to Dean, who was delighted to win the role. Dean's enthusiasm for Stevens and *Giant* eroded rapidly once he arrived in Marfa, Texas, for location shooting in June 1955. Although they continued to butt heads over their creative differences when they returned to the soundstages at Warner Bros., Stevens refused to speak ill of Dean after his death and remained circumspect about the difficulties he experienced directing him in recalling him for this article, published in the January 1956 issue of *Modern Screen*. —Ed.

For nearly two decades tall, affable George Stevens has been a force for artistry in Hollywood. From Gunga Din *to* A Place in the Sun *he has contributed some of the best movies we have had. At this moment he is putting the finishing touches to his latest picture, Edna Ferber's* Giant, *starring Elizabeth Taylor, Rock Hudson and the late James Byron Dean, of whom he wrote this moving story.*

I SPENT SIX HOURS TODAY WITH JIMMY DEAN, as I have most of the days in these past two months. He is always up there on the projection-room

James Dean and director George Stevens discuss a scene while filming *Giant*.
Warner Bros./Photofest © Warner Bros.

screen in front of me, challenging me not to like any part of him in the picture. And there is no part of Jimmy I don't like, no part of him that hasn't always the attraction that goes with complete naturalness. Maybe it is the way he sidles next to someone, chin hugging his chest, then squints up out of the corner of his eye, mumbling a greeting. Or maybe the way he can run a boyish giggle right through his words or, without losing an iota of expressiveness, violate all the dramatic precepts and persistently present only his back to the camera.

When there is this much distinction and force in a personality you can't believe it can ever be destroyed. Certainly for me, as I put together his last picture, *Giant*, the Dean who drove to his death on a cool September evening in northern California is unreal. The real one is the Jimmy I knew and am living with.

"Hey, you know something, Mr. Stevens," I can hear him say, "that part of Jett Rink in *Giant*—that's for me." That was nearly a year ago, when he first read the script and then came searching for me. Now he casts me sidelong glances from the projection room screen, as if saying, "I told you it was for me, didn't I? Man, I just knew!"

Jimmy Was Youth

There are some people who fit themselves colorfully against any sort of background, who always seem to move along a trail of interest so that the eye follows them constantly, speculating on their motives, wondering. Jimmy was like that. On location in Texas I noticed that photographers always kept watch on Jim, knowing that sooner or later he would reward them with a fine picture—maybe silhouetted, lithe and lean on his horse, against a gold and buttermilk sky, or perhaps fooling with a length of rope, making it loop and unloop itself as he talked. Jimmy wasn't a Texan. Jimmy was Indiana born and bred. But Jimmy was youth and he had the free faculty of youth to belong anywhere.

Where do these young people come from, to win identity as our country's best known actors and actresses? Take the three who were together in *Giant*—Elizabeth, Rock and Jimmy. Elizabeth Taylor, a cameo of a girl, gentle and uncomplicated, Rock Hudson—big, handsome, considerate, blending easily into the teamwork of movie-making. And Jimmy Dean. Jimmy, not flattered at all to be considered cooperative. Jimmy, in a hurry about life and career, needing to cut corners. Jimmy, strangely impractical about saying and doing the right things—yet in every word and gesture a poetical presence with an individualized approach that I know is opening up a new tradition of acting in Hollywood.

An Odd Sweetness

Where do they come from and what gives them the sensitivity to bring life to the characters writers imagine and set down on paper? So many have called Jimmy nothing but a small boy with a big ego—and never have so many oversimplified. I used to feel that he was a disturbed boy, tremendously dedicated to some intangible beacon of his own and neither he nor anyone else might ever know what it was. I used to feel this because at times when he fell quiet and thoughtful as if inner-bidden to dream about something, an odd and unconscious sweetness would light up his countenance. At such times, and because I knew he had been motherless

A triumphant Jett Rink (James Dean) strikes oil in *Giant*.
Warner Bros./Photofest © Warner Bros.

since early childhood and had missed a lot of the love that makes boyhood jell right, I would come to believe that he was still waiting for some lost tenderness.

There is a side to Jimmy which may surprise many who have met and known him, an unsuspected, simple relationship to his time and heritage. He hearkened to the kind of mementos old-fashioned sentimentalism feeds on. A friend of mine has seen a scrapbook Jimmy kept. In it were pasted the usual things about the theater, a review of *Hamlet* (it didn't matter who played Hamlet or where it was given—anything pertaining to it he loved), a quotation from another play, a line about himself. But the bulk of the scrapbook was made up of other things altogether, some of them in color. Pasted on one page, the complete marriage ceremony and marriage vows, on another the lyrics to "Love's Old Sweet Song." A full-page picture of a baby's face and under it the following legend: "Watch a child's eye and you will see limitless hope's expectancy." The words to Robert Burns' *My Love Is Like a Red, Red Rose*. The verses of Edgar Allan Poe's *Annabel Lee*.

So Long

Jimmy lost not only a mother's love when she died, but a young mother's love. He was nine and she was only twenty-nine. And Jimmy grew up sentimental, with an intrinsic sadness to him despite all the foolery and wild gags and loud dashing to and fro. I can see him now, blinking behind his glasses after having been guilty of some bit of preposterous behavior, and revealing by his very cast of defiance that he felt some sense of unworthiness. Yet the very next second the glasses come off, a smile flashes and his whole being is transformed. You were disturbed by him. Now you are dedicated to him. It might be because he had a strong sense of fairness, and a deep regard for performance value. He wanted to do all things well even to spitting a cherry pit further than the next fellow—but he bowed to that fellow if to him belonged the victory. Once, on a set, he did an imitation of Charlie Chaplin and afterward a friend of his, Nick Adams, did an impersonation of Marlon Brando. Jimmy roared at Nick's, waved aside his own Chaplin takeoff and begged Nick to repeat his. Once, before his start in pictures, he found himself on Hollywood's Western Avenue and only fifty cents away from missing an already long-delayed meal. But on the way to a hash house he passed a movie showing a rerun of John Ford's *The Informer* and he couldn't resist going in to feed his emotional rather than his physical hunger. The thought of performing, or of seeing someone else perform was a compelling motivation in Jimmy's life. It so caught his mind that I wondered sometimes if he lived unconsciously in resentment of a life thrust at one with the injunction that you *had* to live it. He was fascinated at the thought rather of being able to *select* a life to live.

What would he have chosen? I can't describe it exactly, but no one who ever met Jimmy can forget feeling that he was on his way to that life. I knew it the day we first talked and I knew it the last day I saw him. He blinked at me a couple of times, waved and called out, "So long, I think I'll let the Spyder out." The Spyder was the model name for the fleeting silver scarab that was his beloved Porsche, the car in which he was killed.

END

OUTTAKE

For George Stevens, James Dean Was a
Hell of a Headache to Work With

"Stevens, his last director, said about Dean recently: 'He had the ability to take a scene and break it down; sometimes he broke it down into so many bits and pieces that I couldn't see the scene for the trees, so to speak. I must admit that sometimes I underestimated him, and sometimes he overestimated the effects he thought he was getting. Then he might change his approach, do it quick, and if that didn't work we'd effect a compromise. All in all, it was a hell of a headache to work with him. He was always pulling and hauling, and he had developed this cultivated, designed irresponsibility. It's tough on you, he'd seem to imply, but I've just got to do it this way. From the director's point of view that isn't the most delightful sort of fellow to work with. Anyway, he delivered his performance, and he cracked himself up, and I can't say I'm happy about all that's happening about it. There are some people involved in it who don't show up too well.'"

—Hollis Alpert, "It's Dean, Dean, Dean"
Saturday Review, October 13, 1956

35

Trapped in Marfa

Mercedes McCambridge

On location in the sun-blasted town of Marfa, Texas (pop. 3,600), James Dean and Mercedes McCambridge—who played Luz Benedict, Bick Benedict's (Rock Hudson) sister, in *Giant*—became comrades in arms, united by their hatred of the town and their contentious relationship with director George Stevens. One "disgustingly hot night" in Marfa, mad at Stevens, they ate themselves sick, consuming a jar of peanut butter, a box of crackers, and six Milky Ways, washing them down with twelve Coca Colas. "George Stevens, master editor, director, and not-always-benevolent dictator, had a lot of problems with Jimmy," McCambridge wrote in her 1981 autobiography, *The Quality of Mercy*. "Everybody seemed to have a lot of problems with Jimmy. Nobody had more problems with Jimmy than Jimmy had."

In this excerpt from her autobiography, she discloses some of her more piquant memories of Dean's offbeat behavior. —Ed.

There was nothing to do in good old Marfa. No points of scenic interest. Nothing! There was the mash-feed store downtown, and a couple of real hot-spot storefronts called gin mills. A few tired places where you could buy groceries to take home and fry in grease . . . that was about it for Marfa.

Jimmy Dean and I, and too many other actors, were all languishing at Warner Bros.' expense out there in the Panhandle, where we would likely be kept until our brains burned up and our bones turned to chalk.

The people in the company who were lucky enough to be shooting would leave the hotel at dawn to drive out to the stark grandeur of the mirage-house Warner's had erected in the center of five million acres of nowhere. The house had been assembled in Hollywood, taken apart, each section marked and shipped down to Marfa by rail and reconstructed on its incongruous sight for filming. There were three high walls and an open back and no roof.

Anyhow, the lucky ones who were working out in the brutal sun at the location would leave us unlucky, nonworking ones in town. Day after day after day! It drove us crazy!

Jimmy Dean and I would say to each other, "If you weren't here, I'd kill myself." We got along, maybe because we had to, rattling around out there in the land that God forgot. One day he said, "Listen, Madama!" "Madama" was what he called me in the film. "Listen, Madama, you and me together are more than sixty years old. Twenty-four are mine, the rest are yours. What I mean is, any two people who are as old as we are should be smart enough to figure a way to beat this Marfa rap! They got us nailed in here, Madama! We gotta kick our way out, I am tellin' YOU." He clapped his hands, let out a Texas whoop, and threw his holey straw hat on the dirt and jumped on it . . . hard! "Hooooeeeeeee!"

Before either of us was officially on film in *Giant*, Jimmy tried several times to steal my Stetson hat. He knew that if he switched my hat with his and was photographed wearing it, *I* couldn't be photographed wearing it! Mine was the perfect Texas hat! I had to watch it like a hawk until after the first scene in which I wore it, making it forever identified as *my hat*!

It was originally Gary Cooper's hat. The sweatband inside the brim was taped "G. Cooper."

Back in Hollywood when I was doing wig and makeup tests at Warner Bros., G. Cooper wandered into the makeup department. The hairdresser was placing on my head the never-touched-by-human-hands brand-new Stetson hat.

G. Cooper hooted!

"Where in hell did you come up with that silly-looking headgear?"

We explained that it was my character's hat for *Giant*.

G. Cooper stomped and said, "You mean to sit there and tell me that a Texan woman who spends most of her waking hours in the middle of hundreds of head of cattle would be caught dead in the stupid store hat?"

He was upset, G. Cooper was. He went to the phone and called his wardrobe man. A hat was brought! G. Cooper placed it on my head. He was right! The hat was Texas! Giant! Right!

The hat was also a good bit the worse for wear. There were indications that it had been doused from time to time. I said it must have been rained on quite a bit. G. Cooper said, "Nope. Peed on a lot! That's what makes it such a fine Texas hat. No self-respecting rancher wears a hat that his horse hasn't peed on!"

The hat had surely lost all of its stiffness. It rolled into shape easily at the slightest touch. The discoloration gave it a certain added interest—dark golden streaks, wavering blots of bleach . . . interesting.

Jimmy Dean wanted that hat!

Sometimes as I stood in the blister of the Texas sun, G. Cooper's peed-on hat on my hot, wigged, and perspiring head, the air around me became recognizably ammoniated, but it was a great hat, and I managed to survive the malodorousness.

Jimmy Dean wanted that hat.

Jimmy Dean didn't get it!

Warner's gave us Chevies to drive. Pitted Chevies, stripped raw from sand and wind. Jimmy, on a day of near-to-bursting frustration, drove his little Chevy out of town and, with his BB gun, shot all the windows out of it. The company manager took his car away. Besides, the highway patrol had mentioned several times the indelicate topic of Jimmy's speeding. They found him indelicate on another score. They claimed that he relieved himself against a post in the middle of Main Street. I asked Jimmy about

James Dean and Mercedes McCambridge in *Giant. Warner Bros./Photofest © Warner Bros.*

it. He said he did it because nothing else was happening. I told him the story that Alan Moorehead, the Australian author, had told me about Winston Churchill. Sir Winston was on holiday at [Somerset] Maugham's villa on the French Riviera at St.-Jean-Cap-Ferrat. Each morning the chauffeur would drive Sir Winston along the seawall until a particular scape caught the great man's fancy. There he would set up his easel, palette, paints and brushes and cigars and brandy and soda. He would sit on his stool, hat pulled down to keep the sun's glare from his eyes, and he would paint. Paint and smoke and drink. The villagers of the Midi would stand apart at a respectful distance and observe the Greatest Briton at work.

One morning he felt the need to relieve himself. He put down his palette, his brandy glass, and his cigar, and walked over to the seawall and let spray . . . at great length! When he had finished, the villagers applauded! As he walked back to his easel, they shouted, "*Magnifique!*" and "*Formidable!*" Sir Winston stopped, took off his hat, and bowed!

Jimmy Dean couldn't wait to get back to Marfa's Main Street. He said he would drink a whole tank full of beer, and he would stand there and flood the street. I told him Americans don't know enough to applaud outstanding performances the way French people do.

One morning, after the working actors had abandoned us for still another day, we felt our fuses were getting very short.

We often got up with the working group and waved good-bye to them as the trucks and cars disappeared in all that dry dust. It was likely to be the most excitement we would see until they all streamed in at night: filthy and sore and burned, and ravenously hungry, even for the same old steaks fried in the same old grease.

On the morning we were more than usually jangled, we sat in the coffee shop. At least it was cool. Marfa, in itself, is not a stimulant for good conversation. Porcine grunts will do. I watched Jimmy take a pecan roll from the basket on the table. It was stale, and all the sticky stuff was dried up. Jimmy unrolled it slowly, until it lay stretched out on the table like a brown, bumpy snake. We sat there, looking at it. Then Jimmy took another pecan roll from the basket and did the same thing to it. He laid it down next to its twin on the table. Then he said, "Wanna see a good trick?" I nodded. "Watch this one," he said.

He lifted one of the unrolled rolls and began stuffing one end of it into his left nostril. He packed it in until it held. Several inches of brown, bumpy snake dangled from the nostril. He matched the operation in his right nostril. Then he said, "Shall we go?" He took my arm, and we walked out into the lobby, where three ranchers dropped what was

Edna Ferber, author of *Giant*, converses with James Dean on the set of the film.
Warner Bros./Photofest © Warner Bros.

left of their eyeteeth as we passed. Jimmy said, "If anybody asks you, just say I am so rich I got dough coming out of my nose." Nobody asked me.

Upstairs he sat on the floor and I lay on my belly on the bed. Best thing to do after a Marfa meal is to lie on one's belly for a while. I told Jimmy about a waiter in a sleazy seaside hotel in Alicante, Spain. He was my waiter. He served me every day. I was his princess. His jacket was frayed at the cuffs; his black trousers were as shiny as a waxed Mercedes-Benz; his shoes might not last out the day.

His ministrations which accompanied my breakfast could not have been equaled by any maître d' in the world. It was like my second husband's martini routine, a spiffy performance!

He brought a deep glass bowl full of hot water and placed it on the small serving table. He selected from a fruit tray the finest Valencian orange he could find and speared it with a long-tined fork. In an *arena de toros* he would have been granted both ears and the tail of the bull for such a thrust . . . And he never missed! Then, standing in front of me, holding the speared orange, he dipped it into hot water, swirled it furiously, and lifted it high, as if it were rising from the Rhine. Then he shot his poor frayed cuffs and, holding the fork at eye height, he pierced, as if in surgery, the rind of the fruit. The knife was Toledo sharp. The peeling of the orange was executed in such a way as to keep it in one perfect piece. At the end of the cutting he held the curly cue over a small plate in front of me and let it fall in formation. It stood on its own, a perfect hollow orange! He never missed! ¡Ole! Emotiva!

The Marfa oranges were thin-skinned and not well ripened, but Jimmy Dean bought a bowie knife in town and tried. Jimmy Dean tried anything, sometimes at my expense.

He made me promise to drive him in my Chevy, since his had been taken from him, out into the wasteland to see the jackrabbits jump. He said they jumped the highest at dusk. Out on the potholed road, he made me stop the car, and he got out and straddled the hood like it was a horse. He had his BB gun. He told me to drive nice and easy, "like a slow gallop," and he popped off the jackrabbits. I got very cross and turned the car around and headed back to town. That damned kid up there pow-powing away at the leaping lapins.

There hadn't been any other cars on the road . . . there never were . . . but somebody saw us and the company manager took my Chevy away. Jimmy pleaded our case on the grounds that he was killing the rabbits to save the crops. It was pointed out to him that there were no crops. Also for Jimmy and me there were now no cars. It was good that there was no place to go because if there were, we couldn't go to it.

Another great idea of Jimmy's has marked me for life. On one of the rare days when I actually was called to perform before the camera, the Texas sun melted my makeup, which sank into my open pores and blossomed into serious infection. My face was bad, but my neck and throat were deeply burned. I still have the scars.

The company doctor ordered me to bed, with drawn shades . . . my eyelids were burned, too. He prescribed antibiotics and healing salve and said if it didn't get better, I would have to be shipped back to California. I wanted it to get better because it was hugely painful, but I wouldn't have minded being shipped—anywhere!

My room was, to say the least, air-conditioned. Frigid is a better word. Great gusts of iceberg wind stormed through the grid. The cheesy, sleazy cover on my bed waved back and forth as in a storm on the North Atlantic. Jimmy fixed it.

He sat with me every day. He sat on the floor and practiced his guitar. He was teaching himself how to play it. I kept wishing he had had the opportunity of learning somewhere else than in my dark and icy sickroom in Marfa-for-God's-sake-Texas. He said we would both die of pneumonia in that room, so he went into town and bought a roll of heavy packing tape, and he begged or stole a large piece of cardboard to seal off the wintry blasts. Now there was no breathing in the place. No air at all! Just the guitar plunking away on my nerve ends. Just the burning hide of me.

Jimmy announced that I would never get well in that hellhole with that "crappy medicine." He went downtown again, and this time he came back with some ointment that he knew would turn my hide's tide. It not only would take the heat away, but would shrink the pores, and I would be as good as new. He told me all these lovely things while he smoothed the cool cream onto my parched skin. I whimpered in gratitude. He said he would leave the rest of the tube for me to use up that night. He said not to worry, he would get some more tomorrow; he would bring half a dozen tubes with him, and we would clear this danged thing up in nothing flat! I watched him putting the top back on the tube. Curious thing it was, the top, and small wonder. It was Preparation H. I wanted to tell him his sense of direction was severely impaired, but I waited until he had left, and then I washed, with great pain, the hemorrhoidal remedy from my face and throat. Next day I told Jimmy that the doctor said it was bad for my Irish kind of skin. Jimmy was miffed.

James Dean was a dedicated, perfectionist actor. I watched him develop bits of business until they seemed a part of his nature. He asked cowboys to teach him intricate tricks with a rope. He worked himself bleary-eyed with that rope, but if you watch him as Jett Rink doing tricks with that rope in *Giant*, you will see a Texas boy who has been working with a rope all his cotton-pickin' life! I watched him learn how to let his hat fall from his head, watched it do a complete somersault and land, top side up, on the ground in front of him . . . just the way he wanted it! Every time he did it.

While he was playing Jett Rink, he was inseparable from Jett Rink; he did NOT become Jett Rink, but Jett Rink was his constant companion! I know what it means. You measure everything you do in terms of how the character you are playing would do those things. It's a good game. I know of none better!

OUTTAKE

How James Dean Overcame Elizabeth Taylor's
Intimidating Stardom

"James Dean scandalized bystanders in Marfa with his lout-ish behavior and got away with it. And Dennis Hopper had a ringside seat. Dean's second scene with Elizabeth Taylor in *Giant* takes place when dirt-poor Jett Rink (Dean) invites Les-lie Benedict (Taylor) to tea at his clapboard shack. Plenty of Marfa's locals watched the filming from the periphery of the outdoor location. To create Rink's unease with Leslie Benedict, Dean kept his bladder full before shooting commenced. But his technique didn't work. Intimidated by Taylor's star status, Dean flubbed several takes. He suddenly turned away from her, walked a couple of hundred feet away, unzipped himself, and urinated on the ground in front of about a thousand strangers. Then he went back and got the scene on the next take.

"Even Hopper was aghast. On the drive back to town, he asked Dean why he did it. 'I was nervous,' he said. 'I'm a Method actor. I work through my senses. If you're nervous, your senses can't reach your subconscious, and that's that—you just can't work. It was Elizabeth Taylor. I can't get over my farm-boy upbringing. I was so nervous that I couldn't speak. I had to pee, and I was trying to use that, but it wasn't working. So I thought that if I could go pee in front of all those people, I would be able to work with her.'"

—*Dennis Hopper: The Wild Ride of a Hollywood Rebel* by
Peter L. Winkler (Fort Lee, NJ: Barricade Books, 2011)

OUTTAKES

James Dean and Elizabeth Taylor Had an Extraordinary Friendship

"She went off mysteriously each evening with Jimmy, and none of us could figure out where they went. They would arrive for dinner together, she would sit in the balcony next to him during the rushes, and then they would slip away for what seemed like most of the night."

—*Baby Doll: An Autobiography* by Carroll Baker
(New York: Arbor House, 1983)

"We had an extraordinary friendship. We would sometimes sit up until three in the morning, and he would tell me about his past, his mother, minister, his loves, and the next day he would just look straight through me as if he'd given or revealed too much of himself, given too much of a part of himself away, and it would maybe take, after one of these sessions, a couple of days before we'd be back on friendship terms. He was very afraid to give of himself.

"He was very afraid of being hurt. He was afraid of opening up in case it was turned around and used against him."

—Elizabeth Taylor, quoted in *The Unabridged James Dean: His Life and Legacy from A to Z*, by Randall Riese
(Chicago: McGraw-Hill, 1991)

36

The James Dean I Knew

Bob Hinkle

In 1952, Robert "Texas Bob" Hinkle abandoned his plans to pursue a career as a rodeo cowboy when he realized he just didn't have the makings of a champion rider. He moved to Hollywood to try his hand at acting. A couple of days after showing up for an open casting call for *Giant*, he received a call from the office of the film's director, George Stevens. Elated, he met with Stevens and his coproducer Henry Ginsberg, thinking he'd won the role of Jett Rink. Pouring him a drink, Stevens explained that the role was already taken, but he told Hinkle they wanted the Texas native to teach Rock Hudson, James Dean, and other actors in the film to "talk Texan."

"For the next three months, Hinkle was Dean's constant companion, coaching him on his dialogue and dress," Kirby Warnock wrote in his 1995 article on the making of *Giant*. "He taught Dean a few rope tricks and spent evenings with him shooting jackrabbits with a .22 rifle outside of Marfa [Texas]. Years later, Hinkle would coach another actor, Paul Newman, in the movie *Hud* [1963]."

Hinkle went on to a long and varied career in show business. He wrote, produced, and directed movies; personally managed actor Chill Wills (who played Uncle Bawley in *Giant*) and country singer Marty Robbins; and spent three years promoting daredevil motorcyclist Evel Knievel's exploits.

Hinkle's memoir, *Call Me Lucky: A Texan in Hollywood*, was published in 2009. This article was first published at the website American Legends. —Ed.

O RIGINALLY, I WAS HIRED BY DIRECTOR GEORGE STEVENS to work with Rock Hudson on his accent in *Giant*. I was born and raised in

Brownfield, in West Texas. They wanted Rock to sound like I did. When George Stevens called me into his office, I thought, "They are going to let me do that part of Jett Rink." I was the right age and from Texas. But George and Henry Ginsberg, the coproducer, pulled their chairs up next to me and said, "You think you could teach Rock Hudson to talk like you do?" I told them, "I've been going to a dialogue coach in Hollywood trying to lose this accent." George said, "No don't do that. It sounds great."

They sent me over to meet Rock who was doing a movie at Universal. He handed me the *Giant* script and asked me to read a couple of his lines. Rock wanted to know, "How do you say this or that?" Then he called George and told him it was perfect. George put me on salary and said, "I've got a couple of young kids I want to put in the movie. I want you to work with them for a few days before I test them." One was Dennis Hopper, the other was Carroll Baker. So I started to work with them.

Then, one day there was a knock on the door, and it was James Dean. He said, "You Bob Hinkle? I seen you over at the studio restaurant a couple of times." Well, I'd seen him, but I never had met him. He was kind of a loner, quiet. He ate by himself. He said, "I'd like to work with you in playing Jett Rink. I'd like you to help me create that character." He offered to pay me out of his own pocket but I said that's not necessary. I asked him when he wanted to start. He told me, "I'd like to start today." So we went to dinner that night at Barney's Beanery over on La Cienega.

Giant was really something. I was on the picture seven or eight months. It was a wonderful experience. Everybody bonded, except maybe Rock and Jimmy were a bit jealous of each other. Jimmy was jealous of Rock because Rock had all the good dialogue, and Rock was jealous of Jimmy because *East of Eden* had just been released and Dean was getting all the attention from the media. They never had words, but you could feel the jealousy. It would come out when Rock would say, "How is Jimmy to work with?" or Dean would say, "How do you like working with old Rock. You know, has he ever come on to you?" We all knew about Rock, but on the set he was as straight as could be. There never was any inkling. He was a very nice guy, very easygoing, always prepared.

George Stevens had problems with Jimmy only a couple of times and that's been blown way out of proportion. I was there when George shot

Bob Hinkle, James Dean's dialogue coach on *Giant*, looks on approvingly as Dean demonstrates his lassoing skills. *Warner Bros./Photofest © Warner Bros.*

that scene where Jimmy paces off the property that he inherited from Bick Benedict's sister. We were shooting on a ranch, in Marfa, Texas, on location. There were just four of us there that day including the cameraman. It was like a second unit. George told Dean what he wanted: "I just want you to walk right straight for that fence post," indicating that Jimmy should measure the land with his boot steps. Dean said okay, and Stevens told the cameraman to roll it.

Jimmy hardly got a few feet when Stevens yelled, "Cut." We all kind of stood there for a minute. Nobody said anything. Then, George took a page from the back of the script and started tearing it up into little pieces. Without saying a word, Stevens threw a little piece of paper down and put a rock on it. Then he went about ten feet and did the same thing. "What the hell is he doing?" Jimmy asked me. I said, "I don't have any idea."

Stevens made this trail out to the fence post, then walked back, and said to Jimmy, "Do you think you could follow that line?" Dean replied, "Yeah, I think I can." The camera started to roll. Jimmy walked over to the first rock, picked it up and tossed it away. Stevens yelled cut but Jimmy ignored him—he kept walking, picking up every one of those pieces of paper. Then he came back and dropped them right in the director's lap.

Bill [William C. Mellor], the cameraman, and I were dumbfounded. Dean stared at Stevens and said, "Look, if I need marks, I'll put down my own marks. All you need to do is to tell me what you want me to do, like a director is supposed to. Then I'll do it. Otherwise, I'm going to get my ass on a plane and go back to California."

Stevens reacted real calm. He said, "Well, okay, let's just shoot it." The camera began rolling again. But this time Jimmy Dean was pissed off. He reared back, and began strutting over to this windmill instead of heading toward the fence. I realized Dean was improvising, but the director wasn't angry. He told the cameraman, "Stay on him, Bill. Stay with him." George Stevens was excited by Dean's reaction, even though none of this was in the script.

Dean climbed up on the windmill, crossed his legs, and sat up there. All the time, Stevens kept telling the cameraman, "Hold on to him. Keep on him. You got him, haven't you? That's perfect, perfect. Oh, man."

I think George set up the whole scene. He got the reaction from James Dean that he wanted. It was part of this reverse psychology that made him so good as a director.

After Jimmy died, they came out with all these stories about him burning himself with cigarettes and things like that. It's horseshit. People didn't know him that well. He wouldn't hardly talk to the press. He didn't trust them.

One day we were coming out of the commissary, and a writer for the trade papers asked for an interview. Jimmy said, "Ah, no. Fuck it. You're going to write whatever you want to anyway, so go ahead and write it."

The whole legend thing came about because of the way he died, in that car crash. Dean had just finished *Rebel*, and the studio rushed it out to take advantage of all the press he was getting.

The kids who saw the movie associated themselves with Jimmy Dean, and he became big overnight. The same thing had happened with Hank Williams. No one paid any attention to him until he died. Then everybody wanted to record his songs. That's when he became a legend.

37

Some Unsentimental Memories of James Dean by Rock Hudson

Ray Loynd

Rock Hudson, one of the last big stars created by the Hollywood studio system, was the crowning achievement of gay star-making agent Henry Willson. Willson was notorious for his stable of handsome, vapid actors with stage names like Tab Hunter (born Arthur Gelien) and Troy Donahue (born Merle Johnson Jr.), but only Hudson enjoyed career longevity. In 1947, twenty-one-year-old truck driver Roy Scherer Jr. sent photographs of himself to Willson, then in charge of talent for producer David O. Selznick. Willson, fond of saying "the acting can be added later," saw the prerequisites for stardom in Scherer's looks and physique. He put him under contract, renamed him Rock Hudson, and put him through his personal finishing school. "Willson fixed his teeth and his grammar, showed him which fork to use, how to walk and talk and dress," Louis Bayard writes in his 2005 review of a Willson biography. Willson also went to great lengths to neutralize attempts by blackmailers to expose Hudson's homosexuality, arranging his widely publicized marriage to Willson's secretary Phyllis Gates.

At Universal-International Pictures, Hudson progressed from playing small parts in films like *Winchester '73* (1950) to leading roles in a series of glossy melodramas directed by Douglas Sirk, beginning with *Magnificent Obsession* (1954). He graduated to the major leagues when George Stevens cast him as cattle baron Bick Benedict in *Giant* (1956), for which he received his only Academy Award nomination.

Thirteen years after starring in *Giant*, Hudson offered his impressions of James Dean to show business journalist Ray Loynd while he was filming *Darling Lili* (1970) for director Blake Edwards in France. The *Hollywood Reporter* published Loynd's interview with Hudson on August 9, 1968. —Ed.

James Dean, Rock Hudson, and
Elizabeth Taylor on the set of *Giant*.
Warner Bros./Photofest © Warner Bros.

PARIS.—ROCK HUDSON, REMINISCING ABOUT JAMES DEAN, shot a few
arrows into the fading Dean myth while recollecting his location shooting 13 years ago on George Stevens' "Giant."

Hudson, the last actor to work with Dean before Hollywood's brood-
ing rebel died in a car crash 13 years ago, considered the Dean mania and
the emotional necrophilia that later went with it and casually replied, "I
didn't like him particularly. He and I and Chill Wills lived in a rented
house together for three months while we were doing 'Giant' in Texas,
and although we each went more or less our own way, Dean was hard to
be around.

"He hated George Stevens, didn't think he was a good director, and he
was always angry and full of contempt."

Dean, of course, was never groomed nor bent as a locker room personality, but Hudson still recalls that Dean "never smiled. He was sulky, and
he had no manners. I'm not that concerned with manners—I'll take them
where I find them—but Dean didn't have 'em.

"And he was rough to do a scene with for reasons that only an actor
can appreciate. While doing a scene, in the giving and taking, he was just
a taker. He would suck everything out and never give back."

Hudson, whose major performance before he did "Giant" in 1955 was
"The Magnificent Obsession," [*sic*] admitted that "actually Dean was hotter
than I was in '55, although he had been an extra in a movie in which I had

starred for Universal some five years before." (That film was so forgettable Hudson couldn't recall it.*)

Hudson noted that when Dean was killed, "Dean hadn't yet looped his lines for the scene in which he played an older, white-haired man. So they brought in Nick Adams to dub Dean's old man scene in 'Giant.'"

Hudson made the comments while lounging in his suite at the Plaza Athénée, his momentary home while shooting "Darling Lili" on the outskirts of Versailles.

The complaints about Dean that Hudson voiced in 1968 seem mild today, but concealed a seething resentment of him. In public, Hudson restrained himself. In private, the mere mention of Dean's name made him spitting mad.

In 1974, James Sheldon, who had directed Dean on television in the 1950s, was directing Hudson in an episode of his TV series *McMillan & Wife* (1971–1977). Trying to make small talk with him, Sheldon said, "I used to be a friend of Jimmy Dean's."

"That prick!" Hudson shot back.

Sheldon directed Hudson's show on and off for three years. After he got to know Hudson better, he inquired, "Why was he a prick?" "He was so rude, so unprofessional," Hudson said.

Hudson could never tell Sheldon or Loynd what really provoked his contempt for Dean. To do so, he would have had to reveal that he was gay, which would have spelled professional suicide.

During one of his appearances on David Letterman's late night TV show in the late 1980s, Dennis Hopper related a story that provides a clue to the origin of Hudson's antipathy toward Dean. Hopper, who played Bick Benedict's (Hudson) son in *Giant*, idolized James Dean and hung around him during filming, witnessing his antics. One day, Hopper watched as Dean emerged from his trailer just as Hudson walked by. Dean suddenly pounced on Hudson and French-kissed him. When Hopper asked him why he did it, Dean said, "Aw, he's a fairy."

Dean's action threw a scare into Hudson, reminding him just how narrowly he had averted two recent attempts to blackmail him by threatening to make his homosexuality public knowledge. He may have feared what a loose cannon like Dean might do, and harbored a lingering hatred of him for years afterward. —Ed.

---

* The film whose title Rock Hudson could not recall was *Has Anybody Seen My Gal?* (1952), a comedy starring Charles Coburn, Piper Laurie, and Hudson. James Dean played the bit part of a character who orders a chocolate malt at a soda fountain with overly detailed directions. —Ed.

38

This Was My Friend Jimmy Dean

Mike Connolly

Mike Connolly was the daily columnist for the *Hollywood Reporter* from 1951 to 1966. In August 1955, he spent an eventful afternoon interviewing James Dean at his home for this profile of the actor published in the December 1955 issue of *Modern Screen.* —Ed.

I WROTE THIS STORY TO CORRECT AN IMPRESSION—a bad impression that a lot of people had about a guy named Jimmy Dean, who was a friend of mine. Not a close friend, but I knew him and liked him, and I didn't like what people said about him. Not because it was uncomplimentary, but because it wasn't true—at least, it wasn't true of the Jim Dean I knew.

Now he's dead. There'll be a lot written about that, but not by me. And I suppose no one will have anything bad to say of him anymore. You don't speak ill of the dead. No one will call him rude and neurotic now; at worst they'll say he was a nonconformist. He was.

So I am glad I wrote this story while he was alive. I think it has more meaning that way. All it really is is the story of a day I spent with him, but now that there won't be any more days with Jim for anyone, it makes a good memory to hold.

I don't imagine many people had seen Jim at home recently. How could they? Jim had just moved into a new place and it was a hideaway if ever one existed. When I drove out there for the first time I missed the place entirely, got lost and had to go back several miles.

It was a nice area to drive through but I hadn't wanted to be late.

The house, newly-rented, is in [the] San Fernando Valley. Jim had taken it on a one-year lease. When I finally got there, half an hour late, I found the windows and doors all wide open. A hi-fi machine was blaring Bach's Toccata in F major. I tripped over an iron doorstop. Jim turned the hi-fi down as I entered the living room, apologized for leaving the doorstop in the middle of the doorway and then, right off, asked, "Hey how about coffee? I've got a pot brewing in the kitchen." I said fine and then made *my* apologies—for being late. Jim said it was okay because he had been up late himself the night before. He had worked with Liz Taylor and Rock Hudson in *Giant* at Warners from 8 a.m. to 8:30 p.m. and then, at home, had stayed up long past midnight reading and listening to records.

I had parked out on the quiet, suburban street and hadn't paid too much attention to the heavy shrubbery that veils the house from the street as I hurried up the long path to the door. Now I was beginning to notice things. I noticed that the living room takes up most of the house. It was one of the biggest living rooms I'd ever seen. The whole place reminded me of a ski lodge.

Then I noticed two strange-looking cellophane cones, each about seven feet long, hanging from loudspeakers hidden in the beamed ceiling. One cone hung from one end of the room, one hung from the other end. Jim, who was wearing a white Mexican jean shirt, blue jeans and sneakers, saw me looking at the cones. He grabbed my arm and said, "Come here," then led me to the center of the room, under an old-fashioned wheel lamp. I found myself facing a tremendous stone fireplace. Perched dead center over the fireplace was the wickedest-looking pair of silver-tipped antlers in the world. Looking down, I saw that I was standing on a white bearskin rug. Jim was like a child, keyed up, enjoying every second.

"Hold That Pose"

He left me standing there—"Just hold that pose!" he said—walked over to the hi-fi and turned it up. The music swirled around me, on all sides. It was like the stereophonic sound you hear in theatres. Jim's eyes danced with excitement as he explained that the music zoomed down from the two ceiling speakers—"And how do you like this—those speakers are only eight inches in diameter and yet they have such tremendous volume!"—through the cellophane cones, out into the room. The cones did something to the music that increased the volume pleasantly yet permitted the tone to remain mellow.

"Quite a gadget," I said.

"Wait'll you hear this one." Jim flipped the Bach record off and put on another. "This one's African music, from Kenya. The record is all beat up. That's because I've played it so many times. But listen and you'll notice that it's delicate, sort of Oriental, music—rather than what you usually think of as African—you know, tom-toms and all that."

He spun the record and there were drums, all right, but they were merely incidental to the singer, a man who sounded like he was chanting, "Hallo, Hallo, Jimmie Rodgers!" Jim explained that that was exactly what the man, an African native, *was* singing. I had never heard of Jimmie Rodgers. Jim elucidated.

"Jimmie Rodgers was one of our greatest cowboy and hillbilly singers. He died in the early thirties. But folk singers today still worship at his shrine. And these African natives, 'way off there in Kenya, somehow got hold of some of Rodgers' old-time cowboy records and made up their own songs based on his songs. Listen to the man yodel!" Sure enough, the African was yodeling.

Jim then played one of Rodgers' old yodeling records, dug up in a second-hand record shop, to show the similarities.

The native chant droned on and on. Jim Dean seemed hypnotized by it. I noticed a bar there in the living room, obviously installed by the original owner. Jim wasn't using it as such. It was loaded with books and bundles. He had moved in only the week before.

I noticed the shelves were already crowded with books—fiction, philosophy, Aztec culture, the theatre, history, art, music. There were more record albums, too—hundreds, seemingly. Also bullfight posters and ropes, crash helmets and racing car trophies, stacks of photos, not professional photographs but snapshots.

Back upstairs we went. "Is this the whole house?" I asked. Jim said, "This is it." I asked, "No bedrooms?" Said he, "Nope. Just a little old kitchen and dining room and a big, big living room. Who needs more than that?" I asked where he sleeps. He pointed up to a balcony hanging over the high-ceilinged living room and demonstrated how he got to his bed up there by crawling up a flight of steps built over the fireplace—most ingenious and certainly most unusual!

"Who in the world would build a house like this?" I asked. "And how could they ever expect to rent it or sell it again?"

"Well, you're looking at the guy who rented it," Jim said. Then he explained that the house belongs to a friend, Nick Romanos [Nicco Romanos]. Nick was once a ballet star with Diaghilev's Ballet de Monte Carlo. This was many years ago. The great Nijinsky had also danced for Diaghilev. Nick's wife had a heart ailment and her doctor suggested that Nick take her to live as close to the ocean as possible. "So now they're living in a trailer down at the beach and I'm here," said Jim.

"How did you meet Nick?"

"He manages the Villa Capri for Patsy D'Amore, Frank Sinatra's friend. Marlon Brando eats there a lot, too. So do I. One night I went in and asked Nick, 'What's good on the menu tonight?' He said, 'How should I know? I *hate* Italian food! Go down the street to Don the Beachcomber's if you want a good meal!' I've been very fond of Nick ever since."

Now I noticed a hangman's rope hanging from one of the living room beams. A sign—"We Also Remove Bodies"—hung next to the rope. Jim said the rope was part of his knot-tying studies—"After all, roping and bullfighting." And the sign? "Oh, I guess you can chalk that up to my macabre sense of humor."

More records, all stacked around the hi-fi, spilled all over that end of the room. "What kind of music do you like best?" I asked. "Just about everything," Jim said. "I collect everything from Twelfth and Thirteenth Century music to Wanda Landowska's harpsichord recordings of Bach's *Well-Tempered Clavier* to the extreme moderns—you know, Schoenberg, Berg, Bartok, Stravinsky. I also like Sinatra's *Songs for Young Lovers* album."

He picked up a record. "See if you can recognize this. I feel the same way about this one that the teenagers feel about Sinatra and Eddie Fisher." He spun the disc. Through the cellophane cones poured the magnificent strains of Puccini's "One Fine Day" aria from *Madame Butterfly*. Jim was delighted when I identified the singer first as the late Claudia Muzio. But his face fell when I immediately corrected myself and said it was Renata

Tebaldi of Milan's La Scala opera company. I thought to myself, "Jim must think he has an exclusive on Tebaldi!"

But then he was raving over the record. "Listen to this woman's modulation," he rhapsodized. "And such expression! Wonderful taste, too, and a truly great sense of proportion. Overtrained opera singers usually go overboard—haven't you noticed how they hit a good note and then drive the listener nuts holding onto it? They don't want to let go of it, it's so good. But not Tebaldi. She is a great artist—greatest we've ever had." I gave him an argument, claiming Muzio as greatest. Jim shrugged.

I noticed Eugene Ormandy's *Ports of Call* in the pile of records. Jim said, apologetically, "A friend left that. It's not quite my cup of tea. Too chapter-headingish, too twelve-string-ish—you dig me? But pleasant, if you're in the mood."

"Tchaikovsky?"

Jim dismissed Tchaikovsky and the other Romantics as he had dismissed my favorite opera singer—with a shrug.

Now he was putting Bela Bartok's suite from *The Miraculous Mandarin* on the hi-fi. While we listened to the wild, sensuous music he said, "Someday I would like to direct a movie short of the ballet Bartok wrote this for. It's about a girl of the streets who was forced by two hoodlums to lure men. She's the come-on. The hoodlums beat up the men and rob them. Finally the girl lures a rich mandarin. The men beat him, rob him and try to kill him. But he won't die, because he has fallen in love with the girl, even though she's evil. His love is stronger than their murdering hands. The men finally plunge a sword into his heart. Then they hang him from a chandelier! But his eyes remain wide open, glued on the girl he loves! And then she suddenly realizes that this is the only good man who has ever loved her and that she loves him, too! She throws her arms around him. It is only then, when he knows his love has been returned, that he gives in and lets death take him. Beautiful story, isn't it?"

I agreed. I also wondered to myself which of the big studios would be interested in letting Jim direct it for them. I could think of none.

"Hey, the coffee!" he exclaimed suddenly remembering, jumping up. The Bartok continued to swell from the cones as he went to the kitchen, puttered around, returning finally with a tray holding a coffee pot, cups and saucers, cream and sugar, raisin-and-honey bread and a plate of cream cheese. Meanwhile, Jim had gotten off on another subject: the trees in his front and back yards. He reeled them off for me: peach, plum, lemon, lime, orange and apple. He did all the gardening.

"You Asked Me"

I sat on the floor, leaning against his TV set, as he talked. The TV set was flanked by his bongo drums. I said, "I don't understand how you find time for all this. Acting, collecting hi-fi records—and playing them, too!—roping, bullfighting, carpentry, photography, reading, racing, drumming, gardening, cooking. You play the piano and guitar, too, I've heard."

"Yep. I also study singing and dancing. Some day I want to make a musical. I also sail, play tennis, fence, do gymnastics and also a little boxing. I'm a farmer, too. I know how to milk cows and I'm a great hand at feeding the chickens. I also study body movement and foreign languages and I like to work on sports cars, in addition to racing them. I ride, too. When I first came to California I bought a Palomino named Cisco.

"But don't make me sound like I'm bragging about all this, because I'm not. You asked me and I'm telling you. I keep busy because I think that's part of being an actor. I think actors should spend their lives investigating things, learning what makes things tick. They should try to know every facet of living. Walt Disney's Jiminy Cricket said it in *Pinocchio*, remember, when he sang, 'Hi diddle dee dee, an actor's life for me!' It's a great life.

"But an actor would be selfish if he didn't try to learn everything life has to offer. He should seek the truth—he should try to learn what is valid in life and what isn't. It takes time, time when he could be goofing off, but it's worth it, when and if he finds it."

"How old are you, Jim?"

"I was born February 8, 1931."

"For a twenty-four-year-old, you know a great deal about life."

"I don't know anywhere near what I should know, but some day maybe I will." He looked around at his books, his records, TV set, bongo drums. He smiled.

Two young girls stuck their heads in the front door. One of them said, "We just wanted to say hello to our new neighbor and see what he's been doing to Nick's house." She was the "cool" type. The other, younger girl said, somewhat breathlessly, "Oh, and we heard the music, too—we're just on our way back from market—and we thought you were having a jam session and we thought we'd see what it was all about!" The words gushed out. Neither girl mentioned his name, although it was obvious they knew very well who Jim was. The first girl was eighteen or so, the other about twelve.

Jim smiled and said, "Come on in and look around." They needed no further invitation. They came in and looked around. Jim said to me, "It's really too much house for me, when you stop to think of it." I said, "I should think so—the gardening and all. Why don't you have someone come in and help?" He said, "I guess I'll have to. If I ever get around to phoning an employment agency!"

A little neighbor boy came in, followed by another. They were about nine and seven. They had apparently followed the girls. Jim was just as considerate with them. He told them to have a look around, too. "Make yourself at home." Then, to me: "It's a mess because Nick had to move so quickly and I moved in in a hurry and haven't had time to fix it up. But I will."

The girls came in from the backyard. The older girl said, "That's a beautiful peach tree you have out there. Are you going to eat the peaches or give them away?" Jim said, "Both. You can have some." She said, "Gee, thanks, that'll be wonderful!" She beamed at the younger girl, who beamed right back. "That Jimmy Dean is *real* dreamy," I could imagine them telling their other girl friends later. "He practically invited us to come back and load up with his peaches whenever we want to!"

The girls started looking through the records. The boys were out in the back yard, looking things over.

Neighbors

I had heard that Natalie Wood, the starlet whose name has been linked romantically with Jim's, is a neighbor of his. I asked him about it. He said, "No, I don't think so." That was all.

He added, "But I do know one of my neighbors and I suppose you know him, too. He's George Gobel." I said yes, indeed, I knew George well—George and I both hail from Chicago and I had been visiting the set of his first movie, *The Birds and the Bees*, at Paramount, the day before. George had been doing a love scene with Mitzi Gaynor. "Nice guy, isn't he?" Jim asked. "The nicest," I said.

One of the little boys sauntered in from the yard, swinging a branch he had picked up. He asked Jim, "Hey, do you still have those snakes Nick had? They were sure cute, those snakes."

I had never heard of "cute" snakes. Jim explained to me that they were imitation snakes that Nick had bought in a tricks-and-magic store in Hollywood. To the boy he explained, "Nick took the snakes when he moved to the beach."

Girls

The older girl, somewhat resentful of the boy's intrusion of her session with Jim (I was interviewing Jim for MODERN SCREEN but *I* obviously didn't count!) said, "I think I'll enroll at UCLA this year." Jim said, "I went there. I took pre-law. It's a good school." The girl asked, "Why did you leave?" Jim replied, "The school decided I should leave." The girls and the boy giggled.

The younger girl commented on the clarity of Jim's hi-fi set (it was playing an old Chaliapin record now)—"It's real cool!" she said—and Jim started explaining how the cones worked. The other little neighbor boy returned from the yard, unbidden. Jim and I still had some bread and cheese left on our plates. The four youngsters started whispering about something among themselves so I whispered to Jim, "Don't you find it strange to have so many people walking in and out of the house?" He smiled and whispered right back, "Why not—the door's open."

Then I remembered a sign I had seen at the gate: "Beware of Dogs." I asked Jim about it. He said, "That's left over from Nick. Nobody pays any attention to it."

And this, I thought, is the James Dean they've been calling a hermit!

The older girl was talking to Jim again. She was a very pretty girl. She wore pedal pushers and a plain white blouse and ballet slippers. She said she liked Tchaikovsky and Victor Herbert. Jim said, "It's my opinion that Victor Herbert was a musical imposter. I like creative artists, the ones who don't borrow from others."

She asked, "Do you like Sauter-Finegan?* They play modern jazz."

---

* The Sauter-Finegan Orchestra was a swing jazz band formed in 1952 by big band arrangers Eddie Sauter and Bill Finegan. —Ed.

Jim said, "Well, if you're going to listen to atonal music don't you think it's better to listen to something good, like Bartok? They also copy Berg and the other moderns." She said she would listen to Bartok and the others.

One of the boys asked, "Do you like real fast music?" (Not one of the youngsters had called Jim by his name yet.)

Jim said, "Fast or slow, if it's good."

Surprises

I went out in the kitchen to get more coffee. Dirty dishes were stacked all over the place. Typical bachelor, I thought. Jim left his inquisitors and came out after me. "I cooked some steaks night before last," he apologized, "and had to get up early yesterday, as I told you, and I worked late last night, as you know, so I haven't had time to clean up."

Then Jim pulled one right out of the air and popped it at me: "Would you like to know a good recipe for onions? Well, you put some onions in a pan with butter, let them roll around in that awhile, then put some sugar and cinnamon on them and cook them some more—fabulous!"

We went back to the kids. They were getting ready to leave. He didn't dismiss them. They bade him affectionate goodbyes as they left. The youngest boy said, "Goodbye, Jimmy." The rest of the youngsters picked it up and called him Jimmy, too. Then they were gone.

I complimented him. He said, "I was a counselor at a boys' camp in Glendora, California, for a year, just before I started at UCLA in 1949. So I know a little about getting along with youngsters."

I said, "That was a pretty girl."

"Yeah, real collegiate. You keep getting onto that subject, don't you? You trying to pump me about girls?" He grinned.

"Well—"

"Three gossip columnists had me out with three different girls one night—and all the time I was sitting in the Villa Capri with my insurance agent!"

"That older girl seemed very interested in you."

"A lot of them are, at first."

"And?"

"They're curious. But the percentage of lasting relationships between fellows and girls based on curiosity is limited. There have been a number of these, not only where I'm concerned but where other actors are concerned, and the more of these there are the more one's discretion is taxed. You know what I mean? So where does an actor who wants to be serious with a girl go from there?

"Oh well, I guess that's the position we put ourselves in when we get into this business!"

"How do you find being famous, Jim? Have you lost anything that you had before *East of Eden* made you a star?"

"It's hard to say. I fought it for a long time. I didn't think I was famous—I thought I was more infamous! But after a while I think I started learning what so many actors have learned—about that certain communicative power we have that so few people are privileged to have. We find that we can reach, through the medium of motion pictures and television, not only the people with whom we work on the soundstages here in Hollywood but people all over the world! And then we start thinking, 'I'm famous, all right, and I guess this is what I wanted, so now how do I face it?'

"And then the responsibilities come. And you have to fight against becoming egotistical. It's tough, here in Hollywood. You have reached so many people, and you think they are interested in you personally and that you must have answered some need of theirs, in some small way. There's a great satisfaction in this, you know—to have answered a need in another person.

"You know what I think? I think the prime reason for existence, for living in this world, is discovery! It's part of knowing your Maker and loving Him. Look around you, at children and animals. They're always looking for and discovering new things. That's what I like to do.

"On the other hand, I know there are many people in the world who give up the search. They quit because they're afraid of failing, of being rejected, when they near their goal. This world we live in is dominated, I think, by an idyllic interpretation of success. This, in turn, manufactures fantasy. People become involved with the fantasy and stop looking for their own success. They find it, instead, in the success of movie stars and other celebrities. They live in a dream world.

"People have too much time here. I think it's because of the vastness of the place and the distances. When you drive all the way from Warners to 20th Century-Fox you have too much time to think. You think, think, think, all the way. If the people in Hollywood kept busier at their arts and crafts they would be more productive and not so destructive. I'm talking about the gossipmongers now."

"A Masterful Woman"

I thought this would be a good time to interrupt him: "When are you going to get married?"

"When I find the right companion."

"Are you looking?"

"Every man looks. But looking in itself is superficial. Looking can be an inward thing. It can have nothing to do with actual physical and emotional involvements. Oh sure, I'm looking.

"But—oh, I don't know. I think it would take a masterful kind of woman to tolerate my shenanigans!"

"Maybe," I said, "you could compromise, if the right girl came along."

"It would be a very delicate setup—marriage I mean," Jim said. "I have a lot to learn. I fall short in the 'human' department. I expect too much of people. Tolerance, somebody said, comes with maturity, and I guess I'm sort of a baby where women are concerned.

"Besides, there's no rush. I think thirty is a good age to get married, don't you? So—I've got five more years to look!"

That's what he thought then.

I had heard about his dates with Ursula Andress, a lovely young German actress signed by Paramount.* I asked about Ursula. Jim said, affectionately, "She's a nice girl, a wonderful girl. And she has a great deal of talent, acting talent, that is. It may not be fully realized yet, but she's growing in stature." He laughed, remembering something. "I'm talking in circles. Do you really want to know about Ursula and me? Well, we fight like cats and dogs! No, on second thought—like two monsters!

"But then we make up, and it's fun. Ursula doesn't take any baloney from me and I don't take any from her. I guess it's because we're both so egotistical.

---

* Ursula Andress (1936–) was born in Switzerland. —Ed.

"Did I tell you about the foreign language I'm studying? German. I want to travel. I've never been to Europe. Ursula has stimulated this yen. I want to see France, Italy, Spain, Germany, Switzerland, the Scandinavian countries, England, Iceland. Sandy Roth, our still photographer on *Giant*, keeps egging me on, too. He keeps telling me how wonderful it is over there."

He walked over to his bongo drums and gave them a loving pat-pat-pat or two.

I said, "Jim this has been one of the best interviews I've ever had with an actor. Thanks."

"I'm glad."

"But one thing bothers me."

"What's that?"

"Well, I've learned so much about you I'm not sure which angle I'll take when I sit down to write the story. Maybe I should just write about it from the beginning—you know, my arriving late and all that. It might be tough writing it any other way, because it has a million angles."

Jim laughed and said, "That's me, too—a million angles!"

END

39

—◆—

Along Came a Spyder

Alec Guinness

Alec Guinness arrived in Hollywood in late September 1955, there to perform in his first American film, *The Swan* (1956), starring Grace Kelly and Louis Jourdan. After enduring a sixteen-hour flight from Copenhagen, Guinness wanted one thing above all: a good meal. After Guinness and his host, screenwriter Thelma Moss, were turned away by three restaurants because she was wearing slacks, they arrived at the Villa Capri, only to be told there were no tables available. The restaurant was so busy that evening that James Dean and his dinner companion, Lew Bracker, had to settle for a table in the least desirable part of the Capri, facing the front entrance. As the disappointed Guinness walked away, Bracker told Dean that he'd just seen none other than Alec Guinness in the restaurant. Guinness recalled what happened next in his 1986 autobiography, *Blessings in Disguise.* —Ed.

I BECAME AWARE OF RUNNING, sneakered feet behind us and turned to face a fair young man in sweatshirt and blue jeans. "You want a table?" he asked. "Join me. My name is James Dean." We followed him gratefully, but on the way back to the restaurant he turned into a car-park [parking lot], saying, "I'd like to show you something." Among the other cars there was what looked like a large, shiny, silver parcel wrapped in cellophane and tied with ribbon. "It's just been delivered," he said, with bursting pride. "I haven't even driven it yet." The sports car looked sinister to me, although it had a large bunch of red carnations resting on the bonnet [hood]. "How fast is it?" I asked. "She'll do a hundred and fifty," he replied. Exhausted, hungry, feeling a little ill-tempered in spite of Dean's kindness, I heard myself saying in a voice I could hardly recognize as my own, "Please, never get in it." I looked at my watch. "It is now ten o'clock, Friday the 23rd of September, 1955. If you get in that car you will be found dead in it by this time next week." He laughed. "Oh, shucks! Don't be so mean!" I apologized for what I had said, explaining it was lack of sleep and food. Thelma Moss and I joined him at his table and he proved an agreeable, generous host, and was very funny about Lee Strasberg, the Actors Studio and the Method. We parted an hour later, full of smiles. No further reference was made to the wrapped-up car. Thelma was relieved by the outcome of the evening and rather impressed. In my heart I was uneasy—with myself. At four o'clock in the afternoon on the following Friday James Dean was dead, killed while driving the car.

Lew Bracker disputes some of the details in Guinness's account. Dean's Porsche Spyder wasn't delivered to the Villa Capri's parking lot wrapped in cellophane with a ribbon and a spray of carnations on the hood; Dean had already been driving it for several days when he met Guinness.

Although Bracker didn't leave the restaurant to witness Dean and Guinness's conversation in the parking lot, he still vividly remembers one detail from that evening that lends credence to Guinness's claim that he uttered a prophetic warning to Dean: Guinness looked visibly stricken when he returned to the restaurant. —Ed.

40

———◆———

The Rebel and the Mogul

DORE SCHARY

Dore Schary was the president of Metro-Goldwyn-Mayer from 1951 to 1956. This piece is excerpted from his 1979 autobiography *Heyday*. —Ed.

JAMES DEAN WAS SLATED TO PLAY Rocky Graziano in *Somebody Up There Likes Me*. When we had lent Elizabeth Taylor to Warners for *Giant* we had obtained the services of James Dean for one picture and had elected *Somebody* for that one.

Dean had read the book and came to see me on a Friday afternoon to discuss the project and his possible participation in it. We had never met. He entered my office wearing large, dark sunglasses, moccasins, a short brass-buttoned denim jacket, a dark blue shirt, and clean light-blue jeans.

He waved a hand at me, said nothing, and peered intently at an old Italian puppet given me by my sister, Lillian. After eyeing it, he said, "Old." I nodded. He proceeded from the puppet to other things in the office: some pictures painted by Miriam, a few odd ashtrays, an antique typewriter, an embossed copy of Satchel Paige's *Rules for the Good Life* (including one I've never forgotten, "Don't look back, something might be gaining on you"), and a lovely kaleidoscope Miriam had given me.

During this survey, he'd slide his glasses up to his forehead to closely examine each item, nod his head in a pleased manner, and yet say not a word except, "Old."

I broke the silence.

"I wish you'd tell me what role I should play. Should I be in back of the desk with a fat cigar—or should I swing a golf club or polo mallet—?"

Dean looked at me and smiled, walked over, thrust out his hand to me, and over our handshake sat down and said, "How are you?" Apparently I'd passed a test of sorts.

We spent an hour together. He had liked the book but had worries. What about the makeup? Could he learn to box well enough? Could he get the "dese, dem, and dose" accent so it wouldn't appear phony?

The makeup was a cinch. Johnny Indrisano would teach him the boxing and make him look good. The accent was easy. I demonstrated and said, "If I can do it, you can." But best of all, Graziano would be around—all Dean would have to do would be to listen to Rocky.

We agreed that he would come in Monday morning to meet the makeup people and make some tests. He'd meet the writer, Ernie Lehman; Charlie Schnee, the producer; and Robert Wise, the director. We talked about movies and plays and careers. Before leaving he said, as he pointed to the puppet, "I love that." I told him if he was good as Rocky I'd give it to him as a present.

Then he was gone.

The next day, Saturday afternoon, he was killed in his Porsche while driving to see some auto races.[*]

---

[*] James Dean was killed in an auto accident on Friday, September 30, 1955, while en route to Salinas, California, where he was scheduled to compete in auto races there that weekend. —Ed.

41

The Assignment I'll Never Forget: Jimmy Dean

Sanford H. Roth

In 1947, Brooklyn-born Sanford Roth quit his job managing a chain of retail stores in Los Angeles and moved to Paris with his wife, Beulah, and their Siamese cat Louis XIV to pursue his passion for photography. Roth's photographs of artists, intellectuals, and celebrities soon began appearing in prestigious publications like *Time, Life, Look, Fortune, Paris Match, Elle, Der Stern, Harper's Bazaar,* and *Vogue.* The English-language edition of Roth's collection of photographs, *The French of Paris,* with text by Aldous Huxley, was published in 1954.

Roth befriended James Dean while on assignment from *Collier's* magazine to cover the actor during the production of *Giant.*

On September 30, 1955, Roth and stuntman Bill Hickman (Dean's friend) were following him in his Ford station wagon when he was killed while driving his Porsche to a racing event in Salinas, California. A controversy exists over whether Roth photographed Dean in the wreck of his Porsche. "The ambulance came and I instinctively began taking pictures," he wrote in "The Assignment I'll Never Forget: James Dean," which was published in the July 1962 issue of *Popular Photography.*

An article in the September 1956 issue of *Life* mentioned "the two shots [Roth] got of the dead actor in the smashed Porsche" and quotes him as saying, "They will never be released. And nobody will ever see them. I took them for one reason—if there was a question by the insurance companies or police as to who was driving." Beulah Roth maintained that no such photos existed. Sanford Roth suffered a fatal heart attack in 1962 while he was in Rome to cover the production of the film *Cleopatra* (1963). —Ed.

Like Jimmy Dean, whose untimely death he photographed, Sanford Roth also passed away at the height of his creative powers. He died in Rome last March at the age of 55 following a heart attack. A talented and widely traveled pro, Roth had come to photography at the age of 41, after giving up a highly successful career as a merchandising executive. Although he had photographed many celebrities in all fields the world over, the one he remembered best was the irrepressible young actor, who had won Hollywood fame but not happiness.

IN THE EARLY FALL OF 1955, I was working overseas when I received a trans-Atlantic call from the noted director George Stevens wanting to know when I could get to Hollywood for a magazine assignment from *Collier's.* They wanted me to photograph a new young star on the set of the movie *Giant.*

So when my work in Morocco and London was finished, I flew to Hollywood to begin work on the Jimmy Dean story. Stevens, Liz Taylor, Rock Hudson, and the whole cast and company of *Giant* welcomed me when I arrived on the sound stage.

They took it for granted that I knew Jimmy Dean, but I did not, for his first film, *East of Eden,* had been released while I was in Africa. I hadn't even seen a photograph of this newcomer who had been described to me as a most promising actor.

On the set that day I noticed a young man playing with a lariat. He looked as if he had spent his young life close to horses and cattle. This was Jimmy Dean. He watched me as I approached him.

"Hello, I'm Sandy Roth," I said. "I'm to do the special photography—looking forward to working with you."

Jimmy looked up over his thick-rimmed glasses and replied, "I'm glad you're here." Then, with a puzzled look, he asked: "Are you *Sanford H. Roth?* Did you do the book on Paris with Aldous Huxley?"

I replied yes, pleased and surprised that he knew of my work.

"That book makes me realize I've never been anywhere," Jimmy went on. "I want to be in Paris before this year is out. I want to see the Paris theater—to see Pierre Blanchard and Gérard Philipe. I want to see the great artists—to see Rome—to buy shoes and crazy clothes in Capri. I want to live!"

Later that day after he finished a scene, he strolled over to me and asked if I had any works of the artists I had photographed in Europe. Anything of Picasso? Cocteau? Chagall? Afro?* Dame Edith Sitwell? Miró?

James Dean on the set of *Giant*.
Warner Bros./Photofest © Warner Bros.

"Yes, some of the people have given me a few things," I told him.

"When can I come and see you?" he asked.

That same night he came for dinner and stayed until five in the morning. So it was on that first day we met that we became close friends.

Throughout the next few weeks as the picture neared completion, we worked together each day on the set. On weekends, we shot off-stage material. I needed a story on the youthful Dean for my assignment. *Collier's* was aware of my close friendship with him and was interested in all aspects of his life. And Jimmy's many interests naturally led us to oil field workers, auto races, the countryside, beaches, art galleries, music, children, and animals.

Photography did not escape his interest either, for he knew and understood cameras. Often when I was occupied, he would slip a camera from one of my cases, and with a telephoto lens, shoot a few frames. They generally were well composed and exposed. Later, as my film was being processed, I discovered some shots I could not identify. They had been taken by Jimmy, whom I dubbed "sneaky eye."

Jimmy was also a rabid racing car enthusiast. Before *Giant* began, he had driven in two races. He had won a first and a second prize with his Porsche within two weeks, something that other racing men often take years to achieve.

He had been kept off the tracks during the shooting of *Giant* by a special "no-racing" clause in his contract. But he had bought a new Porsche

---

* Italian painter Afro Libio Basaldella (1912–1976) was known by the single name Afro.

Spyder and had passed his requirements for the big race at Salinas, Calif., scheduled to take place after he completed his work on the film.

When Jimmy was finished with *Giant*, he asked me to go with him to the big races in Northern California. Even though this would take four or five days away from editing pictures, I decided to go. *Collier's* agreed that a fitting close for my story of Jimmy would be a picture of him driving in a big race.

On the morning of September 30, 1955, he came to my house with his racing Porsche atop a trailer attached to his Ford station wagon. With him was his mechanic, Rolf Wütherich, who was to be in the pit at the races. We were happy and enthusiastic at the prospect of the seven-hour drive up the beautiful coast, the races, and the weekend to follow in San Francisco.

The day was magnificent, and Jimmy thought it a pity to sit cooped up in the station wagon for the long ride. They took the Porsche off the trailer and Jimmy and his mechanic set out in the car. I followed behind in the station wagon, hauling the empty trailer.* They soon outdistanced me as they tested the car's engine and handling.

Thirty miles south of Paso Robles the road is straight as an arrow. At this part I could see for many miles ahead, and I noticed what seemed like some kind of a roadblock far off in the distance. As I came closer, the obstruction took form. It was a sedan, not badly damaged, in the middle of the highway. I strained to look around the immediate area—I was looking for the other car.

Off in a ditch to the right, I suddenly saw what had been the sleek, silver Porsche—now it was like a crumpled pack of cigarettes. But where was Jimmy? My heart screamed. I leaped from the car, only to be confronted by a highway policeman asking questions.

Then I saw it all. Rolf had been thrown clear of the car: Jimmy was dead in his seat. The impact had thrown his head back too far.

The ambulance came and I instinctively began taking pictures. I begged the attendant to keep Jimmy under oxygen on the way to the hospital, but it was no use. Neither was the fifteen-mile race against time to the hospital. Jimmy was dead.

---

* Bill Hickman, Dean's friend and fellow sports car enthusiast, drove Dean's station wagon en route to Salinas on September 30, 1955. —Ed.

42

Death Drive

ROLF WÜTHERICH

Former Luftwaffe glider pilot, paratrooper, and aircraft mechanic Rolf Wütherich became a skilled mechanic working on high-performance German sports cars after World War II. He joined the racing department at the Porsche factory in 1950. In April 1955, Porsche sent the twenty-eight-year-old Wütherich to Los Angeles to maintain their cars at John von Neumann's Competition Motors, the Porsche dealership in Hollywood patronized by James Dean. When Dean traded in his Porsche Super Speedster for one of five newly arrived Porsche 550 Spyders on September 21, he insisted as a condition of the purchase that Wütherich accompany him as his mechanic to the races he competed in.

Wütherich was Dean's passenger on September 30, 1955, when his Porsche collided with an oncoming car driven by college student Donald Turnupseed, who made a sudden left turn in front of Dean. Dean died almost instantly in the crash. Wütherich was thrown clear of the car. He required months of hospitalization to recover from the severe injuries he suffered in the accident. He returned to Germany in 1959 but suffered lasting psychological traumas in the aftermath of the accident. Wütherich was driving his Honda Civic too fast on the evening of July 20, 1981, when he missed a tight turn and slammed into the wall of a house, killing him instantly. "Death Drive," his account of the events of September 30, 1955, appeared in the October 1957 issue of *Modern Screen*.* —Ed.

---

* In "Wie es wirklich war mit James Dean" ("How It Really Was with James Dean"), an article published in 1960 in *Christophorus*, a German magazine for Porsche enthusiasts published by the company, Wütherich attributed "Death Drive" to his ex-wife, who, he said, had spoken to the media without his consent. Although the article in *Christophorus* was informed by Wütherich's cooperation, it differs surprisingly little from "Death Drive" in its account of the events of Dean's trip, and contains factual errors. —Ed.

In memoriam—this second year since Jimmy Dean's death—
MODERN SCREEN prints this story by the man who was with
him at the end . . .

When Dean, on September 30, 1955, raced to his death in
his Porsche car, he was not alone. His mechanic, Rolf Wüthe-
rich, was in the seat beside him. Miraculously, Wütherich sur-
vived. He had to spend many months in the hospital. Here, for
the first time, he tells the story of what really happened on that
fateful day when his friend Jimmy Dean was killed . . .

I DON'T THINK I SHALL EVER FORGET THAT DAY in September, two years ago. That was the day I rode with Jimmy Dean to his death.

I was a service mechanic for Porsche cars, and I was a very busy man indeed—film stars like fast cars, and I was experienced as a racing car mechanic in major European motor races.

That's how it happened that I was James Dean's last passenger, on that awful day when he rode to his death.

When I first met Jimmy Dean, he owned a Porsche *Speedster*, a somewhat smaller sports car than the Porsche *Spyder* he crashed in. The *Speedster* had carried him to victory at Bakersfield, Santa Barbara and other races. It was at one of these races that I first met Jimmy. I was looking over the Porsche cars—that was my big job as a mechanic—and Jimmy and I got to talking.

I had seen him driving in another race—he hadn't been racing long, but he was a good driver: he had that essential feel for fast cars and dangerous roads. He had that sixth sense a racing driver can't do without. We talked about his car for a couple of minutes, and then he took off—for a win.

Two weeks later, I was walking along Hollywood Boulevard when I saw Jimmy Dean coming toward me.

This particular sunny afternoon opened the last chapter in the life of this boy whom millions loved—and still love . . .

He was walking with that slow gait of his, a toy monkey on a rubber band hanging from his wrist, hopping up and down with each movement of Jimmy's arm. Jimmy was in a completely carefree, happy mood. We shook hands, and we talked about—sports cars, what else? Jimmy wanted to enter the big-car class in his next race—the class for cars with the large, powerful engines. That was Jimmy's big dream. And he told me about the big Bristol car he had ordered.

That was when I remembered about the Porsche *Spyder* we had on sale. I told Jimmy about this car—told him about how powerful it was and that it might be just what he wanted to make his dream come true. Next day Jimmy was at the shop to look it over. It was September 19, 1955. He drove it once around the block. And really liked it. He made one condition before buying the car—he made me promise that I would personally check it before each and every race he took part in, and that I was to ride with him to all the races. Naturally, I said *yes* because I couldn't think of anything I'd like better.

The Last Ride . . .

The filming of *Giant* was scheduled to end that same week. Jimmy's contract didn't allow him to enter car races during the shooting of a picture, so Jimmy wasn't free to drive in a race till the following weekend—the fateful weekend of October 1, 1955. He was going to take part in an airstrip race about three hundred miles from Los Angeles. But time was running short, and before entering such a race a driver should really get acquainted with his car. The *Spyder* should have been driven by Jimmy for at least five hundred miles. That's why Jimmy told me, "We won't take the car by trailer to Salinas. We'll drive there. You come along, and on the way you can check things." We met that Friday morning of September 30, in my workshop at Competition Motors. It was only eight in the morning when I went to work checking Dean's *Spyder*—the motor, oil pressure, ignition, spark plugs, tires—and all the rest of it. Jimmy paced the floor. Once he thought I was taking too long and he came over and tried to help me. I said "No thanks. You'll only complicate things!" He walked away, with that grin of his, and thumbed through a newspaper. But several times he came back and asked a thousand questions which I had to answer very exactly and in great detail. When the *Spyder* was all ready I fixed a safety belt for Jimmy on the driver's seat. I didn't fix one for the passenger's seat: Jimmy would be alone in the car during the race. He sat in the car and tried the safety belt.

It was just before ten a.m. when Jimmy's friends, film extra Bill Hickman and photographer Sandy Roth, showed up. They were to go with us to Salinas in Jimmy's station wagon, a 1955 Ford. Jimmy's father and his uncle Charles Nolan walked in and Jimmy drove his uncle around the block a couple of times. Charles put his arm around Jimmy's shoulder and said jokingly, "Be careful, Jim. You're sitting on a bomb!"

Around noon we were ready. Jimmy wearing light blue trousers and a white T-shirt, threw his red jacket behind the seat in the car and fixed sun lenses to his glasses. At one-thirty we said goodbye to his friends, his father and his uncle, and I sat down beside Jimmy in the *Spyder* as Jimmy took the wheel. Someone took a last snap of us. Jimmy gripped my hand and pulled it up in some kind of salute. This was the very last picture that was ever taken of James Dean. The last picture of him . . . alive.

Traffic was very heavy at this time of day. We went out to Ventura Boulevard, filled up the gas tank and reached Highway 99, which cuts through the mountains between Los Angeles and Bakersfield. Sometimes we were leading, sometimes the station wagon with Bill Hickman and Sandy Roth took the lead. The sun was high in the sky. I listened to the sound of the Porsche's motor—and it was purring. Jimmy kept nudging me again and again. "What's the rev number?" "How's the oil temp?" "You sure this is the right road?"

A Warning to Jimmy

Jimmy Dean was very happy. We whistled and sang, cracked jokes, and Jimmy laughed loudest at his own jokes—in that way of his. We smoked one cigarette after the other, and I lit them for Jimmy, hunching low under the windscreen as the wind tore along—almost taking the glowing tip of the cigarette away with it. Jimmy was in high spirits, and we felt like we had been very close friends for a long time. The setting was ideal—a very fast car on a sunny day with a long stretch of road ahead of us.

A few minutes before three we stopped at a roadside snack bar. Jimmy ordered a glass of milk for himself and would not rest until I had an ice cream soda. I began to feel uneasy about the race—felt as though maybe I'd better warn Jimmy—"Don't go too fast!" I said, my face dead serious. "Don't try to win! The *Spyder* is something quite different from the *Speedster*. *Don't* drive to win; drive to get experience!" "Okay, Rolf," he said with a smile, a sort of smile that laughed at me and my fears for him.

September 30, 1955: Behind the wheel of his new Porsche Spyder, James Dean hoists the arm of his passenger, Rolf Wütherich, in a gesture of victory before taking off for the sports car race he expected to win that weekend in Salinas, California. He was killed later that afternoon when his car collided with another driver's vehicle. Wütherich survived the accident. *Editor's collection*

A Gift of Friendship from Jimmy

"Give me the signs when I'm going over the rounds!" he said. Then he hesitated for a moment. He pulled a ring from his finger. It wasn't an expensive ring—just some little souvenir he had picked up, but I knew he had a sentimental attachment to the ring. He handed it to me.

"Why?" I asked.

"I want to give you something," he said. "To show we're friends, Rolf."* I was touched. The ring just fitted on my small finger. My hand was much bigger than Jimmy's.

---

* In the article published in *Christophorus*, Wütherich recalled Dean telling him, "Come, Rolf, you are my guardian angel; you get this ring from me." —Ed.

After a while Jimmy's two friends arrived in the station wagon. "Don't let him drive too fast," they said half jokingly, half serious, as Jimmy climbed behind the steering wheel again.

A few minutes later, there was a police car chasing us. They stopped us and handed Jimmy a summons—he was over the speed limit of fifty miles per hour. The police handed another summons to the driver of the station wagon. The funny thing was that Officer O. V. Hunter seemed to be much more interested in the gray Porsche than in his summons, and Jimmy answered all his questions as if they were two drivers gabbing over a cup of coffee. Before we took off again, Jimmy told his friends, "We'll wait for you at Paso Robles. We'll have dinner there." Paso Robles was about a hundred and fifty miles along the road.

"Nonstop to Paso Robles"

It was late afternoon. The road was one gray line cutting through a monotonous landscape—here and there a very slight bend, otherwise straight ahead. It felt like driving on an endless ruler. The only break in the monotony was at Blackwell's Corner—a service station with a small store attached to it, in the middle of nowhere. When we reached Blackwell's Corner a sleek, gray Mercedes was parked in front of the store, another of the racing cars on the road to Salinas. Jimmy stepped on the brake and we got out of the car. He took a close look at the Mercedes and chatted with the owner, Lance Reventlow, the twenty-one-year-old son of Barbara Hutton, until the station wagon caught up with us again. "How do you like the *Spyder* now?" Jimmy's friends asked him. "Grand!" Jimmy replied. "I'm going to treat it well. I'm going to keep this baby for a *long* time." Jimmy bought a bag full of apples, and hopped back into the car. He was raring to go. "Non-stop to Paso Robles!" he shouted and jammed down the accelerator without fastening his safety belt. Blackwell's Corner was our last stop.

We had been on Highway 466 ever since we went through Bakersfield and now it was deserted. No car except our *Spyder* and the station wagon as far as we could see. Jimmy went faster now—a very natural thing to do when you are all alone on a good road in a racing car. It was just past five in the afternoon. The sun, a ball of fire, shone directly in our eyes. It was still very hot and the heat flickered and danced on the sandy brown road. To the right and left of us was desert; in front of us, an endless ribbon of a road.

Jimmy Dean—Beyond Help

"Everything okay?" Jimmy asked.

"Everything okay," I answered, half dozing. The monotonous hum of the engine was like a soft cradle song.

We were not talking now—not of Pier Angeli or of Dean's mother or of anything. The only thought on Jimmy's mind was winning that race. There was no doubt of that: that's all he talked about. I felt a little uneasy again. I glanced at Jimmy but could see no shadow of fear cross his face. He had no premonitions of his death.

A few minutes before six o'clock it happened.

We were near Cholame.

A 1950-model Ford was coming at us.

Suddenly the car swung out toward the center of the highway to turn onto Highway 41, its left wheels over the center line.

Then we hit. My head slammed against the dashboard, and my body was thrown out of the car, yards down the highway. I passed out instantly.

Dimly I remember being lifted by ambulance workers. I came to when the ambulance—racing along at top speed with sirens screaming—lurched to miss a passenger car and I was almost flung from my upper-berth stretcher. Then I thought, *Jimmy! Where was Jimmy? What had happened to him?* I saw him as though I were looking through a leaden haze. There he was—my friend Jimmy—lying limp, covered with blood, bones fractured, his neck broken. He was beyond help—anyone's help.

James Dean was dead . . .

Again and again, during the months that I lay in the hospital in plaster casts with my face lost in weird wire structures, I tormented my memory to recall those few seconds before Jimmy's death . . .

Was there an instant before he died, when he knew that he was dying . . . Did he know pain . . .

I do not know. The only thing I can remember is the soft cry that escaped from Jimmy . . . the little whimpering cry of a boy wanting his mother—or of a man facing his God . . .*

---

* Wütherich didn't know that Dean had died until he was told several days after the accident. —Ed.

The driver of the other car was a young student named Donald Turnup-seed. When Donald found out that he was responsible for the crash, he broke down in tears. "I didn't see him; my God, I didn't see him," he wept. Donald himself suffered almost no injuries.

Rolf Wütherich left the hospital on crutches. Three months later, he underwent a bone grafting operation, connecting his hip bones with an eight-inch silver nail and screws.

The ring Jimmy gave Rolf at Ridge Route was torn from Rolf's finger when he was thrown out of the car. He still has a scar where the ring was. This ring—Jimmy's gift of friendship to him—lies buried somewhere in the desert where Jimmy died . . .

END

"GOOD NIGHT SWEET PRINCE:
AND FLIGHTS OF ANGELS SING THEE TO THY REST!"
—William Shakespeare, *Hamlet*

ACKNOWLEDGMENTS

———◆———

I would like to express my appreciation to the following individuals who graciously contributed their assistance in bringing *The Real James Dean* to fruition.

Yuval Taylor, my editor at Chicago Review Press, who shared my enthusiasm for this project and waited patiently for me to finish it. Without him, you would not be holding this book now.

Erica Marlowe, my literary agent, for her persistence and perspicacity.

Brian Apthorp, the late William Bast, the late Budd Boetticher, Lew Bracker, Frank Corsaro, Susan Cooper Cronyn, Mitch Douglas, Larry Frascella, the late Samuel Fuller, the late Curt Gentry, John Gilmore, Val Holley, Paul Huson, Jay Hyams, Melissa Hyams, Kristine Krueger at the National Film Information Service of the Margaret Herrick Library, David Loehr at the James Dean Gallery in Fairmount, Indiana, Geoffrey Massey, Martha Millard, Barrett Moore, the late Neyle Morrow, Robert R. Rees, Jill Schary Robinson, Judie Rosenman, Toni Lee Scott, Kitt Shapiro, Martin Sheen, George Stevens Jr., Carole Stuart, Stuart Swezey at Amok Books, Liz Weller, and Sheila Weller.

I would also like to give special thanks to James Dean biographer extraordinaire Ron Martinetti and his website American Legends (www .americanlegends.com), which I encourage readers to visit.

Acknowledgment is also given for use of the following material in *The Real James Dean*:

Excerpt(s) from *Elia Kazan: A Life* by Elia Kazan, copyright © 1988 by Elia Kazan. Used by permission of Alfred A. Knopf, an imprint of the Knopf Doubleday Publishing Group, a division of Penguin Random House LLC. All rights reserved. Any third party use of this material, outside of this publication, is prohibited. Interested parties must apply directly to Penguin Random House LLC for permission.

Excerpt(s) from *The Quality of Mercy: An Autobiography* by Mercedes McCambridge, copyright © 1981 by Mercedes McCambridge. Used by permission of Times Books, an imprint of Penguin Random House LLC. All rights reserved. Any third party use of this material, outside of this publication, is prohibited. Interested parties must apply directly to Penguin Random House LLC for permission.

Selected text excerpted from *A Terrible Liar* by Hume Cronyn beginning on page 155 is credited as follows: Excerpt from pp. 276–9 [1,198 words] from *A Terrible Liar: A Memoir* by Hume Cronyn. Copyright © 1991 by Hume Cronyn. Reprinted by permission of HarperCollins Publishers.

CREDITS AND PERMISSIONS

Chapter 4

"Grant County's Own" by Adeline Nall as told to Val Holley is reprinted by permission of Val Holley.

Chapter 5

"The Man Who Would Be 50: A Memory of James Dean" by Gene Nielson Owen is reprinted by permission of Barrett Moore.

Chapter 9

"The Great White Way" is excerpted from *Laid Bare: A Memoir of Wrecked Lives and the Hollywood Death Trip* by John Gilmore (Los Angeles: Amok Books, 1997). Used by permission of John Gilmore and Stuart Swezey.

Chapter 10

"Blindside" is excerpted from *Laid Bare: A Memoir of Wrecked Lives and the Hollywood Death Trip* by John Gilmore (Los Angeles: Amok Books, 1997). Used by permission of John Gilmore and Stuart Swezey.

Chapter 12

"James Dean at UCLA" copyright © 2001–2014 by American Legends Inc. All rights reserved. Used by permission of Ronald Martinetti and American Legends.

Chapter 14

"Life with Rogers: James Dean's Gay Mentor Tells All" is excerpted from *The James Dean Story: A Myth-Shattering Biography of an Icon* by Ronald Martinetti (New York: Birch Lane Press, 1995). Copyright ©1975, 1995 by Ronald Martinetti. Used by permission of the author.

Chapter 17

"The Little Prince" is excerpted from *Maverick: A Director's Personal Experience in Opera and Theater* by Frank Corsaro, copyright © 1978 by Frank Corsaro. Used by permission of Vanguard Press, an imprint of Penguin Random House LLC.

Chapter 19

"Drawing Blood" is excerpted from *Shelley, Also Known as Shirley* © 1980 by Shelley Winters. Used by Permission. All rights reserved.

Chapter 21

"Just Lousy with Rapport" is excerpted from *A Hundred Different Lives: An Autobiography* by Raymond Massey (Boston: Little, Brown, 1979). Used by permission of Little, Brown and Company, The Permissions Company, Inc., and Geoffrey Massey.

Chapter 23

"I Was James Dean's Black Madonna!" by Vampira as told to Robert Rees is used by permission of the author. Copyright ©1989 by Robert R. Rees. All rights reserved by Robert R. Rees. No part of this article may be reproduced without written permission from Robert R. Rees.

"Vampira and James Dean: Cult Vs. Occult" by Robert R. Rees is used by permission of the author. Copyright ©1994 by Robert R. Rees. All rights reserved by Robert R. Rees. No part of this article may be reproduced without written permission from Robert R. Rees.

Chapter 24

"Kindred Spirits" is excerpted from *Alone with Me: A New Autobiography* by Eartha Kitt (Chicago: Henry Regnery, 1976). Used by permission of Kitt Shapiro.

Chapter 26

"James Dean: Rebel with a Cause" is excerpted from *Mislaid in Hollywood* by Joe Hyams (New York: Peter H. Wyden, 1973). Copyright © 1973 Joe Hyams. Reprinted by permission of Melissa Hyams.

Chapter 27

"An Unforgettable Day with Jimmy Dean" by Gene Nielson Owen is reprinted by permission of Barrett Moore.

"James Dean's Ghost Wrecked My 2 Marriages, Says Pier Angeli" by Roger Langley is reprinted by permission of American Media Inc.

Chapter 28

"A Kind of Loving" is excerpted from *A Kind of Loving* by Toni Lee Scott, edited by Curt Gentry (New York: World Publishing Company, 1970). Used by permission of Toni Lee Scott and Curt Gentry.

Chapter 29

"Jimmy Dean: Giant Legend, Cult Rebel" by Leonard Rosenman is used by permission of Judie Rosenman.

Chapter 30

"Chickie Run on the Sunset Strip" is excerpted from *Shelley II: The Middle of My Century* © 1989 by Shelley Winters. Used by permission. All rights reserved.

Chapter 34

"A Tenderness Lost" by George Stevens is reprinted by permission of George Stevens Jr.

Chapter 36

"The James Dean I Knew" by Bob Hinkle. Copyright © 2009 by American Legends. Used by permission of Ronald Martinetti and American Legends.

Chapter 37

"Some Unsentimental Memories of James Dean by Rock Hudson" by Ray Loynd. Copyrighted 2015. Prometheus Global Media. 120007:1015AT

Chapter 40

"The Rebel and the Mogul" is excerpted from *Heyday: An Autobiography* by Dore Schary (Boston: Little, Brown, 1979). Used by permission of Little, Brown and Company, The Permissions Company, Inc., and Jill Schary Robinson.

BIBLIOGRAPHY

———◆———

Allen, Jane. *Pier Angeli: A Fragile Life*. Jefferson, NC: McFarland, 2002.

Associated Press. "Arthur Loew Jr. Film Producer, 69." November 13, 1995.

Ayyar, Raj. "Val Holley on Hollywood's Top Gossip: Mike Connolly." GayToday.com. March 1, 2004. http://gaytoday.com /interview/030104in .asp.

Bast, William. *James Dean: A Biography*. New York: Ballantine Books, 1956.

Bast, William. *Surviving James Dean*. Fort Lee, NJ: Barricade Books, 2006.

Bayard, Louis. "The Celluloid Closet." *Washington Post*. October 9, 2005.

Dalton, David. *James Dean: The Mutant King: A Biography*. Chicago: Chicago Review Press, 2001.

Dalton, David, ed. *James Dean Revealed!: James Dean's Sexsational Lurid Afterlife from the Scandal and Movie Magazines of the Fifties*. New York: Delta, 1991.

Ferris, Jan. "Adeline Nall Sits Erect in a Wheelchair in Her Nursing . . ." *Chicago Tribune*. September 29, 1995.

Guinness, Alec. *Blessings in Disguise*. New York: Knopf, 1986.

Haas, Jane Glenn. "James Dean: An Up-close Look Back." *Orange County (CA) Register*. January 15, 1993.

Holley, Val. *James Dean: The Biography*. New York: St. Martin's, 1995.

Hutchings, Harold. "The Woman Behind James Dean." *Chicago Tribune*. March 3, 1957.

Kashner, Sam. "Dangerous Talents." *Vanity Fair*. March 2005.

Langdon, Verne. "Maila Nurmi." Findagrave.com. January 12, 2008. http://www.findagrave.com/cgi-bin/fg.cgi?page=gr&GRid=23914415.

Langley, Roger. "James Dean's Ghost Wrecked My 2 Marriages, Says Pier Angeli." *National Enquirer.* September 1, 1968.

Lipton, Michael A. "An Affair to Remember." *People.* June 24, 1996.

Manso, Peter. *Brando: The Biography.* New York: Hyperion, 1994.

McLellan, Dennis. "Joe Hyams Dies at 85; Former Hollywood Columnist, Bestselling Author." *Los Angeles Times.* November 12, 2008.

Mogg, Diarmid. "Beverly Wills." *The Unsung Joe* (blog). January 31, 2010. http://morethanyouneededtoknow.typepad.com/the_unsung _joe/2010/01/beverly-wills.html.

Moore, Sally. "Good Heavens! X-Rated Opera Director Frank Corsaro Claims Mozart Would Have Loved It." *People.* April 3, 1978.

New York Times. "Adeline Mart Nall, James Dean's Drama Teacher, 90." November 22, 1996.

Poole, W. Scott. *Vampira: Dark Goddess of Horror.* Berkeley: Soft Skull Press, 2014.

Reading (PA) Eagle. "Davis Kin Die in Fire." October 24, 1963.

Riese, Randall. *The Unabridged James Dean: His Life and Legacy from A to Z.* Chicago: McGraw-Hill, 1991.

Rothstein, Mervyn. "Elia Kazan, Influential Director, Dies at 94." *New York Times.* September 28, 2003.

Sarasota (FL) Herald-Tribune. "Actress Pier Angeli Divorces Vic Damone." December 18, 1958.

Schumach, Murray. "Raymond Massey, Famous For His Portrayal of Lincoln." *New York Times.* July 31, 1983.

Sessums, Kevin. "Elizabeth Taylor Interview About Her AIDS Advocacy." *The Daily Beast.* March 23, 2011. http://www.thedailybeast.com /articles/2011/03/23/elizabeth-taylor-interview-about-her-aids -advocacy-plus-stars-remember.html.

Spoto, Donald. *Rebel: The Life and Legend of James Dean.* New York: HarperCollins, 1996.

Stewart, Jocelyn Y. "Actress, TV Horror Film Hostess Vampira." *Los Angeles Times.* January 16, 2008.

von Frankenberg, Richard. "Wie es wirklich war mit James Dean" ("How It Really Was with James Dean"). Translated by Leon Worden. *Christophorus,* no. 43 (1960). Accessed May 11, 2015. http://www .scvhistory.com/gif/galleries/christophorus1960jamesdean/.

Warnock, Kirby F. "Going Hollywood." Big Bend Quarterly. 2010.
    http://bigbendquarterly.com/giant/index_giant_story.htm.
Whitney, Grace Lee, with Jim Denny. *The Longest Trek: My Tour of the
    Galaxy*. Clovis, CA: Quill Driver Books, 1998.
Ziaya, Christine. "Elvira Vs. Vampira: Tale from the Crypt." *Los Angeles
    Times*. October 25, 1987.

INDEX

———◆———

ABOUT THE AUTHOR

———◆———

Peter L. Winkler is the author of *Dennis Hopper: The Wild Ride of a Hollywood Rebel* (Barricade Books, 2011), the only comprehensive biography of the actor. "I knew Dennis Hopper in his wild days and his sober days, and this book captures the man in his many incarnations," writes filmmaker Philippe Mora. "Winkler's deeply researched biography is the definitive book on this live wire who lived on the high wire."

James Dean biographer Val Holley calls Winkler "a genuine Hollywood historian and that rarity, a James Dean fan with a triple-digit IQ."

Peter Winkler has written about movies for *CineFan, Crime Magazine, Filmfax*, the *Los Angeles Review of Books, Playboy, Pop Matters, Spiked, Video Theater*, and *World Cinema Paradise*. He has also written for the *Huffington Post, PC Laptop Computers Magazine, PICO-Laptops and Portables*, and *Smart TV & Sound*. He was the subject of a feature story in the *Los Angeles Times* in 2011 and has been a guest on talk-radio shows in the United States and Europe. Winkler graduated with honors from the University of California at Los Angeles. He resides in Valley Village, California.